NEW YORK REVIEW BOOKS
CLASSICS

THE WAY OF THE WORLD

NICOLAS BOUVIER (1929–1998) was born near Geneva. His father
was a librarian, who encouraged his son both to read—among the
books Bouvier devoured as a child were those of Stevenson, Jules
Verne, Jack London, and Fenimore Cooper—and to travel. Bouvier
studied for some years at the University of Geneva, but in 1953 he
left without a degree to join his friend Thierry Vernet in the voyage
to the Khyber Pass that is described in *The Way of the World*, published eight years later. Subsequent journeys took Bouvier to Sri
Lanka (his experiences there inspired his one novel, *The Scorpion
Fish*), Japan, and the Aran Islands (described in the books *Japanese
Chronicles* and *Journey to the Aran Islands and Other Places*). Bouvier
worked for many years as a photographer and as a picture researcher,
spending much of his time hunting down obscure images in various
libraries and archives. He was also a founding member, along with
Max Frisch and Friedrich Dürrenmatt and others, of Gruppe Olten,
an informal organization of Swiss writers on the political left, and
the author a slim book of poems, *Le Dehors et le dedans* (1982).

THIERRY VERNET (1927–1993) was born in Grand-Saconnex
in the canton of Geneva. He studied painting and stage design with
Jean Plojoux and Xavier Fiala, and worked as a stage designer for
productions throughout Europe. He was married to the painter
Floristella Stephanie.

ROBYN MARSACK has been director of the Scottish Poetry
Library since 2000. She has degrees in English literature from
Victoria University (New Zealand) and Oxford, and has worked
as an editor for the Carcanet Press. She won the Scott Moncrieff
Prize for her translation of Nicolas Bouvier's *Le Poisson-scorpion*
(*The Scorpion Fish*).

from Chris Bondy
June 2020

THE WAY OF THE WORLD

NICOLAS BOUVIER

Translated from the French by
ROBYN MARSACK

Introduction by
PATRICK LEIGH FERMOR

Drawings by
THIERRY VERNET

NEW YORK REVIEW BOOKS

New York

THIS IS A NEW YORK REVIEW BOOK
PUBLISHED BY THE NEW YORK REVIEW OF BOOKS
435 Hudson Street, New York, NY 10014
www.nyrb.com

Originally self-published in Geneva, Switzerland, in 1963 as *L'Usage du monde*

Library of Congress Cataloging-in-Publication Data
Bouvier, Nicolas.
The way of the world / by Nicolas Bouvier ; illustrations by Thierry Vernet ;
introduction by Patrick Leigh Fermor.
     p. cm. — (New York Review books classics)
 Originally published: Marlboro, VT : Marlboro Press, 1992
 ISBN 978-1-59017-322-0 (alk. paper)
 1. Bouvier, Nicolas. 2. Voyages and travels. 3. Bouvier, Nicolas—Travel.
I. Vernet, Thierry, ill. II. Title.
 G490.B76213 2009
 910.4—dc22
                    2009021401

ISBN 978-1-59017-322-0

Printed in the United States of America on acid-free paper.
10 9 8 7 6 5

CONTENTS

Entabran.
Savrobi NOURRISTAN.
—— Dreholahah.

Kerra Naphani.

Temps très net, soleil — 7 heures du matin
peut-être. La route — une énorme plaine de
zone terminée par les collines brunes — un
plan de montagnes noires — A — Derrière
tout près les énormes massifs blancs de
Nourristan. Pas d'aller depuis ici — Les gens
d'ici pensent que les Nourristani parlent
le langues sont l'anglais — Ce n'est pas à nous
d'où ça indiverses. Personne ne

sait rien ici sur les gens de ces montagnes.
Pourtant les vieux de la Tchaïkhane il y en a
un qui s'est baladé là-bas quand il était
enfant. Ils s'en souviennent à peine. A gauche un
grand marais et les Kostchi très rouges et bleu.
Lumière admirable. J'ai les mains assez
brûlées. Santé très bonne. La route n'a
pas l'air mauvaise. A coup de pié je m'achète
un "porteur" la batterie est à plat. Rien
dormi à côté de la voiture, réveillé par la pluie.
Je suis rentré sous le channe.

On prend moins de photos seul qu'à deux.
Il y a déjà trop de choses auxquelles il
faut penser. Ça viendra, un pli à prendre.
Manqué ce pont très émouvant qui est
la seule entrée du Nouristan. Mais la voiture
marchait si miraculeusement bien que je n'ai
pas osé l'arrêter.

A page from the notebook used by Nicolas Bouvier to write *The Way of the World*

Introduction

When do journeys like this really begin? When the author is very young, like the Baudelairean child in love with lamp-lit maps and prints? Nicolas Bouvier thinks that in his case it must have been between the ages of ten and thirteen; lying flat, chin propped in hands, gazing down at the mountains and rivers unfolding across the carpet and letting himself fall under the spell of their names. Time passes, ties are loosened, at last he is ready to cast off. Then, at the nudge of some chance signal, he is away.

The signal which launches *The Way of the World*—I feel sure Congreve wouldn't grudge the use of his title for *L'Usage du Monde*—is a letter from a painter friend who had wandered to Bosnia, describing the market in Travnik:

> ... sacks made out of entire goatskins, sickles that made one want to scythe acres of wheat, fox skins, paprikas, whistles, shoes, cheeses, tin trinkets, sieves of woven rushes, still green, which mustachioed men were just finishing, and reigning over all this a collection of one-legged, one-armed, wheezing men hobbling on crutches.

In no time at all, the author is in Zagreb on the way to join his friend in Belgrade. Then the two of them set out in a patched-up Fiat Topolino, heading south. It was early summer in 1953; they were in their early twenties, low in cash but high in expectation. 'I thought of a cat's proverbial nine lives', he wrote at the time, 'it seemed to me that I must be starting on my second.'

It is hard to determine exactly what makes the books and the journeys of Nicolas Bouvier so distinct from the work of other writers. He has all the gifts that come to a traveller's help, his wide erudition, rooted in the classics, appears only when something in the journey evokes it. The patronising approach of the old hand and the credulity of a neophyte are both absent, but not the capacity to admire and assess. Passionate curiosity, appropriate seriousness and a comic sense are kept in balance by a wise, tolerant and most unusual cast of mind. He has the intuitive gift of capturing landscapes, atmospheres and personalities in a flash, and he finds himself totally at home in the heart of heterodoxy and strangeness. His scope ranges from the hilarious to the tragic, with a fondness for the eccentric and the grotesque and he catches scenes and atmospheres with a painter's eye and a poet's ear. He sets them down in live and vivid language of great subtlety and beauty. The narrative is scattered with sudden fireworks. It is easy to *see* why *The Way of the World*, and his other books on Ceylon, Japan, and the Aran Islands, have won such celebrity in the French-speaking world. The style is racy, meditative, allusive, elliptic and expansive by turns—a stiff task for a translator, which Robyn Marsack has carried out with great skill. Nicolas Bouvier's background—the French-speaking cantons around Geneva—adds, in English, another fortuitous slant to the narrative, referring us back as it does to a different literature and a less familiar spectrum of historical landmarks. The painter and the writer must have been an irresistible partnership. It was just as well that they were ready for anything, for their journey was beset with ordeals and hardships and dangers, all of them compensated in the end by an almost delirious profusion of marvels. The book that emerged is nothing short of a masterpiece.

Macedonia, Thrace, Constantinople, the southern shores of the Black Sea, Trebizond and Erzurum—one after the other the stages of the author's early lamp-lit geography spring up all round them. When they feel like it, or when lack of cash holds them back, they settle, for a month or two in battered lodgings, or in a shabby-genteel Polish *pension* in Istanbul, where down-at-heel émigrés gather nightly for bridge; or they doss down, under ambiguous semi-arrest, in a provincial Persian prison; or take paupers' rooms for half the winter in back-lanes and then sink, fascinated, into the low life of the Levant. Humble Armenians, stray Zoroastrians, Kurdish mountain-folk and the like are their companions. ('The gun is a cousin', a Kurdish smuggler earnestly informs them, but 'the dagger is a brother.') The painter would unpack his easel, and later on organise exhibitions in Tehran; the author would write all day and give French lessons; or, tidying himself up, persuade French Institutes and nuns to allow him to lecture on Molière and Stendhal to the Tehran smart set, with princesses in the offing, and fox-terriers; or, if Stendhal was too much for the nuns, Pascal. (In advanced Tehran circles, Larbaud and Proust were all the rage.) They moved painlessly up and down the social scale, but the lower rungs attracted them the most: the villagers, the craftsmen, and the nomad tribes, with haunting suggestions of sorcery and ghouls, djinns and afreets. The intrigues and feuds of the Sunni and the Shia flicker in the background; and the ululating frenzy of Muharram scanned by the blades of zealots falling on their own limbs and skulls. Unforgettable picaresque sequences would come to rest in long sessions among the hookahs and tea-glasses in the *tchaïkhanes* of down-and-outs and blind beggars. Starting at sunset, these inspired scarecrows would recite Firdausi and Saadi and Hafiz to each other in exquisite and learned poetical trances until long after daybreak. At moments like these, the travellers felt the age-old civilisation of Iran surfacing through the fanaticism and the rags, unconcernedly outsoaring the materialistic cultures of the West.

Terrible stretches of breakdown and disaster in the deserts of Yazd and Lut assailed them as they moved east. They broke into Baluchistan at a point on the border which is so seldom crossed that the most recent signature in the frontier log-book was Sir Aurel Stein's on his last journey. The sun became a mortal enemy; nobody moves there after dawn; flies keep up a merciless black siege and the nights choke with opium-smoke from which there is no escape.

In Quetta, all is suddenly different. With the mountains of Waziristan along the skyline, the Baluch regiment, though it is long after Partition, swings on to the parade-ground behind leopard-skinned bandsmen and massed pipers on the kilts of the Robertson tartan; battle honours from the Great War—Ypres, Neuve Chapelle, and the Ardennes—still flutter on the colours. The two travellers find sanctuary here at the Saki Bar, which is run by Terence, one of the book's most winning characters, an intensely civilised ex-Guards officer who has gone a bit to seed. The young waiters nibble each others' ears whenever they get a chance. By mistake, a servant elsewhere throws away the author's manuscript, covering more than a year of their travels. The seemingly unending hunt for it, half-fainting under the haze of sizzling miles of rubbish, with the sun thrashing down and the vultures crowding back in a ring each time they are driven off, is worse than anything Dante invented.

Baluchis and plethoric British officers who have stayed on, sip their drinks at the Saki Bar cheek by jowl with the Pathans whom, in the old days, they would have only seen on the frontier crags through field-glasses. The walls of an Indian café are frescoed with wonderful *Vie Parisienne* art-deco murals, painted there by the author's versatile partner to keep up with the superannuated march of local fashion; at the Saki Bar on gala nights they even manage to bash out old-fashioned jazz. Terence, deep in *Le Côté de Guermantes* in a frayed edition, or listening to Gluck's *Orphée* in his den, breaks off to amuse his guests with tales of heartier pre-war days: young ensigns, writing a cheque in Mrs Fitz's discreet *maison de rendez-vous* in South Audley Street, were asked to make it out in guineas rather than pounds (how unlike the Baluch red-light quarter the author so brilliantly conjures up). They leave him at last, having pored over maps of Savoy and Haute-Provence; he wonders whether to start all over again among the trout and the plane-trees. Too late, perhaps.

Beyond the Afghan sierras the author—alone now; his companion has flown to Ceylon to join his girl—shakes off malaria, and Kabul and the Hindu Kush are his next moves. In a very skilful way he conducts us through another score of encounters—the tribes, the nomads, the snows, the willow-trees, the streams, the woods, the migrant birds, the gypsies, the camel-drivers, the glens where he is woken by pheasants and hoopoes and the soaring maze of passes are woven into a kind of summing-up of these nineteen extraordinary months. At last, in the middle of his second December, he turns south to join his friend beyond Cape Comorin. The hot wind of the Indian sub-continent is blowing up the Khyber, and he is a shade reluctant to leave his wintry fastness. We too! we too! It is an unforgettable journey, and one longs for it never to end.

Patrick Leigh Fermor
March 1992

Acknowledgements

I am grateful to Danielle Piovano, Mark Thompson and Patrick Leigh Fermor for their assistance and advice; also to Nicolas Bouvier for his encouragement and lively interest in the process of translation. I owe thanks to the Scottish Arts Council for a grant that enabled me to work through the translation with the author, and to the Bouviers, Lydia Wevers and Alastair Bisley for their kind hospitality in Geneva.
R.M.

THE WAY OF THE WORLD

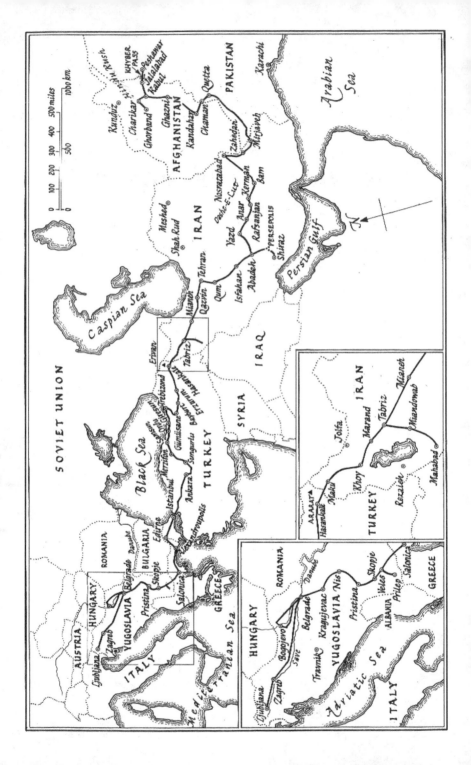

Preface

> I shall be gone and live, or stay and die.
>
> *Shakespeare*

Geneva, June 1953 – Khyber Pass, December 1954

I HAD LEFT Geneva three days previously, and was making my way at a leisurely pace when I found a letter from Thierry at the poste restante, Zagreb.

Travnik, Bosnia, July 4ᵗʰ

This morning, brilliant sunshine, heat; I went up to the hills to draw. Marguerites, young wheat, serene shadows. Coming down, met a peasant on a pony. He got down and rolled me a cigarette, which we smoked squatting beside the path. With my smattering of Serbian I gathered that he was taking bread home, that he had spent about a thousand dinars on finding a girl with sturdy arms and big breasts, that he had five children and three cows, and that one should watch out for thunder, which had killed seven people the year before.

Then I went to the market-place. It was market day: sacks made out of entire goatskins, sickles that made one want to scythe acres of wheat, fox skins, paprikas, whistles, shoes, cheeses, tin trinkets, sieves of woven rushes, still green, which mustachioed men were just finishing, and reigning over all this a collection of one-legged, one-armed, wheezing men hobbling on crutches.

This evening, had a drink under the acacias while listening to the gypsies, who surpassed themselves. On the way back, bought a large slice of almond paste, pink and greasy. Is this the East or what?

I looked at the map. Travnik was a little town encircled by mountains in the depths of Bosnia. He was planning to go back to Belgrade, where the Association of Serbian Painters (ULUS) had invited him to exhibit. I was to join him there towards the end of July, with the luggage and the old Fiat we had fixed up, and we'd go on to Turkey, Iran, India, perhaps even further… We had two years in front of us, and money for four months. The programme was vague; the main thing was just to get going.

From ten to thirteen I had stretched out on the rug, silently contemplating the atlas, and that makes one want to travel. I had

dreamed of regions such as the Banat, the Caspian, Kashmir, of their music, of the glances one might meet there, of the ideas that lay in waiting... When desire resists commonsense's first objections, we look for reasons – and find that they're no use. We really don't know what to call this inner compulsion. Something grows, and loses its moorings, so that the day comes when, none too sure of ourselves, we nevertheless leave for good.

Travelling outgrows its motives. It soon proves sufficient in itself. You think you are making a trip, but soon it is making you – or unmaking you.

On the back of the envelope he had scribbled: 'My accordion, my accordion, my accordion!'

He'd made a good start; me too. I was in a café on the outskirts of Zagreb, in no hurry, a flute of white wine in front of me. I watched as night fell, a factory emptied, a funeral procession passed by – barefooted, black-shawled, carrying brass crosses. Two jays were squabbling in the branches of a lime tree. Covered in dust, a half-eaten pepper in my hand, I listened to the day joyfully crumbling away like a cliff inside me. I stretched out, gulping litres of air. I thought of a cat's proverbial nine lives: it seemed to me that I must be starting on my second.

A Scent of Melons

MIDNIGHT WAS CHIMING when I stopped the car in front of the Café Majestic. A friendly silence reigned over the still warm street. Through the lacy curtains I saw Thierry sitting inside. He had drawn a life-size pumpkin on the tablecloth, and was killing time by filling in tiny pips. Obviously the Travnik barber hadn't seen him very often. With his sideburns over his ears and his little blue eyes he looked like a jolly, if worn-out, young shark.

I gazed through the window for a long time before joining him at the table. We clinked glasses. I was happy to see this old project taking shape, and he to have a companion. He had found it hard to tear himself away. At first he had walked too far, without being in training, and weariness made him gloomy. Trudging along, sweating, through a countryside populated by incomprehensible peasants, he had questioned the whole enterprise. It seemed absurd, idiotically romantic. In Slovenia, an innkeeper who noticed his defeated look and his top-heavy rucksack hadn't helped matters by saying kindly, '*Ich bin nicht verrückt, Meister, ich bleibe zu Hause.*'*

The month he'd spent drawing in Bosnia, however, had restored his balance. When he arrived in Belgrade, his drawings under his arm, the painters of ULUS had welcomed him as a brother and unearthed an empty studio in the suburbs, where we could both stay.

We got into the car, as it was quite a way from the city. After crossing the Sava Bridge, you had to follow two ruts along the river bank as far as a patch of land overgrown with thistles, where several dilapidated houses stood. Thierry made me pull up in front of the

---

* 'I'm no fool, Meister, *I* stay at home.'

largest. In silence, we lugged the bags up a dark staircase. The smell of turpentine and dust caught in our throats. The heat was stifling. A powerful humming came through the half-open doors and echoed round the landing. In the middle of an enormous, bare room, Thierry – a methodical tramp – had settled down on a bit of swept floor, well away from the broken tiles. A bedding-roll, his painting materials, a gas lamp and, leaning against a primus stove, sitting on a maple leaf, there was a melon and a goat cheese. It was frugal, but so natural that I felt it had been waiting for me for years.

I spread my sleeping bag on the floor and went to bed without undressing. The umbels of hemlock climbed right up to the casement, open to the summer sky. The stars were very bright.

Loafing around in a new world is the most absorbing occupation.

Between the tall arch of the Sava Bridge and the confluence with the Danube, the suburb rose in clouds of dust in the fiery summer. It owed its name – Saïmichte (the fair) – to the remains of an agricultural showground, turned into a concentration camp by the Nazis. For four years, Jews, resistance fighters and gypsies had died there in their hundreds. When peace returned, the municipality roughly restored these lugubrious 'follies' for artists on state bursaries.

Ours – with its warped doors, smashed windows and capricious toilet flush – numbered five *ateliers*, ranging from the absolutely bare to the opulently bohemian. The poorest tenants, those on the first floor, were to be found every morning, clutching their shaving brushes, queuing for the washbasin on the landing. The concierge would be there too, his cap pulled down tight over his head; he had been wounded in the war, and his skin had to be stretched at the chin by some helpful soul while he carefully shaved with his one hand. He was a sickly man, more suspicious than an otter, with nothing to do but watch over a nubile girl, and pick up bits and pieces from the toilets – built in the Turkish style, so one emptied one's pockets before squatting down – handkerchiefs, lighters, pens that distracted users might have forgotten. Milovan the literary critic, Anastasia the potter and Vlada, a peasant painter, occupied the *ateliers* on the ground floor. They were always ready to help us, serving as interpreters, lending a typewriter, a bit of mirror, a handful of rock-salt or, when they had sold a watercolour or an article, inviting the whole house to a noisy feast – white wine, peppers, cheese – followed by a collective siesta on the sunny, bare floor. Heaven knows they lived on meagre rations, but the black years of occupation and civil war had taught them to value the good things in life, and Saïmichte, although stark, had a bonhomie all of its own.

It was a jungle of poppies, blueberries and wild grasses which had laid siege to the crumbling buildings, and drowned in its green silence the shacks and stray encampments that had sprung up all around.

A sculptor was living in the house next to ours. Stubble on his chin, his hammers slung from his belt .45s, he used to sleep on a mattress at the foot of the statue he was working on: a bare-chested partisan, fist clenched round a machine gun. He was the richest man in the neighbourhood. Times had been kind to him; with monuments to the dead, red granite stars, effigies of resistance fighters battling against 125 mph winds, he had at least four years of commissions. It wasn't surprising; at first the business of secret committees, revolutions become established, ossify, and rapidly become business for sculptors. In a country like Serbia, which was constantly in turmoil, there was already a large heroic repertoire on which he could draw: horses rearing, swords brandished, comrades-in-arms. But this time it was more difficult. The liberators had changed their style; they went on foot, their hair cropped short; they were wary, unprepossessing, and the spoonful of jam that the sculptor offered when we visited him, as was the Serbian custom, suggested a less martial, gentler world.

At the other end of this wasteland, an icebox beside a bar served as postbox and rendezvous for those who lived there, between the sky and the undergrowth, with their chickens and cooking pots. One could take away solid, gritty blocks of coarse ice cream and sorbets made from goat's milk, their sour taste lingering in the mouth until evening. The bar had only two tables; when it was hottest, the rag-and-bone men of the area gathered around to sleep or sift their pickings. They were old men, with red, roving eyes; because they'd always sniffed the dirt together, they were like ferrets from the same burrow.

Behind the icebox lay the domain of a Ukrainian secondhand dealer, who had made a very clean niche for himself amidst his treasures; a big man, sporting a cap with ear flaps, he owned a mountain of worn-out shoes, another of light bulbs (some of them burning, others fused), and conducted his affairs on a large scale. A heap of battered flasks and empty oil drums completed his stock. The astonishing thing was the number of clients who left his depot with their 'shopping' under their arms. Past a certain degree of poverty, there was nothing that couldn't be sold. In Saïmichte, *one* shoe – even with a hole – could make a deal, and the Ukrainian's mountain was often scaled by the bare-footed, scanned by the sharp-eyed.

Westwards, along the Zemun road, Novi Beograd rose up above a sea of thistles, the foundations of a satellite city that the government had been determined to build, against geologists' advice, on badly drained soil. But even so august an authority could not prevail against spongy land, and Novi Beograd, instead of rising out of the ground, persisted in sinking into it. Abandoned two years before, its false windows and twisted girders stood between us and the countryside. It was a frontier.

At five o'clock in the morning, the August sunshine pierced our eyelids and we would go off to bathe in the Sava, on the other side of the Saïmichte bridge. Soft sand beneath our feet, a few cows among the scattered bushes, a little girl in a shawl watching over goslings, and a tramp asleep in a shell hole, covered with newspapers. When day broke, the bargees and inhabitants of the area came to wash their clothes. We cheerfully scrubbed our shirts together, squatting in the muddy water, and all along the river bank, across from the sleeping town, there was nothing but the sound of clothes being wrung out, brushes, and snatches of song as masses of soapsuds floated away towards Bulgaria.

In summer, Belgrade is a morning city: at six o'clock the municipal watering cart sweeps away the refuse left by the market-garden trucks and the shops' wooden shutters bang open; at seven, all the cafés are jumping. The exhibition opened at eight. Every other day I would go along to hold the fort while Thierry badgered recalcitrant purchasers all the way home, or went sketching in town. The entry was twenty dinars, for those who had it. The cash box contained only a handful of coins and Valéry's *Variétés V*, left behind by the last exhibitor – its mannered style took on an exotic attraction in those surroundings, which added to the pleasure of reading. Under the desk, half a melon and a flask of wine awaited the friends of ULUS who would come along at the end of the afternoon and suggest a dip in the Sava, or translate a few lines of a review that had appeared in the evening paper.

'…M. Verrnette… has certainly seen a lot of our countryside and his sketches are amusing … but he is too sarcastic and lacks some … lacks some … – how would you say this?' said the translator, clicking his fingers. 'Ah, I've got it, he isn't really serious!'

Indeed, seriousness is the preferred mode of people's democracies. The journalists of the Communist press, who arrived very early in the morning to work on their paper, had enough and to spare. They were young officials with squeaky shoes, who had mostly emerged from Tito's resistance and whose new importance gave them legitimate enough satisfaction, though it also made them both arrogant and uncertain. Frowning, they would move from one drawing to the next, severely disapproving yet puzzled, for who was to say whether irony was retrograde or progressive?

Between eleven and twelve the poster at the door – a yellow sun in a blue sky – would attract all the kids from Terazié Avenue, on their way home from school. An exhibition of bread and jam couldn't have been more successful: urchins with gap-toothed grins hopped along the picture cordon; dusty gypsy kids paid up with a scowl, and ran yelling from room to room, leaving their tiny bare footprints on the polished parquet floor.

From five to six, the blank hour would bring some ghosts from elegant neighbourhoods. Pathetic, gentle *ci-devants*, whose fluent French and retiring, respectful manner betrayed their bourgeois origins: old men with quivering moustaches carrying enormous shopping-bags, and matrons in tennis shoes, as tanned as peasants, would draw up chairs to the cash desk, extend a dry handshake and carefully sound us out, searching for an echo of their melancholy ruminations. Many of them, having returned after the October 1951 amnesty, were now living in the smallest rooms of their former residences, and in totally unforeseen circumstances. A music-loving former lawyer was copying out parts for a jazz orchestra, and an erstwhile muse of the salons would cycle off at daybreak to teach *solfège* or English in distant council flats. They would merely glance distractedly at the walls and, too lonely to go away immediately, but too proud to say so, they would launch into exhausting monologues – prone to last until closing time – on the tomb of King Alexander or on the ruined convents of Macedonia which we, who *would understand*, absolutely must see. And they would linger there, pressing, wearisome, confiding, giving more and more advice. But their hearts were no longer in it. They made an effort of will, but the spirit had gone out of them.

At dusk the whole street would go past the exhibition. The inhabitants of Belgrade had too few amusements to let any slip. Life was still frugal enough for people to be hungry for everything, and this appetite led to all sorts of discoveries. Theologians followed motor races, peasants – after a day's shopping in Marshal Tito Street – would come along to discover watercolours. They would leave a sack of fertiliser, a new halter, or a sharp, oiled billhook at the door, peer at the tickets and take money from under their belts or caps. Then they strolled from drawing to drawing, with long strides, hands behind their backs, gazing at each one, determined to have their money's worth. Used to the pasty clichés of the *Mostar Daily* or the *Cetinje Echo*, at first they were hard put to understand line drawings. Then from a familiar detail – a turkey or a minaret, the handlebars of a bicycle – they would work out the subject and would suddenly laugh, or look thoughtful, craning their necks to see whether they could recognise their station, their hunchback, their riverbank. Faced by someone sloppily dressed, they'd check their own flies. I liked the way they related everything to themselves, looked at things slowly, patiently, weighing up the work. Usually they would stay to the very end, quite at ease in their baggy breeches and farmyard aroma, then they would come politely to the cash desk to shake the artist's hand or roll him a cigarette, which they stuck down with a single sweep of the tongue. At seven o'clock Prvan, the manager of ULUS, would arrive with the news. No, the state purchasers who constituted his main clientèle had still not made up their minds.

'Oh well,' he'd say, 'tomorrow we'll go and chew their ears...,' and he would take us off to eat spinach flan at his mother's. If we didn't have customers, friends sprouted from under our feet. There was an immense store of personal generosity in Serbia, and though lacking so much, people were warm-hearted. France may well be – as the Serbs liked to tell us – the brain of Europe, but the Balkans are its heart, and there can never be too much of that.

They invited us into dark kitchens, into little, ugly, comforting sitting-rooms for enormous bellyfuls of aubergines, kebabs, melons which sprayed open under a pocketknife. Nieces and frail old relatives – because at least three generations would be sharing these cramped quarters – would have already, excitedly, set the table. There would be introductions, low bows, phrases of welcome in charming, old-fashioned French, and conversations with these old bourgeois who were passionate about literature, who killed time by re-reading Balzac or Zola, and for whom *J'accuse* was still the latest literary scandal from Paris. Spa waters, the 'colonial Exhibition'... when they reached the end of their recollections, there would be silence, and then the friend who painted would go off in search of a book on Vlaminck or Matisse. All the dishes would be cleared from the table, and we would leaf through the book while the family looked on in silence, as though a ceremony they couldn't participate in was taking place. This gravity touched me. During my years as a student I had earnestly potted 'culture', done my intellectual gardening, analyses, glosses, taken cuttings; I had dissected various works of art without grasping their dynamic value. At home the stuff of life was so well cut, distributed, cushioned by habit and institutions that there was no space for invention, it was confined to decorative functions and only thought of as something 'agreeable' – that is, immaterial. In Serbia, things were quite different; being deprived of necessities stimulated, within certain limits, an appetite for what was essential. Life was still demanding and greatly in need of form, and artists – by which I mean any peasant who knew how to hold a flute, or daubed their wagons with sumptuously mingled colours – were respected as intercessors, or bonesetters.

Thierry had not yet sold anything. I had written nothing. As frugal as our life was, our dinars were rapidly diminishing. I went to the newspapers in search of work and, thanks to our Saïmichte neighbours, was able to place a few jottings. The editors didn't pay much, but they gave me a warm welcome. I was swiftly put at ease by finding in most of their buildings a grand piano, prominently placed

with its lid up, for emergencies – as though the need for music was as imperious there as any natural need – and a refreshment room where, in the bracing aroma of Turkish coffee, one could freely discuss things. There was no prior censorship, and in principle the most heterodox opinions could be published... and sanctioned. The editor-in-chief, however, would prudently remove from the press anything with a whiff of heresy, and at least half the copy was never used. Sometimes, in order to create a good impression, the people in charge recklessly exaggerated the latitude they were given.

'In your country, women don't have the vote. Give us a page on that – your feelings. Be quite blunt about them.'

I had no firm opinion, nevertheless I wrote that the situation was fine as it was, perhaps because after several weeks in Yugoslavia I could have wished to see the women a little less militant, and a little more intent on pleasing. I even called La Fontaine to my aid: 'grace, which is something even more than beauty'. The ladies – it was for a women's magazine – were certainly flattered; if they weren't all beautiful, they were certainly graceful, but it wasn't the kind of writing they were looking for.

'We had a good chuckle,' the editor said to me, somewhat embarrassed, 'but the line you take is rather... how shall I put it ... frivolous. There might be trouble.'

I suggested writing a fairytale.

'That's an idea: a fairytale without a prince.'

'With the devil?'

'If you like – but not a saint. I've got to keep my job.' She shook her black locks, laughing amiably.

Belgrade is nourished by a rustic magic. Although it's in no way a village, an influx of countryfolk pass through it and make it mysterious. It's easy to imagine the devil behind the features of a well-off horsedealer, or a waiter in a threadbare waistcoat, wearing himself out weaving his weft and setting his traps, constantly thwarted by the formidable candour of the Yugoslavs. All afternoon I wandered along the Sava, searching for a story on such a theme, without success. As the deadline was tight, I spent the evening typing up a little fable in which the devil didn't figure at all, and went off to deliver it to the editor, on the sixth floor of a dilapidated building. Although it was late, she let us in. I can't recall the conversation at all;

what struck me was that she wore high-heeled mules and a superb red dressing-gown. In Belgrade, such things were eye-catching. I was grateful to her for such a pretty outfit because, of all the aspects of poverty, one of the most distressing to me has always been the way it makes women ugly: cheap shoes as big as surgical boots, chapped hands, flowered materials whose colours run and blur. In that context, such a dressing-gown was a triumph. She warmed our hearts, like a standard flying. I wanted to congratulate her, to drink a toast to frivolity. I wouldn't have dared to be so explicit. We left with such profuse thanks that she seemed rather surprised.

Four thousand dinars. We needed ten times that before we could leave the city, but it was something towards our hoped-for retreat to Macedonia. We needed to go away in order to work; Belgrade was beginning to overwhelm us.

Little factories lined the quays on the Sava. A peasant, his forehead pressed against a shop-window, endlessly contemplated a new scythe. In the upper town there were white buildings crowned with the red Party star, and onion domes. There was a heavy smell of petrol from the evening trams, packed with wide-eyed workers. A song floated out from a café, *sbogom Mila dodje vrémé* – goodbye, my darling, time is flying … Haphazardly, as we became used to it, dusty Belgrade got under our skins.

There are cities whose histories are too pressing to allow them to be carefully presented. When it was promoted to capital of Yugoslavia, the big fortified town was suddenly enlarged by entire streets, in that administrative style which was already not modern, and didn't look as though it could be ancient. Up went the main post office, parliament, acacia-lined avenues and residential areas, where the villas of the first deputies sprang out of ground watered by bribes. Everything had gone ahead too fast for Belgrade to evolve the hundreds of details which make urban life enjoyable. The streets seemed occupied rather than inhabited; the mesh of incidents, gossip, encounters was rudimentary. There were none of those shady, concealed nooks that real cities provide for love or meditation. Elegant objects had disappeared along with bourgeois customers. Shop windows displayed merchandise that was scarcely finished: shoes gaping open like split logs, blocks of black soap, nails by the kilo or talcum powder wrapped up like fertiliser.

Occasionally a diplomat would drop by the exhibition and invite us to dinner, enabling us to rediscover that city patina which the town so lacked. Around seven o'clock we dumped the day's dust in the Sava, hastily scraped our faces in front of the mirror on the landing and, dressed in faded suits, we strolled blissfully towards the handsome houses, their chrome taps, hot water and cakes of soap, which we'd make use of – under pretext of having to leave the room – to wash a stock of handkerchiefs and socks. When the person charged with this task eventually returned, beaded with sweat, the hostess would say maternally:

'You aren't well? It's the Serbian food... nobody gets away with it, all of us... and recently...'

'I myself –' the minister would add, raising his hands.

We only half-heard the conversation, devoted to bad roads, incompetent departments, in short to the trials and tribulations which didn't affect us at all; all our attention was focused on the smooth brandy, the texture of damask napkins, the scent of the lady of the house.

A traveller's social mobility makes it easier for him to be objective. These excursions beyond our suburb enabled us, for the first time, to form a dispassionate judgement of that milieu; one had to be at a distance to distinguish its contours: its conversational habits, its absurdities and humour, its gentle ways and – once one had passed the test – its naturalness, a rare flower in any soil. It was sleepy too, and lacked curiosity; its life was already furnished in every nook and cranny by preceding generations, who had been more avid and inventive. There was a world of good taste there, and often of goodwill, but basically it was a world of consumption, where the heart's virtues were certainly maintained but, like the family silver, were reserved for special occasions.

Returning, we would find our shack white hot from the day's sunshine. Pushing open the doors, we came down to earth. Silence, space, just a few objects and those very dear to us. The virtue of travelling is that it purges life before filling it up.

We had a new neighbour – French, of Serbian extraction. Anastase found life in Montparnasse too hard, and chose to return to Yugoslavia. He had just settled in with a sweet Parisian wife, whom everyone in the house secretly hoped would be a pushover, and who wasn't. Anastase knew scarcely any Serbian. He had difficulty adapting to Saïmichte and its ways. A strong Parisian accent and a sort of shyly cheeky humour served him for aplomb. For fear of seeming bourgeois, he wouldn't discard his scruffy jersey and his wife made herself a sackcloth dress of an austere cut that was very surprising there. She wasn't able to wear it for long. After a week, *papadaci* (the fever-mosquito) had bitten her, and there she was lying on her bed, melting before our very eyes, in floods of tears, surrounded by gruff, helpful neighbours.

In short, Anastase went from one unexpected setback to another. Even the women completely disconcerted him: confident that his French style would make him irresistible, he had gaily assailed the concierge's daughter in the shower. She had practically knocked him out.

'If I'd got my hand between her legs...' he said resentfully. Milovan laughed at him.

'Haste will be your downfall, Anastase. Poor girl... French, French... she must have expected something wonderful, a little courtship, sweet nothings, a siege! And you fell on her to make love on the spot, just like everyone else!'

For the first few weeks, Anastase felt the ground give way beneath him. Everything was so different, right down to the politics. At the beginning, in order to pass the test and show he was right-minded, he gave vent to ferocious criticism of the Vatican – without raising the slightest interest. Why the Vatican? No one asked him much, and the subject concerned no one in Saïmichte; journalists in the extreme left-wing press in Belgrade were paid to do that sort of thing, so why do their work for free? His listeners regarded him with an astonishment that cut him off in mid-flow, and kindly invited him to calm down and have a drink. Confusion and loneliness are things the Serbs recognise at once, and they immediately come forward with a bottle, a few shrivelled pears, and their kindly presence.

Like us, Anastase benefitted from their generous dispositions; Milovan, Vlada the naïve painter and the ULUS people had fraternally kept his head above water. When he realised the kind of gang he'd stumbled on, he threw himself on them with frantic gratitude. Then he desperately wanted to distribute the coffee he'd brought back from France. You'd see him going down the corridors, carrying a steaming tray: this would earn him love. At last he'd hit on the right thing; coffee was rare, and Anastase made it perfectly. People did like him. It was as simple as that.

Friday service in the little church concealed behind the post office: a few sunflowers against a worm-eaten fence, and rabbit-skins stuffed with straw propped against the sacristy wall. Inside, a dozen old people in dusty sandals chanted the liturgy behind a screen. Two candles stuck in a bucket of sand feebly illuminated the altar. It was gentle and shabby. The dimness, the quavering, frail voices made the scene almost painfully unreal; I had the impression that a careless stage designer had flung it together a few minutes beforehand. This church seemed moribund: it would not be able to adapt, it could only suffer. The role it had played in the formation of the Serbian kingdom and the help it had given to the resistance prevented its being persecuted, but if the Party had done nothing to finish it off, it had done even less to succour it. Everyone knew that assiduous church attendance would do nothing to advance their careers.

At least it could flourish among the dead without fear of harm. In the cemeteries of Belgrade, families would go to place crosses made of purple beads on the tombs of partisans surmounted by the red star, or on Sundays to light tiny candles, their flames guttering yet not extinguished. The competition between emblems was carried on in silence, even as far as this. The Party's emblem was flaunted everywhere: at the very least on fences, at the entrance to shops, stamped on gingerbread; sometimes even in villages in the depths of Bosnia, where a squad from the neighbouring headquarters would come and put up a 'co-operative triumphal arch' right opposite the mosque, a gross cardboard fake which rapidly lost its fresh paint and fell into peeling decrepitude. At the end of the week the peasants would hitch their wagons to the uprights; soon they would dismantle the arch piece by piece to patch their broken roof-tiles, the varnish sparkling under a leaden sun, and the clumsy totem would wilt like a cutting that hadn't taken.

It's very odd how revolutions which profess to know the people take so little account of their sensibilities, and fall back on slogans and symbols that are even more simple-minded than the ones they're replacing. Although designed by the most brilliant Enlightenment minds, the French Revolution rapidly deteriorated into an inane parody of the Roman republic, with its Pluviose, ten-day 'weeks', the goddess of Reason (a street-walker being chosen to personify her at the ceremonies in the Champ de Mars). The same deterioration was observable passing from the warm, thoughtful socialism of Milovan to the Party machine: loudspeakers, straps and buckles, Mercedes full of ruffians, bouncing over the potholes – the whole apparatus already curiously old-fashioned, and as arbitrary as the heavy stage-machinery which brings down the flies at the play's end, with dead gods and clouds in *trompe l'oeil*.

Nobody in Saïmichte talked about the past. Doubtless it had been difficult everywhere. Like old nags with short memories, the little inhabitants of the area drew from their forgetfulness the courage to live again.

In Belgrade, influential people were silent about the past, as though it were a dubious old man whose trial had brought too many people's actions into question. Nevertheless, there existed a glorious Serbian history, Croatian and Montenegrin chronicles, Macedonian epics full of Machiavellian prince-bishops, conspiratorial philologists, partisans with many notches on their blunderbusses; there were splendid individuals, shadily employed, still unfit for consumption – like meat that needs stewing for a long time to lose its bitter taste – since they had generally profited from the brief respites allowed them by their Turkish or Austrian adversaries to fall on them in their turn.

While waiting to recover this patrimony, still 'under seal', official history began with the Nazi invasion. The bombing of Belgrade that had killed twenty thousand, the partisans, Tito's insurrection, the civil war, the revolution, the breach with the Cominform and the development of a national doctrine had all occurred in less than nine years. It was from these brief, violent episodes that all the examples, words and myths necessary to nationalist sentiment had been taken. Obviously that period had not been lacking in authentic heroes, or in martyrs; there had been enough of both to re-name all the streets in the country, but nothing resembled one partisan so much as another, and eventually we got sick of perpetual references to the resistance – especially as the Serbs hadn't waited until 1941 to acquire the qualities we found so attractive.

When we missed this truncated past, it was enough to open our *Manuel de conversation franco-serbe* to be sent right back to a bygone world.

Let me take this opportunity to malign these little tourist phrase-books. I had several of them during my travels, all equally unhelpful, but none went as far as the *Manuel de conversation franco-serbe* by Professor Magnasco, published in Genoa in 1907. It was anachronistic to a dizzying degree, and its playful dialogues were of the kind imagined by an author who dreamed of hotel life without stirring from his own kitchen. It consisted entirely of phrases about ankle boots, redingotes and minute tips, plus unnecessary remarks. The first time I went to use it – in a barbershop on the Sava quay, amongst cropped heads and workers in overalls – I opened it at: *Imam, li vam navostiti brk?* – 'Should I wax your moustaches?' – a question to which one was supposed to reply promptly: *Za volju Bozyu nemojte pustam tu modu kikosima* – 'No, thank heavens! I leave that fashion to the ladies' men.'

If that was already a glimpse of the past, the splendid antiquities in the Belgrade museum offered plenty of other resources for historical inquiry. It's true that you paid for the pleasure by first walking through a gallery devoted to the works of the old sculptor Meštrovič, all on heroic subjects or in heroic attitudes: tormented, hopeful, stunned. The musculature was Michelangelesque, reinforced by a diet of double fat and cabbage, tensed to the very temple as though to expel that little kernel that would prevent these athletes from thinking.

After that, however, there were astonishing things: a series of busts from Hadrian's era – consuls, prefects of Mesia or Illyria – with a wonderful presence. Classical statuary is so often rhetorical and frozen, I had never seen it this explosive. To make them lifelike, the sculptors had marvellously rendered the sly precision of the Romans, their acidness and cynicism. Bathed in honeyed light, a dozen wily old magistrates, lively as tomcats, revealed themselves in silence. With set foreheads, sarcastic crow's feet, and the lower lips of men who had lived well, they paraded sickness, slyness or greed with fantastic impudence, as if their sojourn in these foreign hills had relieved them forever of the burden of pretence. Even so, despite the wounds and scars collected on the Danubian frontier, these faces were basically serene. One felt they had come to terms with the twists of a life to which they must have clung, avidly, and the Mithraic altars found in southern Serbia showed that nothing had been neglected in order to get the supernatural on their side in this struggle.

Then we would find ourselves outside in the sunny street again, with the scent of melons, the big market where horses bore children's names, and houses scattered in a disorderly fashion between two rivers – a very old encampment, which today is called Belgrade.

In the evenings, to preserve some essential moments of solitude, I would prowl on my own. I would go past the water, a book under my arm, and climb up Nemanjina Avenue, dark and deserted, as far as the Mostar, a pleasant café, lit up like a steamer, where all the Bosnian natives gathered to hear their magnificent music on the accordion. Scarcely had I sat down than the owner would bring me a pot of purple ink and a rusty pen. From time to time he would come and peer over my shoulder, to see how I was getting on. He was amazed to see a page being covered at one sitting. I was too. Since life had become so entertaining, I was hard put to concentrate. I would jot down some notes, rely on my memory, and gaze around me.

There would be bossy Muslim farmers' wives, snoring on the banquettes among their bags of onions; truck drivers with pock-marked faces, officers sitting ramrod straight in front of their drinks, fiddling with toothpicks, or leaping up to offer a light and trying to engage in conversation. And every night, at the table by the door, four young whores would be chewing melon seeds, listening to the accordion player caressing delirious arpeggios on his brand new instrument. They had lovely, smooth, tanned knees, a bit dirty when they had just come in from practising their trade on a nearby embankment, and well-defined cheekbones where the blood throbbed like a drum. Sometimes they suddenly fell asleep, and sleep made them look extraordinarily young. I would look at their sides, covered in purple or apple-green cotton, lifted by their regular breathing. I found them beautiful in a harsh way, and troubling, until they shook themselves, cleared their throats with an abominable sound, and spat into the sawdust.

On my return, the sentry on the bridge would sometimes pick a quarrel. Although he knew perfectly well who we were, our

insouciance made him bitter, and he would take the only revenge he could: delaying passers-by. He would shake his cropped head, breathing garlic and rakia, and demand imaginary permits. My foreign passport enabled me to get round this and to cross the bridge, but his rage would not be subdued and Vlada, who crossed much later and often tipsy, would suffer the consequences. He would be leaping from one strut to another, like a boy, thinking about the marvellous picture he could paint if he weren't Vlada, if he hadn't grown up here, if... when the sentry's voice brought him rudely back to earth. They would both get angry and their quarrel echoed as far as the atelier.

'Five hundred dinars fine,' the soldier would yelp, and Vlada would yell back, suggesting he return to his mother's belly. The world was too tough for the soldier to leave it at that. We'd hear him shout 'Five thousand!' A dead silence would follow this figure, then the slow footsteps of Vlada, sobered up, returning to the house through the high grass and coming to knock at our door. He cursed his temper; with what he earned in a month, he'd never be able to pay. Tomorrow he would have to go back to the sentry-box, apologise, make an idiot of himself, arrange things with a peasant's finagling and a bottle of plum brandy in his pocket.

We would comfort him after a fashion, but on those evenings the city weighed us down. One would have liked to sweep away with the flick of a hand the miserable shacks in the area, the militia's bad breath, the tragic squalor of the one and the wary torpor of the other. We suddenly needed happy looks, clean nails, urbanity and fine linen. With a stencil, Thierry painted two crowns on the enamel mugs we clinked together. It was our only form of sedition. Henceforth, we would be kings.

Bačka

The exhibition had closed. We now had enough money to dream of a trip north. Our friend Mileta, a young ULUS painter, had offered himself as interpreter and spurred us on; if we wanted to record gypsy music, we would have to go to the northern part of the country.

There are about a hundred thousand gypsies in Yugoslavia today; less than there used to be. Many had perished in the war, massacred or deported by the Germans. Many others, with their horses, bears and cooking-pots had settled in the poor suburbs of Niš or Subotica, and became town dwellers. There were still a few gypsy villages, however, hidden amidst the provinces along the border with Hungary; villages of clay and straw which appeared and disappeared as if by magic. One day their inhabitants packed up, abandoned them and went off to live somewhere else, in a more isolated patch. But no one in Belgrade could tell us where.

One August afternoon, the owner of an open-air café on the main road from Belgrade to Budapest, deftly grilled by Mileta, gave us the name of one of those phantom encampments: Bogojevo in Bačka, south of the Hungarian border, some sixty miles from the arbour where we were sipping tokay. We downed our wine and took the road for Bogojevo, Bačka. Summer was gently turning into autumn, and the last storks wheeled above the fields.

The Bačka roads belong to ferrets, to venturesome geese, to ramshackle carts covered in dust; they are the worst roads in the Balkans. So much the better for Bačka which, protected by its ruts, had been bypassed by the war; just as well that we were in no hurry to see the end of that countryside. The plain already belonged to horses, green pastures stretching out, broken here and there by a solitary walnut-tree or the antennae of a wellshaft with its pendulum. This is a province where they speak Hungarian. The women are lovely, and on Sundays wear a costume of melancholy opulence; the men – small, talkative, helpful – smoke slender, lidded pipes and still go to mass in silver-buckled shoes. The atmosphere is capricious and sad. It takes only an afternoon to be spellbound.

It was night by the time we reached Bogojevo. The village, prosperous and silent, huddled round a heavy, freshly whitewashed church. There were no lights, except at the inn, from which came the muffled sounds of a last game of billiards. Inside, three peasants in black suits played in silence, devising rapid and astute shots, and their enlarged shadows danced on the white wall. An old portrait of Lenin in a cravat hung above the counter, opposite a crucifix. Alone at a table, a shepherd in a cloak dunked bread in his soup. It was a singular gathering, but there was no trace of gypsies. We were mistaken about Bogojevo. There were two neighbouring villages: peasant-Bogojevo and gypsy-Bogojevo – pastoral and mountebank –

who apparently didn't get on very well. The three billiard players, questioned on the doorstep, gestured vaguely towards a loop in the Danube, sparkling a stone's throw away. Our slip would be held against us. We had time to book the only room, then we were off again.

Behind the river bank, gypsy-Bogojevo was already asleep, but a few steps from the encampment, at the edge of a tumbledown bridge, in a shelter covered with bindweed, we discovered a few of the men who were spending the night drinking and singing. From the kitchen, lit by an oil lamp, came flashy, gay music. We stood on tiptoe to peer in the window: near the lamp, a fisherman was gutting eels while a buxom country lass revolved barefoot in the arms of a soldier. Sitting in a row behind a table covered in half-empty litre bottles, five gypsies in their forties, five dirty, tattered, wily, distinguished gypsies, strummed their patched instruments and sang. Flat, black hair, long at the nape. Asiatic heads, but rubbed by all the byways of Europe, and hiding the ace of clubs or some getaway key beneath their moth-eaten felt hats. It is very rare to surprise gypsies at home; this time we couldn't complain, we had found their lair.

When we appeared in the doorway, the music ceased. They put down their instruments and stared, astonished and suspicious. We were newcomers to a country where nothing came; we had to say the password. We sat down at the table, ordered wine, smoked fish and cigarettes. When the soldier left with his girl, they became more relaxed, understanding that we were all vagabonds, and set to cleaning their plates very carefully. Between rounds we talked, in French to Mileta who spoke in Serbian to the owner who translated it into Hungarian for the gypsies, and back again. The atmosphere loosened up. I brought out the tape recorder, and the music started up again.

Gypsies usually sing the folksongs of whatever province they're in: *czardas* in Hungary, *oros* in Macedonia, *kolo* in Serbia. They borrow their music, like so much else, and doubtless music is the only thing they return. It goes without saying that there is also a real gypsy repertoire; they are very discreet about that, and it's rarely heard. But that evening, in their hideout, they played that very music on their battered instruments, the old melodies that their village cousins had long since forgotten. Crude, rousing, vociferous songs in the Romany tongue, which told of the ups and downs of ordinary life, poaching, small windfalls, the winter moon and empty stomachs.

Jido belku peru rošu
Fure racca šiku košu
Jido belku peru kreč
Fure racca denkučec
Jano ule! Jano ule!
Supileču pupi šore...

The Jew with the mop of red hair
Stole a red hen and a duck
The scarlet Jew with his little curls
Disrobed a duck in the corner.

You have plucked their legs
For your mother to eat
More tender than the heart of red roses
Hola Janos! Hola...

We listened. While Janos made off with his plucked poultry and the gypsies chanted his flight on their squeaky violins with childlike exuberance, an old world emerged from the shadows: nocturnal and rustic, red and blue, full of succulent, cunning animals. A world of lucerne, of snow, and of ramshackle cabins where the rabbi in his caftan, the gypsy in rags and the priest with his forked beard whispered their tales around the samovar. A world whose mood they would alter quite casually, without warning passing from wild gaiety to agonizing shots from a bow...

Tote lume ziši, Simiou fate de demkon šie... – all the same, the whole world told me: marry your neighbour's daughter...

Did the new bride go off with someone else? Was she less of a virgin than had been promised? The story didn't matter; they suddenly wanted to be sad, no matter the theme. In the time it took to smoke a few cigarettes, they made their strings sob for the simple pleasure of turning one's soul upside down.

Merely a temporary slowdown. A minute later, the two fiercer men whom we – for recording purposes – had relegated to a place behind their colleagues, led off at a furious pace. A return to the liveliest style was to be feared and indeed took place as we departed, with no regard for the fisherman and proprietor of the shack, who was yawning in the corner, rubbing his eyes.

It was late when the bells for High Mass pealed out and woke us. Doves were pecking round the inn courtyard; the sun was high. We had café au lait in the square, in large white bowls with gold rims, while looking at the women on their way to the church adorned with flags. They wore flat shoes, white stockings, embroidered skirts like corollas puffed out over lace underskirts, laced-up bodices and on top of their chignons, a flutter of ribbons fixed on to a little cap. Beautiful and slender, they were drawn in a single, flowing line.

'They lace themselves so tight,' whispered the innkeeper, 'that every Sunday two or three of them faint before the Elevation.'

He lowered his voice respectfully. It had to be a flourishing civilisation to speak about women in that tone of mystery. With its tanned daughters, its fresh starched linen, its cows out to pasture and the neighbouring gypsies as leaven in the dough, peasant-Bogojevo had plenty to be pleased about.

Around midday we went back to the cabin by the bridge, where two of the previous evening's virtuosi were waiting to take us to the encampment. They were sitting, fresh as daisies, beside an old Hungarian peasant to whom they were trying to flog a horse. We played back the recording to them. It was excellent: their voices timid at first, soon lapsing into rustic bellows, irresistibly gay. They listened with their eyes closed in pleasure, smiles on their hatchet faces. At the end of the table, the old man's face began to light up. The tape-recorder and our presence made him listen to the familiar music with a new heart. When it stopped, he got up and introduced himself to everyone in a composed manner; he also wanted to sing, Hungarian songs. He had picked up the gauntlet: he condescended to compete. We no longer had a band? No matter – he simply wanted to sing. He undid his top button, placed his hands on his hat and with a strong voice chanted a tune whose development was quite unpredictable yet seemed – once we'd heard it – perfectly clear. The first verse told of a soldier who, on returning from the war, requested a pancake to be kneaded until it was 'as white as this man's shirt'; the second told how

> The cock crows, the dawn breaks
> I long to enter the church
> The candles have been burning for a long time
> But neither my mother nor my sister are there
> Someone has stolen the wedding rings...

Absorbed in his song, the old man assumed a miserable expression while the gypsies were convulsed with laughter, as though they were not unconnected with this disappearance.

Gypsy-Bogojevo is below a dyke, in a solitary meadow kept green by a stream. Around the village, ponies are tethered beneath clumps of willows or sunflowers. Two rows of little cottages form one wide, dusty street where a litter of black piglets were charging about and tumbling over, sunning themselves belly up. Something had just been butchered; on each doorstep a bundle of blue entrails smoked in a stoneware pot. The village was silent but in the middle of the

deserted street three chairs had been set out for us, around a rickety table covered with a red kerchief, like a splash of fresh blood. We set up the machine and looked up to meet a hundred pairs of magnificent eyes; the whole tribe was on tiptoes around us. Grubby faces, naked children, old women smoking pipes, girls covered in blue glass beads, adjusting their dirty, gaudy rags.

When they recognised the voices of their husbands and brothers, the violin of the 'President', there was a great murmur of surprise then several shouts of pride, swiftly suppressed by cuffs from the old people. Bogojevo had never heard its music issuing from a machine; enveloped in great affection, the camp's artists basked in their hour of glory. Naturally everyone had to be photographed, especially the girls. Each one wanted her photograph taken on her own. They pushed and pinched. Soon a scuffle ensued – nails, curses, slaps, split lips – which ended up in a whirl of gaiety and blood.

The 'President' with his violin and a young, weaselly acolyte accompanied us as far as the dyke. They walked along slowly, a dahlia behind their ears, totally absorbed in their surprise concert. In Serbian, they asked us to come back.

At peasant-Bogojevo, everyone must have been dining or sleeping behind their blue shutters. Nothing moved in the square, except a tall column of red dust which danced upwards and then crashed into the wall of the church. We crawled along the road leading to the Backa Palanka ferry. The silent countryside drowsed in the heavy, fruity light of summer's end.

One day I would return – on a broomstick, if necessary.

Bačka Palanka
On the other side of the Danube, beyond the ferry landing stage, the country became hilly again. On a steep slope bordered by wheat fields, a man with the ruddy complexion of a butcher sprang out of the wheat and barred the road. He was shouting something in Croatian. We gestured to him to get in. He hurled himself between the front seats and the back and set about covering himself with everything in reach – bags, quilts, raincoats – until he was almost completely concealed.

'He wants to be driven to the police station,' said Mileta. 'He has deflowered a girl and as he's a married man, the family has been after him for two weeks. They're Montenegrins – there are lots of them around here, the government gave them land. He's been on the run since sun up.'

Indeed on approaching the village, we came across a small band of wiry, weather-beaten, moustached men, with guns slung across their backs, who were pedalling along on high bicycles and scanning the fields. We exchanged polite greetings, which had our fugitive in agonies. When we drew level with the station, he leapt from the car, knocking Mileta aside, and dived for the doorway. Once our man was safe, I began to feel sympathy for the Montenegrins, the squad of uncles and cousins showing solidarity, going about their business, resolved to comb the countryside; I liked their slightly distant, correct manner of greeting. I longed to go down south.

On our return to Saïmichte, we spent half the night looking at the map. South-west of Niš, a road lined with rasping, sunlit names descended towards Kosovo and Macedonia. We would take that one.

Return to Belgrade
Going from the upper city to the Sava quays, the road went past a hillside covered in wooden houses, wormeaten fences, sorb-apple trees, tufts of lilac. It was a gentle, rustic corner, inhabited by tethered goats, turkeys, and little children in pinafores playing silent games of hopscotch, or drawing on the pavements, with charcoal that didn't work very well, shaky graffiti, full of experience, as if drawn by old people. I had often been there, following the setting sun, empty-headed, light-hearted, scuffing the stalks of maize, breathing in the odour of the town as if I might die the next day, giving in to that power of dissipation so often fatal to those born under Pisces. At the foot of the hill a tiny café set out three tables along the river. There they served a fragrant plum brandy which trembled in the glass with each passing cart. The Sava flowed peacefully on its brown way under the nose of the drinkers, waiting for night. Across the water you could make out the powdery scrub and the shacks of Saïmichte, and when the wind blew from the north I could sometimes even hear Thierry's accordion, *Ça gaze* or *L'insoumise*, airs from another world whose frivolous sadness was somewhat out of place.

I went back on the last night. On the quay two men were cleaning out enormous barrels which reeked of sulphur and sediment. The scent of melon was certainly not the only one you inhaled in Belgrade. There were others just as prevalent: the odour of heavy oil and black soap, of cabbages and shit. It was inevitable: the city was like a giant sore that had to run and stink before it could heal, and its robust blood seemed strong enough to heal, come what may. What she could give already counted for more than what she still lacked. If I didn't manage to write anything substantial there, it was because being happy took up all my time. Besides, we cannot judge as to whether time is lost.

The road to Macedonia

The road to Macedonia passed through Kragujevac in Šumadija, where our friend Kosta the accordionist was waiting for us, with his parents. Šumadija is Serbia's land of Cockaigne: a sea of hills planted with maize and rape seed, wheat, orchards where glowing plums fall in circles on the dry grass. It is a province of rich farmers, stubborn and spendthrift, who paint *sbogom* – goodbye – in gold on the back of their wagons and distil the best plum brandy in the country. Walnut trees tower over the centre of the villages and the bucolic atmosphere is so strong that it infuses even the sons of the bourgeois who go to the main secondary school in Kragujevac. Kosta was thus always rustically pigheaded, and moved his neck or shoulders in a rural expression of embarrassment. His silences were rustic too. We didn't know much about his family: his father was a doctor at the local hospital – talkative, he added, before lapsing into his muteness – and his mother large, gay, and practically blind.

At Kragujevac, however, everyone seemed to know who was expecting us. A bunch of urchins, perching on the car, directed us right to the door. With exclamations of welcome, handshakes, very blue eyes and some spluttering, we were ushered into a big, shabby room. Plush, a black piano, a portrait of Pushkin and a laden table – and, sitting in a shaft of sunlight, a grandmother bent with age who took our hands in a grip of iron. A moment later the doctor sprinted in: a warm man, this doctor, and lyrical, with forget-me-not blue eyes and a naïve moustache. He knew Geneva, spoke stentorian French and thanked us for Jean-Jacques Rousseau, as though we had created him ourselves.

*Beer to whet the appetite, salami, cheese-cake
covered in sour cream*

We hadn't been at the table an hour when Kosta strapped on his instrument and the doctor joined in with his violin. Next to the sideboard where she had piled the plates, the maid began to dance, clumsily at first, the upper half of her body immobile, then faster and faster. Kosta went slowly round the table, his blunt fingers flying over the keys. He inclined his head, listening to the keyboard as though it were a stream. When he stopped walking, just his left foot kept time, his placid face seeming scarcely concerned with the rhythm. Such restraint marks out real dancers. We, who didn't know how to dance, felt the music creep over our faces and dissolve in vain. The doctor made his violin sing its utmost; the bow was drawn scarcely an inch across the strings, while he sighed, perspired, swelled with music like a mushroom in a downpour. Even the grandmother, although completely crippled, bent one arm behind her neck and stretched out the other – in the dancer's position – and nodded her head to the measure, smiling with all her gums.

Crumbed cutlets, meat rissoles, white wine

The *kolo* is the circle dance that all Yugoslavia dances, from Macedonia to the Hungarian border. Each province has its own style; there are hundreds of themes and variations, you only have to leave the main roads to see it danced everywhere. Sad little *kolos*, improvised on station platforms, between the poultry and the baskets of onions, for a son going off to join his regiment. Sunday *kolos* under the hazel trees, much photographed by Tito's propagandists, who took great care of this national heritage and sent their 'specialist' officials into the depths of the countryside to collect the cunning rhythms of the peasants, their lightest syncopations and most ingenious dissonances. Obviously this promotion of folklore is to the musicians' advantage, and a good flute or accordion style is real capital here.

Bacon, pancakes with jam, double-distilled plum brandy

At four o'clock, we were still at the table. The doctor had put down his violin and was singing at the top of his voice, rapturously pouring out drinks. He was one of those men of booming amiability who was deafened by his own noise and often ended up being taken for a ride. As for the mother, who could see virtually nothing, she touched our faces with her fingertips to assure herself that we were really there, laughing fit to take off into the air. You would think that she was the guest. During the pauses, I could hear at the end of the passageway water dripping into a bathtub full of flagons and melons, keeping them cool. Going out to pee, I reckoned it up: a month's salary, at least.

The Serbs are not only marvellously generous, they also maintain the ancient sense of a banquet: an occasion for rejoicing that is also an exorcism. When life is lighthearted: a banquet. Is it too heavy? Another banquet. Far from throwing off the old Adam as the Scriptures exhort us, he is comforted by enormous glassfuls, surrounded by warmth, gorged on splendid music.

After the cheese and pie, we thought we had reached the end of our efforts, but the doctor, ruddy-faced in the dusky light, was already sliding enormous slices of melon on to our plates.

'It's nothing but water,' he said encouragingly.

We dared not refuse for fear of bringing bad luck. Through a sort of haze I heard the mother still murmuring '*Slobodno... slobodno!*' – help yourselves, dig in! – and then fell asleep upright in my chair.

At six o'clock we took the road for Niš, which we wanted to reach before nightfall. The air was fresh. We left Serbia like two day-labourers, the season over, money in our pockets, memories full of new friendships.

We had enough money for nine weeks. It was only a small amount, but plenty of time. We denied ourselves every luxury except one, that of being slow. With the top down, the accelerator only just pulled out, perching on the backs of our seats and guiding the steering wheel with our feet, we pottered along at twelve miles an hour. The countryside never changed without warning; there was a full moon, rich and prodigious. Past fireflies, roadmenders in Turkish slippers, modest villages dances under three poplars, calm river banks where the ferryman wasn't up and the silence was so perfect that the sound of our own horn startled us. Then day broke, and time slowed down. We had smoked too much, were hungry – the grocers we passed were still shut – chewing without swallowing a crust of bread discovered among the tools in the boot.

Around eight o'clock the light became lethal, and as we passed through hamlets we had to keep a lookout for the old men in police caps who were dazzled and inclined to dash clumsily across the road, just in front of the car. By midday the brakes, our skulls and the engine were very hot. However desolate the countryside, there was always a clump of willows we could sleep under, hands beneath our necks.

Or an inn. Imagine a room with bulging walls, torn curtains, cool as a cave, where flies buzzed around in a strong smell of onions. The day would find its centre there: elbows on the table, we'd make an inventory, telling the story of the morning as though we'd each seen it separately. The mood of the day, which had been dissipated by the acres of countryside, was focused by those first mouthfuls of wine, by the paper cloth to draw on, by the words formulated then. Appetite was accompanied by emotional salivation, proving that food for the body and the spirit are closely allied in the sediment of travel: plans and grilled mutton, Turkish coffee and memories.

The end of the day would be silent. We had spoken our fill while eating. Carried along on the hum of the motor and the countryside passing by, the journey itself flows through you and clears your head. Ideas one had held on to without any reason depart; others, however, are readjusted and settle like pebbles at the bottom of a stream. There's no need to interfere: the road does the work for you. One would like to think that it stretches out like this, dispensing its good offices, not just to the ends of India but even further, until death.

When I went home, there were many people who had never left who told me that with a bit of imagination and concentration they travelled just as well, without lifting their backsides off their chairs. I quite believed them. They were strong people: I'm not. I need that physical displacement, which for me is pure bliss. Moreover, happily, the world reaches out to the weak and supports them. When the world – as on some evenings on the Macedonian road – is made up of the moon on the left hand, the silvery waves of the Morava on the right, and the prospect of looking for a village over the horizon in which to spend the next three weeks, then I would be sorry to dispense with it.

Prilep, Macedonia

There are only two hotels in Prilep. The Jadran is for Party members, and for unlikely travellers there is the Macedonia, where we spent the first evening haggling over our room. Unless I'm in a hurry, I really like this practice. After all, it's less greedy than fixed prices, and engages the imagination. It is more than a matter of explanations; on both sides there are needs which must be squarely confronted in order to reach a solution neither will wish to go back on. It was easier because the Macedonia was almost empty. It was a Saturday evening, however, and the management had gone to a lot of trouble; the courtyard restaurant was hung with coloured light bulbs and there, among the fallen leaves, a conjurer in a smoking jacket had been produced for a handful of tired, distracted peasants. The evening wind cut off his patter as it left his lips, and the doves bursting out of his top hat didn't raise a smile in the audience – as if this slender miracle were no match for their worries. We waited for him to finish, then took our bags upstairs. Two iron bedsteads, paper flowers, a little table, a blue enamel washbasin and through the open window the smell of stone from the mountains, which lifted their spine against the black sky. Good: we'd wait for autumn in Prilep.

Here in a town full of artisans, having a luggage-rack made for the car should have been easy. Forget it. First of all the ironsmith had to grasp what was wanted, and he didn't understand Serbian. So, draw it. But I'd forgotten my pencil, he didn't have one, and the curious crowd already gathered round the car patted their pockets... they didn't either. Pencils were not something to be carried around lightly. While an onlooker accompanied me to a neighbouring café to enquire, the crowd continued to grow and comment: he's going to draw something... he's twenty-three. Some touched the windscreen with timid fingers, others sniggered at nothing in particular. I launched into a sketch as precise as I could make it, and the black face of the ironsmith cleared, then reddened when he recalled that he didn't have a blowtorch. He drew one on my sheet of paper, put a cross, and looked at me. A murmur of disappointment ran through the crowd, then an old man pushed through to the front; he knew a boy who had returned the previous day from Germany with his van, and he had a blowtorch. So I went in search of this friend at the other end of the village, guided by the old man. He was completely bald, had mad eyes, a hooked nose, and trotted along barefoot in a ragged black suit. He had the air of a miserable, defrocked priest. He spoke American quite well, and said that he was called Matt Jordan. He had lived in California for thirty years. Charlie Chaplin was his schoolmate. As he pattered along, he supported his statements by showing old, sweat-stained American postcards. Nevertheless I had the impression he was lying all the time, and when I realised there was a band of kids fifteen yards behind us, imitating him, I began to fear that his services would not help negotiations. Fortunately the man-with-the-torch spoke intelligible German and we could do without intermediaries. He had been a prisoner of war, married in Bavaria, and had just returned to the country with his wife and children. He had over-celebrated his return the previous evening, held his head in his hands and kept shivering. Not that he had drunk a great deal, he said, *aber er hat gemischt*. His blowtorch was new; he handled it as delicately as an icon, and he agreed to lend it in exchange for some good petrol for his van. Fine. Back to the ironsmith, who seemed to agree. The crowd, still dense, shouted encouragement; they were very pleased to see matters advancing. But when it came to the price, they were let down. The man was asking for five thousand dinars, an outrageous sum which bore no relation to the work involved. He knew it, too, but iron was rare and the State took at least half of whatever he got. He went back into his workshop, crestfallen, and the crowd dispersed. I had lost my morning, he had lost his, but how could I be cross with him? What's to be done when nothing is available? Frugality is one thing, and enhances life, but such continual poverty deadens it. Ours didn't: we could give up the luggage-rack, and obviously we could even give up the car, and all our plans, and go and meditate on top of a pillar...without solving the ironsmith's problems one bit.

Prilep is a little Macedonian town, in the centre of a circle of wild mountains west of the Vardar valley. The dirt road coming from Veles goes through it and is interrupted twenty-five miles south by a wooden barrier covered in bindweed; this is the Greek frontier at Monastir, closed since the war. Westwards, several bad roads lead to the Albanian border, not very safe and hermetically sealed.

Within its belt of cultivated fields Prilep spreads out its cool cobblestones, lifts up two bleached white minarets, façades with bulbous balconies corroded by verdigris, and long wooden galleries where, from August, they dry some of the best tobacco in the world. In the main square, between the white and gold jars of the pharmacy and the tobacconist, a militiaman drowses, a gun at his feet, outside the 'Liberty' shop. The two rival hotels confront each other amidst the racket from the Jadran's loudspeakers, which broadcast the 'Hymn of the Partisans' and the news three times a day, without rousing the peasants asleep in their carts.

The stranger who entrusts his head to the pillows of the Macedonia for a night takes away – besides the familiar flea – the image of a carefree town, with its roaming donkeys, perfumed with drying tobacco and over-ripe melons. If he lingers, he will perceive that things are a great deal more complicated, because over a thousand years Macedonian history has managed to set races and hearts at odds. For generations the Ottomans divided and ruled villagers crushed by taxation. When the Turkish empire weakened, the 'Great Powers' took up the baton; this burnt country was useful, and quarrels could be settled by third parties. You armed the terrorists or the counter-terrorists, the clerical party or the anarchists, and too bad if the Macedonians themselves no longer had breathing space.

In Prilep there were Turks whose settlement went back to Suleiman's time, living in their own communities, sticking to their mosque or field and dreaming only of Smyrna or Istanbul; Bulgarians who had been forcibly enrolled in the *Wehrmacht* during the war, and had nothing left to dream with; Albanian refugees; Greeks from

Markos's army, whose status was uncertain and who hung about in cafés for the day's handout; the Party hacks who sat around under the Jadran's flypapers and didn't stint on alcohol; and dour Macedonian peasants with their crooked backs, who thought – not unreasonably – that they always bore the brunt of everything. To round off this miniature Babel we should add the barracks, at the entrance to the town, where the conscripts from the north understood not a scrap of the local dialect and surreptitiously gazed at photos of fiancées or village parents.

On a sunny slope, fifteen minutes' walk away, there is the site of an old city. It was called Markov Grad. When the water that had fed it dried up, the inhabitants abandoned it to build Prilep. You can see a baptistery there, together with several fourteenth- and fifteenth-century convents. They are almost all locked up, or converted into cheap lodgings with the washing drying outside, but no one in Prilep offers information about the place. It belongs to a bygone era.

After our first meeting, old Matt Jordan was always at our heels. He lay in wait in shadowy porches to cut across our path, or coincided with us in a café to unfold in melancholy slang the memories which never had the ring of truth.

'One day I will tell you my big secret...nobody knows...shhh.'

A political secret, it appeared, enough to set the country alight; he would tug at our sleeves with that greedy look of mythomaniacs who need to see people swallow their whoppers in order to enjoy them to the full. I knew from the hotel keeper that it was the police who had shaved his head so closely; he had just spent a week in the local prison for preaching against the regime. In many respects his bitterness was understandable, but it was not so much on account of the regime as on account of the life he led. With his skull like a lump of sugar, his complexion like pumice stone and his sunken eyes, he simply radiated misfortune; indeed perhaps he fulfilled a sacred function in the town by concentrating every form of bad luck in himself. He had nothing to do all day but warm his bag of bones in the sun. He even had a smidgeon of garden and a house which, by dint of persistence and pleading, he ended up getting us inside.

It was a lugubrious house, surrounded by acacias, and smelling of free dental care. He waited for us on the gravel to shake hands and then, once inside, shook them again, as is the custom there. As soon as I sat down, I regretted coming. The blinds were drawn, the room lit by an oil lamp giving on to a dim kitchen where we could hear whispering and chewing. Neighbours coming in from the garden piled into the kitchen and soon emerged, their cheeks stuffed, to pass in front of Matt, who kept bowing. He was delighted to be at the centre of this stifling coming and going: it was his father's funeral feast, which had already been going non-stop for two days. When he judged that we were sufficiently impressed by this file-past, he clapped his hands and two lurking boys emerged from the shadows to kiss our hands. They were his sons. He poked them until they stammered out some words in English. They were visibly afraid of the old man, and never looked him in the face. The smaller one managed to escape under pretext of laying the table, but the elder didn't have that excuse and remained on the carpet. Because his father prevented his going to school, even though he was over thirteen, he spent his days doing sewing which he was made to produce for us on the spot. It was an enormous Serbian flag on which was written, in letters of felt, *Love thy king ... love thy country.* Clumsy appliqué work in embroidery wool surrounded the motto. Matt was pleased and stroked his head until the boy, ashamed of this girl's task and on the verge of tears, fled with his work under his arm.

We went to the table: sour cabbage, bread soup, gritty potatoes which must have been frozen in the earth under a curse. I could hardly swallow a mouthful; the whole plate stank of death. We had to, all the same, because there were half a dozen old women in the kitchen, with straggling locks escaping their black kerchiefs; they kept a grip on the table for at least two hours, chatting away as they ate the stew. These were the mourners. I didn't understand whether the corpse was still in the house or not, and had no desire to be enlightened. Matt filled our glasses with a transparent liquid and invited us to drink a toast.

'Home-made whisky,' he explained, smiling gummily. It was murderous gut-rot, without warmth or light, again with that sweet stink that flooded the mouth with saliva; the soul instinctively associated it with bad luck. I scarcely dared glance at the kitchen for fear of seeing one of those farting hags astride a broomstick.

Once we had crossed his threshold and eaten his bread, he had us for an hour at least. There was time to show us certain 'confidential' documents, postcards from the turn of the century: green trams below the first skyscrapers, *Garden Party at Belle-Isle, Michigan*, women in ankle boots under orange trees. Then photographs: a young man in uniform against a background of luxurious shadows.

'This is me at West Point.'

But on closer inspection, those stripes could have been mistaken for those of the Salvation Army. Here he was again, in the midst of men in pointed hats at the annual banquet of the magicians' club; the pale face in the second row, a cheek bitten off by shadow, was Charlie Chaplin.

When he thought we were taken in, he no longer bothered with reality. One story followed another, each madder than the last: the police spied on him day and night, he was a conspirator, the real Tito had died long ago. Moreover, he had evidence: in an old biscuit tin he had hidden Christmas cards, and he showed us an example – 'Merry Christmas 1922, from Mr and Mrs Boshman'.

The arrival of a visitor interrupted this painful session. It was a Methodist pastor, who had come to do his duty by the deceased. He took in the situation at a glance.

'I see that our friend Matt is carried away with his crazes,' he said in German.

The pastor had studied in Zurich and seemed to have all his wits about him, or as many as necessary, but age, solitude and the exercise of a barely tolerated ministry had made him more fearful than a cockroach. He had several Methodist families in Prilep and half a dozen others scattered through Kosovo. We asked him about his parish, larger than a province, but couldn't get anything out of him other than a weary allusion to Sodom and Gomorrah.

I wondered whether his competitors fared any better in gathering souls: the Orthodox priest who prudently scrubbed his sermons and paid his Party dues; the Muslim imam who took snuff with the faithful on his doorstep in the evening, cultivating a faith thinned by exile; and the Marxists with their choir, youth group and the new swimming pool, who won recruits without too much difficulty. Each one fought the others' opinions with the means at their disposal, but they all shared one sentiment: *Bog* had departed from the town.

'If you want to know Prilep,' added the pastor, 'here's a local proverb: "Everybody suspects everybody but nobody knows who the Devil is".' And the two old men smothered a laugh in their handkerchiefs.

'Don't go to see the priest,' said the hotel keeper, 'he isn't very bright.'

It wasn't his intelligence that interested me, but his function. He represented the sacred, and the sacred – just like liberty – is not a preoccupation until one feels it is under threat. Besides, the priest traded in candles, whose quivering flames evoked all one's desires,

and kept the keys of a wooden church that was all shadow and silence. To open it, he spent ages chivvying a vast, echoing lock, relieved you of some small change, and then left you in the blue, dark gold and silver. When the eye got used to the gloom, it could make out a puffed-up wooden cockerel above the altar, a touching object, its wings outstretched and its beak open to crow St Peter's betrayal. Its presence was warming yet defeated: as if sin, childhood and human weakness constituted capital on which God, through forgiveness, drew the interest.

The Turkish mosque expressed rather the placidity of adoration. It was a squat building, adorned with two minarets in which storks nested. The interior was roughcast chalk, the paving stones covered in red carpets, the walls decorated with verses from the Koran cut out of paper. There was an agreeable coolness and absence of solemnity, which by no means excluded grandeur. Nothing suggested – as in our churches – drama or absence; everything indicated a natural linkage between God and man, source of the guilelessness in which sincere believers unendingly rejoice. To pause in this place, bare-footed on the rough wool, was like bathing in a river.

There were not many Turks in Prilep, but they were well organised. It was through Ayub, the barber, that we entered their society. He was our age and knew a few words of German. We made friends. Since we'd said that we liked Smyrna, where his family came from, he insisted on shaving us for free. So every other day we went along and stretched out in his cracked leather chairs; covered in soap, we faced the black and white photos of Istanbul surrounding the mirror. Gradually we were accepted and one day Ayub and his friends invited us to spend Sunday outdoors with them. Wine, music, hazelnuts... we'd go in a cart... there would be a chamois, poached by the miller. All this he explained by gestures, his German not being adequate to such marvels.

At daybreak we found ourselves at the exit of the town with a lot of strangers to whom we were known – being 'the foreigners'. Husky *salaams*, blue suits, ties with enormous spots, handsome heads flecked with blood from the morning shave, and an old cart packed with food, amongst which they had squeezed a violin and a lute. Off to one side stood an urchin holding two green and purple bikes, borrowed by Ayub in our honour. Once we were all assembled each person – as was the custom on Sundays – released the dove he'd brought, and we took the road to Gradsko on our multicoloured bikes, followed by a cartload of revellers.

Bicycles were rare in Prilep. They were a luxury only the well-off could afford, and an inexhaustible subject of conversation. In cafés you heard sober men passionately discussing the different makes, the softness of saddles or the hardness of pedals. Those lucky enough to have a bike painted it in several carefully designed shades, spent hours polishing it, kept it beside the bed in their rooms, and dreamed about it.

After a mile or two we passed a hedge of plum trees in a hollow and came out on to a meadow bordered by poplars. At the end of the field, the miller sat cross-legged in front of his mill, finishing the sharpening of his millstone. He was waiting for the group to arrive before replacing the stone, which weighed a good six hundred pounds. Six of us returned it to its socket, the miller set the waterfall, tipped the grain, and the grinding began to whiten the joists. Then he spread out hides on the grass, around a basket of tomatoes and onions, and filled a blue enamel coffee pot with rakia. We began on our feast, sitting on our heels; Ayub had the lute between his thighs, and the veins in his neck swelled with effort as he soothed us with a very high-pitched sobbing. He did well. In the intervals you could hear sighing from the heart of the mill; it was the cooking pot in which the chamois was simmering on a bed of aubergines, sending up puffs of steam into the autumn sky.

The cries, the choruses, the barber's strident *amanes** which could be heard as far as Gradsko attracted all the stray hunters to our meadow. The Muslims joined the circle, soon popped peppers into their mouths and let off several rounds of buckshot as a sign of satisfaction. The Macedonians, somewhat less welcome, gathered by a tree stump a little way off, their guns across their knees, catching in mid-air the cigarettes the miller threw them, and firing off one or two salvos in a timid attempt at togetherness. The *raki* continued to circulate. We had to drink to the Turks' health, to our own, to the horses, to the confusion of Greeks, Albanians, Bulgarians, militia, military, and the godless in general. All the bad temper lingering amid the Macedonian hills was dissipated in remarks of astounding obscenity.

It was a successful Sunday. The inebriated miller had stuffed in several cartridges and fired point-blank on at least half his hens, which he staggered into the mill to pluck, while his friends, with the smiles of the elect, passed around guns which went off in every direction.

---

* Choruses of Turkish origin which ended with the words *aman, aman.*

The chamois having been picked to the bone, everyone lay back in the clover for one of those siestas in which you feel the earth pushing up along the length of your spine. Around six o'clock, as none of the sleepers had stirred, we returned to Prilep. Our bikes struck sparks. Legs aching but clear-headed, we really wanted to work. Our full stomachs swelled in rustic satisfaction; there's nothing like the spectacle of happiness to get one off to a good start.

It was as well that the Turks made the best of Sundays and the fields, because the inhabitants of Prilep gave them a hard time in town. The Macedonians, who felt exploited by Belgrade, turned on Islam which had ground them down before. They were wrong, of course; the few Turks in the town formed a guileless, close-knit family whose soul was less troubled than their own.

Between their minarets and their redeeming gardens, the Turks formed a pastoral island well fortified against nightmares; a civilisation of melons, turbans, gold paper flowers, beards, bludgeons, filial respect, hawthorns, shallots and farts, with a pronounced taste for their plum orchards, which were sometimes invaded by bears seduced by the smell of early fruit, which would give them terrible diarrhoea at night.

The natives of Prilep preferred to keep their distance, depriving themselves of the Turks' help and bullying them on the sly – like all peoples who have suffered too much and then seek justice too late, at cross-purposes, and without regard for their own interests.

The Macedonian dialect includes Greek, Bulgarian, Serbian and Turkish words, not to mention local terms. They speak faster than the Serbs and interlocutors are less patient, which meant that the phrases we had picked up in Belgrade didn't get us very far. When the coffin-maker asked Thierry the time, it was always the same: one indicated that he couldn't say it, but pointed to his wristwatch; the other indicated that he couldn't read it. At least we always reached an understanding as to what was impossible.

While planing his boards, the coffin-maker chatted to his mate in the shop next door, who, by happy coincidence, made guns. Death never entered their conversation, which was studded with bursts of laughter and those words – which by dint of seeing them spelt out in toilets or as graffiti – one couldn't help but know. As for the coffins, they were simply wicker constructions covered in plywood or even cardboard, beautifully decorated: orange, black and blue with great daubs of gold and silver-painted trefoil crosses. It was sumptuous rubbish that a child could demolish with one kick. But where trees were rare, why consign good wood to the earth?

By working with death the carpenter ended up resembling it. At siesta time, he rested on a plank supported on two trestles, his chin in the air, his large hands joined over his stomach. You could scarcely see him breathing. Even the flies were deceived. The plank was narrow: if he stirred, he would fall; if he fell, he would die.

On holidays he would exhibit his wares in the street, like the florist or the confectioner, at all prices and for all ages. The display was a bit macabre, but no one else in town had such beautiful colours. Sometimes a peasant woman dressed in black would come along, bargain vigorously, and then walk off decidedly, a little coffin under her arm. It wasn't so striking because there life and death confronted each other every day, like two shrews with no mediator to mollify their quarrel. Tough countries trying to make up for lost time don't permit such niceties. In Prilep, when someone isn't smiling they are either asleep or gnashing their teeth. Moments that aren't taken up by weariness or anxiety are soon stuffed with satisfaction, like an explosion meant to be heard a long way off. Nothing is neglected that might aid survival; hence the intensity of their music, which is some of the most powerful in the land. Those taut, anxious voices suddenly become sunny and take on a kind of imperious urgency which sends musicians rushing to their instruments. In short, one is perpetually on the alert… it's a war in which one must neither dawdle nor sleep.

I had plenty of time to think about it at night, battling with the fleas. They devoured me. I saw them everywhere in town: the grocer leaned over to slice the cheese… a flea came out of his shirt, crawled over his chin without his flinching, travelled across his Adam's apple and disappeared into the flannel. If I lost sight of it for a moment, I just had to be resigned: that flea was for me. In the evening, turning back the sheet, a red dust cloud flew towards my face; neither DDT nor lashings of water had any effect. At the other end of the room, Thierry had ten hours sleep a night, hands under his head, and not a bite.

Those insects, or the heavy wine I used to drink in an effort to knock myself out, or the happiness of being away, used to wake me before dawn. The room would be bathed in shadow and the smell of turpentine and brushes. I would hear Thierry, wrapped up in his sleeping bag, dreaming aloud: 'Don't shit on my paintings... eh! flies!' I envied the way he had calmly gone back to painting. I was still pretending to write, trembling in front of my notes like a kid in front of a cop. I would go downstairs, shoes in hand. My stomach clenched, my mind sharp, I tramped the cold dust of the streets, swept by gusts of air that bore the scent of stone from the mountains. The sun hadn't risen, but stooped grey forms were already at work in the tobacco fields. You could hear the donkeys braying around the town, the cocks crowing by the roadside, then the pigeons on top of the minarets as the sun touched the first crests. One surprised the town swimming up through the mists of a September dawn in lovely innocence, with a kind of fresh courage. I could easily forgive it the fleas, the apathy, duplicity and fears, and wished it a better future.

Returning through the hotel courtyard, I would come across the maid whose job it was to clean out the toilets. A sturdy, ruddy, strapping girl, firm on her large bare feet, she lugged the shit around and talked to herself, greeting me in the hallway with raucous morning playfulness. One day I absently replied to her in German. She stopped abruptly, put down her overflowing buckets and smiled at me, revealing her chipped teeth. I would have preferred her to put down her load a bit further away, but it was a lovely smile, unexpectedly impish and feminine from such a great sow.

'So... *du bist Deutsch?*' she said, raising her eyebrows.

'No.'

The hands she had crossed on her pinafore had lost their nails, and I noticed that her toenails were horribly squashed.

'*Ich bin Jüdin und Makedonin,*' she said, '*aber Deutschland kenn ich gut. Drei Jahre...*' she raised three fingers '*...während des Krieges, im Lager Ravensbrück... sher schlect, Kameraden kaput. Verstanden?... aber Deutschland kenn ich doch gut,*'* she finished, with a sort of satisfaction.

* 'I am Jewish and Macedonian,' she said, 'so I know Germany well. Three years... during the war, I was in Ravensbrück camp... very bad, all my friends gone. You understand?... so I know Germany very well.'

After that, whenever our paths crossed she made some sign or winked conspiratorially; having both been to Germany – however different the circumstances – we had that at least in common. I have never forgotten that woman, nor her way of coming to terms with her memories. Beyond a certain degree of hardship or misery, life often revives and heals the scars. As time passed, deportation had become a kind of voyage and even, thanks to the almost terrifying capacity of memory to transform horror into courage, a voyage that she could easily mention. Any way of seeing the world is good, as long as one returns. It was a shaming paradox for her erstwhile tormentors: the period in Germany had become her main source of pride, an adventure which might be envied by all those unfortunates in Prilep who had to make do with being tormented at home.

Midday: an onion, a pepper, hard bread and goats cheese, a glass of white wine and a cup of bitter, frothy Turkish coffee. At night: mutton kebabs, and the small luxury of a plum brandy under the sorb-apple trees, which hiked up the price of the meal a bit. Adding the excellent local cigarettes and postage, the two of us could live on seven hundred dinars (about £2) a day.

If one was thirsty, it was best to go for melons, chosen by rattling them against the ear. It was better to avoid the water. The natives didn't make great claims for theirs anyway, they thought it had a poor, common taste. I never noticed that, but who cares in our countries about the taste of water? In Macedonia they were crazy about it; they would urge you to walk five miles to reach a stream where the water was excellent. They didn't much like Bosnia, but honesty obliged them to admit that its water was incomparable, refreshing, etc... a dreamy silence would descend, and they'd cluck their tongues.

There were other things to watch out for: bruised fruit which flies had visited; some bits of fat that instinctively – unless it would cause offence – one left on the plate; handshakes after which one avoided rubbing one's eyes, for fear of trachoma. There were warnings, but no iron rules: it was just a case of listening to the body's music, unnoticed for so long, which gradually returned and with which one needs to be in harmony. Remember too that a local diet contains its own antidotes – tea, garlic, yoghurt, onions – and that health is a dynamic equilibrium, made up of a set of infections that are tolerated to a greater or lesser extent. When they aren't, one pays for a dodgy radish or a mouthful of polluted water with days of cyclonic diarrhoea. With sweating foreheads, we'd rush to the Turkish-style toilets and resign ourselves to staying there, despite hammering on the door, because dysentery grants only brief respites.

When I found myself in this low situation, the town would get me down. It was very sudden: it was enough to have a lowering sky and a few drops of rain for the streets to be transformed into quagmires; then dusk fell and Prilep, so attractive an hour before, would become soggy like cheap paper. Everything in it that was misshapen, nauseating and deceptive would emerge with nightmarish clarity: the sore flanks of the donkeys, feverish eyes and ragged jackets, rotten teeth and those shrill, wary voices moulded by five centuries of occupation and conspiracies – right down to the mauve offal in the butchers' shops, which seemed to be calling out for help, as though meat could die twice.

First, as is only natural, I would defend myself by hate. In my mind I poured acid over the street, cauterising it. Then I tried opposing disorder by order. Retreating to my room, I swept the floor, scrubbed myself down, dealt briefly with pending letters and went back to work, forcing myself to expunge the rhetoric, the patching-up, the tricks. It was a modest enough ritual, probably with a long history, but you make the best of what's to hand.

When I'd got over that, I would see through the window, in the evening sunshine, the white houses still steaming from the downpour, the mountain chain spread out beneath a washed sky, and the army of tobacco plants which surrounded the town with their reassuring, sturdy leaves. Once again I would find myself in a solid world, at the heart of a gilded icon. The town had revived. I could dream. For ten days it would be likeable, until the next bout – the vaccination process continued.

Travelling provides occasions for shaking oneself up but not, as people believe, freedom. Indeed it involves a kind of reduction: deprived of one's usual setting, the customary routine stripped away like so much wrapping paper, the traveller finds himself reduced to more modest proportions – but also more open to curiosity, to intuition, to love at first sight.

So one morning, without knowing why, we followed in the steps of a filly that a peasant was taking to wash in the river. A high-stepping filly, with eyes like chestnuts beneath half-open lids and a faultless coat under which the muscles rippled with seductive majesty: she was the most womanly thing I had seen in Yugoslavia. The shopkeepers turned to look at her in the street. We silently followed her fresh footprints in the dust, like two old lechers, our hearts in our throats. We were literally rinsing our eyes. Because the eye needs those new, whole things that only Nature provides: the swollen tobacco shoots, a donkey's silken ear, the shells of young tortoises.

Nature renews itself with such vigour there that man, by comparison, seems to have been born old. Faces harden and alter suddenly, like coins flattened on a railway track: tanned, scarred, worked on by stubble, smallpox, weariness or anxiety. The most striking, the most handsome, even the boys' faces, look as though an army of boots has trampled over them. You never see, as at home, soft, thoughtful, healthily unformed faces, whose future is yet to be written on them.

Only the old people had some freshness, a second round, wrung from life.

At daybreak, in the allotments surrounding the town, we often came across Muslims with carefully trimmed beards, sitting on a rug amidst the beans, silently inhaling the smell of the earth and savouring the early light with that talent for self-contained moments of refreshment and content which the countryside and Islam develop so soundly. When they saw us, they would hail us and invite us to sit down, take a knife from their trousers and cut one of those slices of melon that would leave a pink, sticky mark from mouth to ear.

In this way we encountered the mullah of the mosque, who knew a bit of German. He rolled us cigarettes and then courteously introduced himself, indicating the minaret. And we...?

'Painter and journalist...'

'*Ganz wie Sie wollen* – just as you please,' politely replied the mullah, to whom these professions were of no account, and returned to his meditation.

Another morning, as I crouched in the public gardens to photograph the mosque, with one eye shut and the other on the viewfinder, something warm, rough and sandy-smelling rubbed against my head. I thought it was a donkey – there were lots around, familiar beasts who nuzzled one's armpits – and calmly went on with my photo. But it was an old peasant, who had tiptoed over to rub his cheek against mine to make his seventy- and eighty-year-old mates laugh. He went off doubled up with laughter; it made his day.

The same day, through the window of the Jadran café, I glimpsed another of those old trolls with a fleecy-lined cap, a few crumbs of *passa-tempo* (toasted sunflower seeds) in his beard, blowing on a small wooden propeller in a charming way. Thank Heavens for such freshness of heart!

Those old jokers were the lightest spirits in town. As they became whiter and more stooped, so they became more distinctive and detached, and came to resemble those stick figures that children draw on walls. Such men scarcely exist in our societies, where the mind is developed at the expense of feelings, but there not a day passed without our meeting one of those pithy, mischievous, rash creatures, carrying hay or patching slippers, who always made me want to hug them and burst into tears.

The accordionist who played for the dances in the Macedonia's garden on Saturday nights wasn't bad, but his instrument's cracked bellows sent a jet of cold air into his face, which made him play with his eyes almost shut. Thierry lent him his own accordion, 'a hundred and twenty bass', powerful enough to raise the dead, and the accordionist had played so much and drunk so much that we had to get together in fits of laughter to take it away, in case he fell flat on his face with it. Here, as in Serbia, music is a passion. It is also a password for a stranger: if he loves it, he'll make friends. If he records it, the whole world – including the police – busies itself touting for musicians.

Thus several days before we left, the singing teacher came early to shout under our window that he had the best bagpiper in the land locked up in his classroom. We followed him, a bit embarrassed. We hadn't meant anyone to go to these lengths, but his catch was quite something: a balding old man, his eyes gleaming with mischief, drowsing beneath the blackboard with his bagpipes between his knees. He was called *Lefteria* – which roughly means 'Liberty' – and for thirty years he had roamed the roads of Macedonia, playing at weddings and baptisms. He looked mortified at having been penned in by the teacher. We had to invite him to the Jadran and offer him four rounds before he'd consider playing. Meanwhile a real court had gathered to hear him: the coffin-seller, the post-office worker, the Party secretary, all the boys in their thirties, who showed him great respect.

The sun was at its zenith and the heat was tremendous. The bagpipe was stinking, its skin and badly tanned leather attracting a horde of flies which formed buzzing haloes around heads beaded with sweat. The bagpipe was an entire sheepskin, finished with an embouchure towards the top, and below, a droner and a pipe with five holes on which his fingers manipulated the acid gusts of air expelled from the sack. He played a wedding song, addressed by the bride to her husband on crossing the threshold of her new home:

'You have parted me from my father and brother
You have taken me away from my mother
Ah! Why did I fall in love with you?'

Macedonian tunes usually have something scholarly and ornate about them, reminiscent of church music. Even in the most vigorous ones there is an air of Christian melancholy. One would think that in the era when there was nothing but scrub, Byzantine monks must have chanted their canticles and psalms in the same harsh, piercing, blood-stained voices. The bagpipe, however, was an exception. It cannot have changed since the time of the House of Atreus. It is antique, the bagpipe, and made to express immemorial things: the cry of the jay, the sound of a downpour, the panic of a girl pursued. And it is really Pan's instrument because the heart of the blower, the skin and the mouthpiece all belong to his reign. The old man played faster and faster. We were carried away. When he came to the final dance, an imperious cackling welled up from the depths of the ages, the room was black with people, and all the backsides and big toes in the café were wiggling.

After that day, the operator of Radio Prilep, who made up the programmes as he pleased, sent a little French music over the loud-speakers in the square to please us. When the sun abandoned the boiling street and the town looked out through half-closed eyes, the quivering of Ravel's quartet stole trembling across the carts and roofs, and we savoured fifteen minutes of dandified capitalist broadcasting, kindly provided by a good Marxist.

There were plenty of militants in Prilep. The most fortunate rose in bronze above the dusty squares, one hand on the book of doctrine, or sat in Skopje in the Macedonian government. The others were several powerful men in the militia, whose names were spoken in whispers, and lots of native children who had bravely thrown themselves into the Resistance and seemed bewildered to have accomplished the revolution.

This wasn't their first one, however. Prilep had always been a recalcitrant town which struck against the state at the level of the commune or the region. Since at least the tenth century men had taken to the maquis under someone or other's heel, and had honourably held the mountains, which sometimes bore their names. Irregular status has always been the recourse of the discontented. Now it was over: since the Maquis had taken power, there was no more question of the maquis. That was the past, and the town's Communists had no truck with the past.

Above all they were concerned with youth, and with their very active propaganda. The choir was theirs. The football team, the Sunday competitions, the buses crammed with aggressive players – all theirs; the new swimming pool as well, worth several points in this burnt, dry land. From six o'clock there was a crush of young people. At first it was good to see them so well-built, muscled to the chin. Then they seemed all too similar, young brutes whom one could already imagine as policemen. Then we murmured to ourselves the words 'state machine', and this hackneyed formula was somewhat soothing... until we realised that it was, after all, very seductive for young people who didn't have machines, or a state.

The eve of our departure for Greece, Ayub, the Turkish barber, invited us to his place – to show us his radio. It was a superb set that he had ordered from Salonika after several years saving; he had covered it, not in gold, but in mirrors. He easily located Suisse-romande for us... It was only six weeks since we'd left, but the well-fed, pedagogic voices of the announcers gave us a start. They were definitely the blackboard voices of home. I scarcely dared open my mouth to speak for fear of hearing myself sounding just like them. I wondered how many roads we'd need to travel and what mischief we'd have to get up to in order to lose that pastoral tone.

Ayub was delighted by our attentiveness; he'd scored a hit, his radio hadn't let him down. For him, however, everything worked well: the coffee was boiling, the donkey in the courtyard was well-groomed, and he assured us that his wife was perfection – which we took on trust since, as a good Muslim, she refused to appear.

'And your father?'

'*Er sitzt und raucht* – he sits and smokes,' replied Ayub, completing the idyllic image of his family.

We returned to the hotel, the moon at our backs. Ayub accompanied us and in the darkness his carefully waved hair gave off whiffs of a flat perfume that was faintly nauseating. Just as we reached the municipal gardens, where the local cinema was showing a Western in the open air, the central fuses crackled and the town went out like a candle, the screen too, and a great sound of frustration rose up from the audience.

'*Elektricität Prilep… extra – prima,*' sighed Ayub.

It was easy for us to chuckle: our bags were packed and we were leaving the next day.

The Road to Anatolia

WHEN YOU LEAVE Yugoslavia for Greece, the blue – the colour of the Balkans – follows you, but its nature changes; you move from a slightly muted night-blue to an intensely gay sea-blue, which affects the nervous system like caffeine. That's just as well, as the rhythm of conversations and exchanges speeds up considerably. You've got into the habit of explaining things slowly – usually twice rather than once – and of pausing over words for comprehension to catch up. Once across the border, this is no longer necessary: a listener will interrupt you in mid-flow with impatient gestures – he's got it – and as you go on talking he gets carried away, having already launched into a kind of pantomime which contains his response.

Indeed the Greeks sometimes understand more than you intend; at the border crossing, because I assumed more authority than my voice usually conveys, I was immediately treated with the special indulgence reserved for the timid.

For the first couple of days this agility caught us unawares. We were at least one response behind, our gestures too, then we became attuned to their receptive awareness and the fun began.

Alexandroúpolis
After the furnace of the road from Salonica to Alexandroúpolis, what a pleasure to sit in front of a white tablecloth, on a little quay with smooth, round cobblestones. For an instant the fried fish gleamed like gold ingots on our plates, then the sun sank below a purple sea and drained the colour away.

I thought of those loud lamentations with which primitive civilisations accompanied the death of light each evening, and suddenly they seemed so appropriate that I was prepared to hear behind me a whole village in tears.

But no, not a one. Apparently they had got used to it.

Constantinople

The very morning we arrived, we ferried the car across to the Asian shore and were prowling through the little streets of the Moda neighbourhood in search of a lodging that would beckon to us, when a frail but imperious voice calling out in French made us turn round. It belonged to a large woman with snow-white hair, wearing a heavy amethyst brooch and elegant mourning. From the top of her steps she gazed thoughtfully at our bags, as if they reminded her of something, and asked what we were looking for. We explained.

'My season ended last week, but I've kept on my servants and I rather like travellers. You can stay here.' With her cigarette-holder, she indicated a little gold plate above the door: Moda-Palas.

In silence our bags were taken across a sombre Victorian dining room. On the sideboard, a mustard cat was asleep between ornate Christofle teapots. The room gave on to a faded garden, and had a light but distinct odour of polish and mildew. Except for a chambermaid, the *maître d'hôtel* and Madame Wanda, the proprietress, the hotel was deserted and, with its shutters closed, more intimidating than a tomb. We already found ourselves lowering our voices, but since the voyage had to pass through the Moda-Palas, there was nothing for it but to acquiesce. On one side the hotel looked out on the Sea of Marmara and the Isle of Princes, where unruly claimants were once exiled. On the other, it backed on to a hill from which you could see the shore of Europe beneath a mauve sky, the Pera Tower and the buildings of the old town with their flowering wisteria and their dilapidated façades the colour of waterlogged wood.

'So what do you hope to sell here?' said the old lady, looking at the tape recorder and the easel.

'Paintings, articles... a lecture perhaps.'

'Have you had a lucky life?'

'So far, yes.'

'Well, you won't have much luck here, believe me. Madame Wanda tells you so.' There was perhaps a hint of pity in her voice.

We spent a week prospecting the town. Thierry was looking for somewhere to exhibit his drawings. I went round the newspapers, the radio, the cultural associations to try to place something. I even tried the Usküdar French lycée in the hope of finding dunces and teaching. Nothing came up. We walked around all day, the sun beating down on our shoulders, in the sweltering flannel suits we thought indispensable to the success of our projects. At night we would meet, harassed and stammering, with Turkey's singular French spelling our only consolation: *Fileminyon... Agno alobergine... Kudefer & Misenpli*, picked up in passing from a restaurant menu or in a hairdresser's window.

Moreover, a popular hit in town seemed to sound the knell for our modest enterprise. This song was entitled '*Kübik Nikel Mobilialar*' – a whole way of life encapsulated. The Istanbul bourgeois didn't care at all for modern painting, nor for articles by foreigners. No, they wanted everyday things: nickel-plated furniture, in fact, and powerful red-haired singers, and interminable games of backgammon under the plane trees, with plenty of arguments. A bit of poetry, plenty of grub, American cars, and a future revealed in coffee grounds. As for art, they were convinced that they had already produced more than their share; they had only to look at their marvellous mosques – Ali, the blue one; Suleiman's, the colour of tobacco, and Ortaköy, in white and gold – to convince themselves; or they could go and look in the windows of the 'Old Seraglio' at the sumptuous porcelain sent by the Chinese emperors, and measure how highly esteemed their country had been at the other end of the world. They thought the time had come to be practical and they set about it in a jolly way. It was up to them, of course, but our business suffered enormously from their self-satisfaction. The city was dear, and after ten days we still hadn't earned a single kurus.

We were thus reduced to corncobs on skewers or cheap restaurants that were far from inviting. There are many of those, on the shore of Asia, and many opportunities to get violently sick. First of all your head burns, then the piss-yellow mounts from your liver to your eyes, then endless vomiting and fever. With just enough strength to cancel the next day's appointment and get to bed, you then spend a week counting the flowers on the wallpaper and racking your brain to identify the poisonous dish. In a way, it was better to fall ill in Constantinople; once on the Anatolian roads for a month or so, it would be impossible.

On the days he wasn't drawing, Thierry bravely continued his rounds like a broken spinning-top. I would see him set out each morning, his carefully laundered shirt drying on his back, under his arm the drawings that were gradually covered with indifferent fingerprints. Because he was showing them in such unappreciative circumstances, he had ended up hating them. He would return beside himself, and while standing and sponging himself down, would recount his day. A gallery-owner whom he'd gone to immense trouble to contact, and on whom he had pinned so much hope, had energetically explained to him why it was that a painter in Istanbul had to starve. The businessmen whom he'd been told were collectors would hold out ten lirettes without even looking at his work; but when Thierry, mortified, offered them a drawing in exchange, they would become animated, put on their glasses, minutely compare them and then cleverly choose the best and most expensive ones. Going door-to-door around the Swiss businessmen whose addresses he'd got hold of was scarcely more successful. They kept him waiting like a pedlar in the pantry, where he'd have tea with the cook – a White Russian or a Ukranian émigré – who would tell him breathtaking stories while gazing at his sketches. This always helped to pass the time, and he could rest his feet. The lady of the house would refuse to appear – a compatriot who came to the door to sell his paintings, three thousand miles away from Berne; one knew where that began but who knows where it might lead – but she would eventually send down some small change, which we would return the same evening together with a very rude note in the style of Corneille, of which those fine housewives wouldn't understand a word.

Our setbacks were no surprise to one person: the chambermaid at the Moda-Palas. A bitter, thin woman, Polish like the proprietress, who wore on her grey hair one of those heavy linen tiaras such as you still see in the grand Montreux hotels, and did all her work with a cigarette in her mouth. Every morning, when she brought the tea, she would sit on the end of the bed and make us rehearse the defeats of the previous day. The room would still be grey, and you could hear the sirens of the boats on the Bosphorus. She would listen with

lowered eyes, knocking ash into a saucer and greeting each lamentable detail with a vigorous shake of the head. It gave her pleasure, though, this litany of misfortune, as though she were hearing again a song she herself had often sung. I don't know what problems she'd had, but to her ours seemed totally commonplace and mild. From time to time she would turn towards us with a gesture of her hands which seemed to say 'Of course'. It was her means of encouragement.

She spent her days in the pantry with Osman, the *maître d'hôtel*, constantly polishing the tumblers, samovars and teapots. At night they both waited on Mme Wanda, who dined alone without uttering a word. Once the washing-up was done, they joined her for a game of whist which would go on until the early hours of the morning. No matter how late we returned, we'd find them sitting up beneath the yellow silk lamp, absorbed in their cards. They didn't raise their eyes except to point to the sideboard and the plate of honey cake prepared for us.

I got better, but our affairs didn't. A long piece on Lapland, with photos, which I'd had to copy out in capitals the size of sugarlumps for the short-sighted translator, brought in only fifteen lirettes. Two meals. Mme Wanda had been right: Istanbul was a hard nut to crack.

And the season was getting on. The west wind brought the pop-pop of hunting guns. In the extensive, brown, fallow lands alongside the Edirne road, vividly painted taxis bristling with guns, gamebags, and braces of woodcock were scattered like coloured pebbles. Shoals of swordfish, glinting turquoise, made their way silently through the Straits on their way south. The wealthy bourgeois of the town went down to their estates in Brousse or Smyrna, in cadillacs stuffed with sweets. On the Asian shore, starlings cawed softly in the greenery of the sorb-apple trees. Along the narrow streets going up to the Moda, in the taverns lit by gas-lamps, porters and drivers, seated in front of their curd-milk, slowly spelled out the newspaper, letter by letter, so that the whole neighbourhood resounded with this extraordinarily sad, murmured incantation. The over-ripe, golden autumn which had taken hold of the town tugged at our heartstrings. The nomadic life makes you sensitive to the seasons: you rely on them, even become part of the season itself, and each time they change, it seems you have to tear yourself away from a place where you have learned to live.

That night, on my way back from the newspaper offices, I stopped in front of Haidarpasha Station to look at the trains sleeping at its platforms. The carriages were marked BAGHDAD, BEIRUT, KONYA-ANADOLU. It was autumn in Istanbul, summer in Baghdad, perhaps winter in Anatolia. We decided to leave the same night.

At the Moda-Palas the servants were asleep for once. We packed in silence. There was still a light in the proprietress's room. Her door was ajar and we peeped in to say goodbye and thanks. Mme Wanda didn't see us immediately. She was sitting motionless in a four-poster bed, a night light next to her, a book open in front of her – Merimée, I remember – but no longer turning its pages. We had never seen her wide-awake and alert, as though there were always ancient voices distracting her. We hardly recognised her. We spoke softly in order not to frighten her. She saw us, saw our travelling gear and said, 'God bless you, my little pigeons... the Madonna protect you, my little lambs...' and then she began to speak in Polish. She continued, without pausing, in tones of such desolate tenderness that it took us a moment to realise that she was no longer looking at us nor speaking to us, but to one of those ancient shadows, loved and lost, which accompany the old into exile and linger in the depths of their lives... We closed the door.

Leaving Istanbul at around two in the morning, unless we encountered rain we thought we could reach Ankara before nightfall.

The Ankara road
October

North-west of Ankara the trail crosses vast plateaux as bare as a hand. You must look downwards to see any crops: they are lodged below, in the rifts cracked open and enlarged by rivers. At the bottom of such green canyons you see glistening willows and vines, some animals – buffaloes and sheep – wandering between piles of dung, a few houses around a wooden mosque, and smoke rising up to the level of the plateau, where it is caught and carried away by the wind. Sometimes the pelt of a bear, freshly skinned, is nailed to a barn-door.

You have to go down there for a siesta, after hours of driving, to the bottom of one of those muffled little Arcadias, to really understand the meaning of the word 'bucolic'. Stretched out on your back on the grass, which is humming with bees, you gaze at the sky – and nothing, unless the speed of the clouds, recalls the autumnal gusts of wind roaring about your ears all morning.

In these coombs the villagers are well-off and the crops well tended. But one hasn't the heart to steal so much as a walnut, nor would anybody offer one: they must be counted on the tree. It was fair enough: agriculture in 'islets', this labouring in miniature, made for very careful peasants, and watchful ones. Moreover it has always been this way: in the Hittite excavations of Hattusas-Bogasköy they found tablets over three thousand years old with touchingly minute inventories of goods, down to the last details of one hop-plant or one newborn pup.

The Sungurlu road

Only a slight difference in texture and the truck-marks distinguished the dirt road from the brown earth surrounding it and stretching out to the horizon. Feet hot in their boots, one hand on the steering wheel, earth as far as we could see, we started out on that vast countryside, saying: this time the world has changed scale, it's really the beginning of Asia!

Sometimes you could make out the lighter beige smudge of a herd on the hillside, or the puff of a flight of starlings between the road and the green sky. Mostly you couldn't see anything... but you could hear – you should be able to tape-record the sound of Anatolia – a slow, inexplicable whining, which began on a shrill note, went down a tone, went back up horribly, and persisted. It was a piercing sound, well constructed for travelling those leathery expanses, sad enough to raise goosepimples and penetrating beyond the reassuring sound of the engine. Our eyes widened, we pinched ourselves, but there was nothing! Then we saw a black spot, and this sort of music grew unbearably loud. Some time later we caught up with a pair of oxen and their driver, who slept with a cap over his nose, perched on a heavy cart with solid wheels, their axles straining and grinding at each turn. We passed him in the knowledge that, at our pace, its dreadful song of a soul in torment would pursue us right into the night. As for the trucks, their headlamps were visible for at least an hour before we met. We would lose them, find them again, forget about them, and suddenly they'd be there. For a few seconds our lights would show their enormous bodies painted in pink or apple green, scattered with flowers, then they would disappear into the distance, pitching over the bare earth like monstrous bouquets.

We also became intrigued by two dear little gold lights which lit up, went out, blinked, and seemed to retreat before us. We thought – because of the width between them – that they must belong to a tourist van... but when we came upon them, they turned out to belong to an owl dozing on the pillar of a bridge alongside the track, and with a cry it rose like a heavy snowflake in the draught from the car.

Those solid-wheel carts looked exactly like the kind you'd find in Babylonian tombs: so their axles had been disturbing the silence of Anatolia for four thousand years. That wasn't bad going, but on the track linking Bogasköy with Sungurlu we came across something even older. The afternoon was getting on, the sky was clear, we were crossing an absolutely deserted plain. The atmosphere was so transparent that you could make out a lone tree standing twenty miles away. And suddenly... tock... tocktock... tack... a hail of light knocks sounding louder as we went on, clear and irritating. A bit like the crackling of dry twigs in a fire, or metal at white-heat expanding and contracting. Thierry stopped the car, going pale, and I shared his fear: we must have lost oil, overheated and stripped the differentials. But we were mistaken, because the noise didn't stop. In fact it increased, just on our left. We went over to look: just across the bank which ran along one side of the road the plain was black with tortoises, who were rapt in their autumn amours and were knocking their shells together. The male used his like a ram to poke his companion and push her towards a stone or tuft of dry grass, where she was cornered. They were a little bit smaller than the females. At the moment of coupling the males would be standing straight up to reach them, stretching out their necks, opening their bright red mouths and letting out strident cries. As we left, we could see tortoises in all directions hastening slowly over the plain to their rendezvous. Night fell, and they were no longer to be heard.

Sungurlu

At six o'clock, before the sun was up, the peasants were already seated at the inn with a glass of tea on a blue enamel saucer. Voices and muddy footsteps mingled. Huge hounds of uncertain breed went sniffing from table to table. When there was a little more light, the studs on their collars and the copper trays began to gleam, picked out, while the ground, old clothes and faces were still in shadow. Brown caps, dull saffron shirts and rags gayer than gypsies' passed through the square. The horses wore a collar made of a peeled bough that made a great hoop behind their ears; teams of horses and some big, peeling trucks were parked around the café. Two old men with woolly beards had just left their table and waded out into the early morning, laughing, squashing a rat which ran alongside the house. In the room you could make out a poster representing a Mexican peasant in a sombrero, with the legend 'Discover the world through Turkish radio!' There was a radio, certainly, but the customers had been fiddling with it for twenty minutes without being able to get Ankara.

Then the clay and mud were lit up by a thousand fires and the autumn sun rose up over the six horizons still separating us from the sea. All the roads round the town were carpeted with willow leaves, smelling good, silently crushed by the teams of horses. Such expanses of land, pungent odours, the feeling that one's best years lie ahead – they increase the pleasure of living, like making love.

The Road to Anatolia

Merzifon
After twelve hours' drive

At nine o'clock at night the only restaurant still open in Merzifon was the Pilots' Club. There was a military base just outside the town. White tablecloths, potted laurel trees, waiters in red uniforms – there is an indirect but sure way of retreating when one has strayed into that kind of trap. We knew what to do, but that evening we decided to treat ourselves to a little luxury. We had been driving since 5 a.m. and we had to push on that evening, to steal a march on the snow. So we ate and each drained a tankard of smooth wine half full of gritty ice cubes, looking at a dozen pilots dancing with each other to the sound of their out-of-tune piano. As they were all more or less the same height, they held their annoying caps in their hands in order to dance closer. I could quite believe that distractions were few and far between here, and dancing partners even scarcer; all the same, their imitation seemed a little too languorous. Those who had seen the accordion and guitar sticking out of our bags asked very politely if we would play something. Waltzes and *javas*: the soldiers swayed their hips, tenderly entwined.

Thirteen to twenty hours' drive

We left around midnight, fed and rested. The roof was open to a sky sprinkled with stars. We crossed two brown passes talking quietly, then one of my questions went unanswered and I glanced over to see Thierry asleep. I drove slowly until dawn, the lights off to husband the battery. On the last pass which separated us from the coast the dirt road was slippery, and the slopes too steep for the engine. Just before it stalled, I shook Thierry who jumped out and pushed, still asleep. At the next ledge I waited for him to catch me up. At the end of the descent a last, very steep slope obliged us to repeat the manoeuvre, which left Thierry far behind. I stopped the car and, trembling with tiredness, went to have a good pee against the willows whose branches caressed my ears. At the top there had been snow, but here it was still autumnal. The dawn was humid and mild. A lemon glow bordered the sky above the Black Sea; mist floated between the glistening trees. Lying in the shining grass, I congratulated myself on being in the world, on... on what, really? When you're that tired, optimism needs no reasons.

Fifteen minutes later, Thierry emerged from the night, drew level with me and went striding ahead, asleep on his feet.

The Ordu road
Twentieth hour of driving

It was my turn to sleep. Sleeping in a car you dream your own life; the dream changes course and colour at each jolt, hurrying the story to its end when a bigger bump shakes you, or there's a sudden change in the motor's running, or silence unfolds when the driver switches off the engine to rest too. You press your bruised head against the window, and through the dawn mists make out a bank, a copse, a ford or a shepherdess in slippers, a wooden staff in her hand, herding buffaloes whose strong, warm breath wakes you up completely; nothing is lost by waking up to this sort of reality.

The girl warily approaches the window, ready to run away. She is twelve or thirteen, with a red kerchief over her head and a silver piece hung round her neck. These ill-shaven, pale bodies – she is flabbergasted.

A little later

On a black sand beach, we grilled a small fish. Its pink flesh took the colour of smoke. We gathered roots blanched by the sea and slivers of bamboo to build up a fire, then ate squatting by the flames, in a gentle autumn rain, watching the sea given over to a few lighters. An enormous mushroom cloud rose far off in the sky over the coast of the Crimea.

The Ordu Pass

On our map it was not half an inch from the village of Fatsa to Babali, and sixteen hundred feet or so in altitude; but at the very first slope we had to get out and push. The narrow, slick track climbed right through the scrub, with walnut and sorb-apple trees. When it got too steep, the driver pulled out the accelerator, jumped out, and pushed with his shoulder while steering through the window. When the engine stalled anyway, he had to quickly pull the handbrake, or put a stone under the back wheels to stop the heavily loaded car from breaking a gear in rolling back. There was no other recourse than to whistle and shout until one or two peasants arrived, hoes over their shoulders. When they grasped that it was a matter of pushing, their faces lit up, they made two holes in the road to wedge their feet, gripped the car and literally threw us up the slope. They wouldn't accept any money: the pushing was what they enjoyed. Having got into shape, they would have been even happier with a few rounds of Graeco-Roman wrestling. Everything we had been told about the strength of the Turks seemed less than the reality. But we didn't find peasants everywhere, and we had to do the worst bits ourselves: six hours to cover fourteen miles.

At the top of the pass, amid a few dilapidated wooden houses, thirty or so villagers were dancing in the mud to the sound of rather shrill music. They revolved slowly in the rain soaking the bush-covered hills, grasping each other by the elbow or the cuffs of their old black coats, torn to shreds. Their feet were wrapped in clumps of hessian or rags. They had hooked noses and stubbly jaws – murderous faces. The big drum and the clarinet neither speeded up nor paused. A sort of pressure was mounting. Nobody uttered a word; I would have been happier if they had. Even an irritated argument suddenly seemed to me the most peaceful of occupations. I had the uncomfortable feeling that they were methodically ramming gun-powder down a barrel. If a rival village existed somewhere in that misty jungle, it would have done well not to sleep more than a wink.

Even the music was full of menace and the thud of flails. When we tried to get closer to see the instruments better, a wave of shoulders and backbones pushed us back. Nobody had replied to our greetings: they had ignored us completely. I had the tape recorder over my shoulder but this time I didn't dare use it. After an hour we retreated into the fog covering the Black Sea.

Let me briefly digress on the subject of fear. There are such moments in travelling when it arises, and the bread you are chewing sticks in your throat. When you are over-tired, or alone for too long, or are let down for a moment after a burst of enthusiasm, it can take you unawares as you turn a corner, like a cold shower. Fear of the month to come, of the dogs that roam at night around the villages, threatening anything that moves, of the nomads picking up stones on their way down to meet you; even fear of a horse hired at a previous stage, perhaps a vicious brute who has just been biding his time.

You defend yourself as best you can, especially if it's a case of getting on with the job. Humour is an excellent antidote, but it takes two to make it work. Often it's enough to take deep breaths and swallow a throatful of saliva. When it persists, you have to give up the idea of that particular street or mosque, taking that photo. The next day you will romantically berate yourself – quite wrongly. At least half of this uneasiness – you understand later – is instinct aroused by serious danger. You shouldn't ignore such warnings. The stories of bandits and wolves, of course, are exaggerated; nevertheless, between Anatolia and the Khyber Pass are several places where poetic protesters, their hearts on their sleeves and ignorant as stones, wanted to risk everything and did not live to tell the tale. No need of brigands for this; all it takes is a poor, isolated mountain hamlet and irritated bargaining over a loaf of bread or a chicken; instead of being accommodating, your gestures become increasingly wild and you look increasingly anxious, and the moment arrives when six cudgels are rapidly raised above one head. And all your notions about the brotherhood of man will not prevent their descent.

Giresun

At the end of the street leading to the sea, big demijohns of amber wine and lemon squash filtered a thundery light. The wisteria smelled strongly and was loosing its petals. From the bedroom window we could see bandy-legged fishermen going to and fro across the square, chatting and linking their little fingers. Great tomcats slept on the cobblestones amidst the fishbones and guts. Stone-grey rats ran along the gutter. It was a world of its own.

In these small coastal towns people were proud of three things: their physical strength, their hazelnuts, and the perspicacity of their police. The 'constable', usually a young man stubborn as a mule and trussed up in a jacket too tight for him, was at the inn and then outside our door fifteen minutes after we had moved in. Stretched out on our beds, or busy trying to scrape off the accumulated mud, we didn't immediately respond to his tapping, which was promptly transformed by frustration into an avalanche of blows. Very annoyed, we finally opened the door to this intruder who clumsily tried to pretend he was a crook and, without even bothering to be furtive, asked us whether we would like him to change our dollars on the

84

black market. (If you weren't a bit of a provocateur in these dull villages, you'd never be heard of in Ankara.) 'On the black market? Of course not,' we replied, indignantly. Reassured on the main point, the cop then said without any ill-feeling, 'I'm the secret police round here.' We complimented him on such an exalted post and ushered him out.

Sometimes he'd hesitantly come to find us in the evening, bringing a bag of apples and his photograph album. Dim banalities, developed by the ironmonger: a coach trip, half a freighter, the statue of Atatürk at Samsun, a brother-in-law or uncle outside his shop in the rain. We had to play at identifying him, with short back and sides, among twenty identical recruits. We were wrong – silly, refreshing laughter. He was our age and knew almost nothing of the world. For a halfpenny he would have told us all the town's secrets. There was no longer any question of his being on duty.

Trebizond

Here our road left the coast, crossed two mountain ranges via the Zigana and Cop passes, and at Erzurum came out at the level of the high plateau of Anatolia.

I went to inquire at the Post Office, where they told me 'It's good as far as Erzurum, the road's dry. Beyond that, we don't know. We could certainly wire but you would lose time while waiting for the reply, and it's expensive... You'd better go and ask at the school; they have boys boarding from all over Anatolia who'll know what the weather's like at home.'

At the school I explained my business and the French teacher interrupted his lesson to ask the class, speaking slowly in French. No one stirred. Rather embarrassed, he repeated himself in Turkish and at once several crumpled letters were produced from beneath smocks and little hands with black fingernails were raised one after another. No snow yet at Kars... nor at Van, nor at Kagizman... only a little at Karaköse, and that hadn't stayed on the ground. The general opinion was that we could get through for a fortnight yet.

In the square, I found Thierry absorbed in fixing the car. He worked without looking up, surrounded by at least a hundred curious people. It had been like that ever since we left Istanbul, so we'd had time to get used to it. The crowd was always the same:

dimwits, ones who gave advice, well-meaning types, old men in slippers who scrabbled in their pockets and offered a penknife or a bit of sandpaper to help us in our work. We had to grease the springs to make them less brittle, unclog the nozzles, clean the spark-plugs and the distributor, and generally tidy up everything that the jolts and bumps of the previous day had displaced. As the roads became worse, we did all this every day to improve our chances a bit. The two passes which still divided us from Anatolia were worrying.

We were mistaken. The road first of all crossed small, emerald green valleys with thatched villages, heavenly olive and hazel groves stretching out behind them. Then there was a gently sloping valley bordered with rounded blue mountains. At the end of the valley, the first slopes of the pass rose up through forests of gigantic beeches whose yellow leaves burst out like fanfares twenty yards above our heads. The undergrowth was red with wild strawberries, but we dared not stop for fear of not being able to start again on the slope. We had done the pass entirely in first gear, standing on the running boards, ready to leap down. Night fell when we had got past the tree-line. Far below us, in vast grassy coombs, we could see herds milling around black tents, and unsaddled camels lying down by the fires of nomad camps.

Gümüsane
The same night

Here was the mountain and the winter. Sturdy stone houses with steeply sloping roofs to withstand the snow, mules whose nostrils were smoking, brown woollen suits and fur hats, and partridges chirping as they drowsed in their cages above gas-lit groceries full of heavy, colourful, shining goods.

We had only just stopped the car when an urchin came looking for us and took us to the headmaster of a school whom the teachers at Trebizond had advised of our coming. He was a large, cordial man, waiting for us in his pyjamas (in Turkey, as in Persia, as soon as the day's business was done men put on pyjamas), between a basket of apples and a red-hot stove. He didn't have a word of German, English or French. We knew scarcely twenty words of Turkish and were too tired to launch into gesticulations and sketches, so we all sat eating apples and smiling at each other. Then he showed us the skin of a bear he'd killed the previous week, and a silver fox. When we admired it, he offered it to us, holding out the fur with trembling hands while his brown eyes pleaded to keep it. We firmly declined it. He got dressed, took us to the inn, found us the best room and as we slept, fully clothed, a dreamless sleep, he paid the bill. The next morning he returned, accompanied by a mis-shapen dwarf from Istanbul, who was up there looking after his bad lungs, and served as interpreter. He wanted to invite us to spend a few days at his school, and to persuade us began to number on his fingers the village's attractions: the air was good, the houses well heated, the silver mines had been worked since Byzantine times and were the best in the country, the court had not registered any complaints of theft since 1921 and finally, the honey was full of fortifying little waxy flakes. All that was true, and I promised to advertise it: now I have done so. All the same, we wanted to winter in Persia.

Cop Pass

A tiny car with two runners steering it from the outside: this was bound to attract attention. The trucks coming from Erzurum knew about us already, having heard from those who had overtaken us the night before. However far off they were, they greeted us by parping their horns. Sometimes, when our paths crossed, those enormous vehicles going downhill would stop fifty yards away with a squeal of tyres and the drivers would get down to offer us two apples, two cigarettes, or a handful of hazelnuts.

The hospitality, the honesty, the goodwill, a guileless, dependable chauvinism – these were the virtues of the place. They were straightforward and quite palpable. One didn't wonder – as in India – whether people were genuine, or if the virtues were real. They were strikingly obvious, and if by chance they went unnoticed, there was always someone who'd tell you, 'You see – all this... this kindness, these good manners etc – these are the Turks' good qualities.'

The Cop road was excellent because the army kept it in good repair. But it was very steep and rose to almost ten thousand feet. We had to push and run all the way; by the time we reached the top our hearts were ready to burst. The sky was blue and the view stupendous: great undulations of land rolling south as far as the eye could see; the clearly traced road disappeared and then re-emerged at

least twenty times; on the horizon, a thundercloud occupied a tiny portion of the sky. It was one of those landscapes that is absolutely convincing by dint of repetition.

A heavy bell hanging from a gibbet marked the top of the pass. They still rang it when the snow fell, to alert travellers who had lost their way. As I approached, an eagle which had been perching on top of it flew off, glancing the bronze bell with his wings. A wild, interminable resonance descended and spread out over the herd of mountains, most of which do not even have a name.

Bayburt

Thierry remarked that up here it was as though the landscape turned its back on human habitation.

All the same, there was a village: straggling, a leprous yellow scarcely distinguishable from the soil of the plateau; black caps, bare feet, scurvy dogs, trachoma, and, emerging from a building like a swarm of buzzing flies, groups of dark little girls. They looked sidelong at us, wearing black stockings, black smocks, tight plaits and big, white celluloid collars – absurdly ugly collars, but reassuring because they represented school. And wretched as they were, these urchins were learning a bit of arithmetic, the alphabet, how to keep tidy, not to rub their eyes with dirty hands, and to take the regular doses of quinine the teacher handed out. These were definitely weapons. One felt that even here, Atatürk had passed by with his teacher's cane, his wolfish air and his terrible blackboard. In the poor tea house where we rested, a fly-swat hung like a sword beside his colour portrait.

Needless to say the people here dreamed only of cars, water on tap, loudspeakers, consumer goods. In Turkey they point out such things, and you must learn to look at them with a new eye. The splendid wooden mosque – which you can find if you search – nobody would think of showing you, being less aware of what they have than of what they lack. They lack technology: we want to get out of the impasse into which too much technology has led us, our sensibilities saturated to the nth degree with Information and a Culture of distractions. We're counting on their formulae to revive us; they're counting on ours to live. Our paths cross without mutual understanding, and sometimes the traveller gets impatient, but there is a great deal of self-centredness in such impatience.

Erzurum

A dirt-coloured town, with heavy cupolas low on the horizon and handsome, eroded, Ottoman fortifications. Brown earth surrounds it on all sides. It swarms with grubby soldiers and strangers have their papers inspected ten times a day. The only colour is provided by a few elderly lavender-blue fiacres, and the yellow plumes of poplars.

At the end of the afternoon we went along to the district high school to see them dance the *bar*. This is a warrior's dance of Turko-Mongolian origin, and each district of Anatolia has its own way of doing it. The partners – dressed in frogged waistcoats, wide red belts and white trousers slashed with black – circle slowly, waving their sabres in a parody fight. In the eastern provinces, where the dance is popular, most boys have costumes and the game can be improvised on the spot.

Five minutes after we arrived, the teams began to dance under the trees in the playground. It was cold, and night was drawing in. The dance was fine because of the strength encapsulated in each gesture, but the music was finer still. There were only two instruments: the *zurna* – an oriental clarinet – to rouse heroic feelings, and above all the *davul*, an enormous bass drum which is struck on the side. It was the same kettledrum that the Parthians had used to open battle, and that the Hiong-Nan had introduced to China. It is an instrument well-suited to the steppes; its deep sound, more sombre than a tugboat's siren, travels like a slow heartbeat to which the heart itself eventually responds, like the feathery flight of great nightbirds – so faint that it verges on silence.

Once the dance was over, we lingered to watch the younger boys whirling round. The teachers, hands clasped behind their backs, surrounded us in silence. Occasionally they would yell to stop a fist-fight. The older ones with their close-cropped, grizzled hair looked like retired policemen. The younger ones seemed harassed. The French teacher went off by himself from time to time to compose a phrase and repeat it under his breath before speaking to us. He stammered a little, and it was hard for him to understand us. Meeting us was worse for him than an exam; rather as if we, with our school Latin, had had to reply to two travellers emerging from the Alexandrian era. Still, given his isolation, a little French learnt almost without books did him great credit.

It was from this class of ill-paid, badly dressed teachers that the new ideas came, the initiatives and realism so necessary after the euphoria of a national revolution. With the obstinacy of artisans they worked on the gnarled, reticent Anatolian peasantry, at bottom avid for learning, who were the backbone of the country. Even further away, other colleagues – young women among them – had the unkinder fate of struggling to wrench the countryfolk out of filth, cruel superstition and poverty. Anatolia was at the stage of village schoolteachers and the primary school. You can't bypass that stage, and such devotion was needed to get everything underway. Perhaps no careers in Turkey were less rewarding or more useful.

The refectory exuded a heavy smell of food. In the dark playground you could still hear shouts and the click of clogs on the sodden ground. We saw horseless cavaliers parading with their wooden swords, and mournful black wool caps on small, shaven heads. It's always disconcerting to hear children speak a foreign language. One has the impression – perhaps not entirely false – that they make it up as they go along. Probably these were the same shrill cries heard in playgrounds the world over: 'Give back my ball', and as they fight each other, 'Hands off my jersey!'

In Istanbul, one didn't hear anything about these obscure educators; indeed, they would have been completely unknown if they hadn't sometimes published in literary reviews bits of Anatolian folklore, with its extraordinary flavour and pungency. Along with a few soldiers and some 'young Turks' in Ankara, these were the last keepers of the austere Kemalist spirit. These Spartans have not really been recognised for what they are: the representatives of an era of merciless drilling that Turkey officially celebrates while hoping it will never return. After Atatürk's death, the brutal but necessary innovations which he had put in train slowed down considerably. Some civil servants, whom fear had made models of virtue, have not been sorry to discover a taste for compromise and for *baksheesh*. In the provinces the clergy have regained influence, and sometimes encourage the faithful to deface or destroy statues of the 'Father of the Turks', leading them back to sordid medical superstitions (quite alien to the Koran) and setting them against the teacher – that enemy of God – and especially the female teacher, that whore without a veil. Of course not all mullahs are like this, but for every good pastor there are many who are ignorant, rapacious and tyrannical, who dream of gutting Turkey of all innovations and getting their revenge. They are quite capable of it: the holy war they launched against Atatürk when they were desperate was short-lived, and in the atrocious reprisals that followed many Anatolian mosques and madrasas heard spines and skulls crack under clubs. Now they have come back, here and there, and many peasants follow them; old habits are sweet, even if oppressive. Better the devil you know than the devil you don't and, on top of that, the back-breaking effort to understand new things at the end of a crushing day.

And it is left to this type of scholar-sergeant, living an indigent, straitlaced life, badly fed and horribly isolated, to prevent such a recoil and to spread the light that's often so unwelcome. Watching them pace the muddy playground, I recalled the despairing reply of one of their Black Sea colleagues when I'd asked what he lacked most in his teaching: 'Twelve dozen Voltaires…'

We had spent the whole evening with two kindly truck-drivers, trying to mend the ignition. By midnight it was done, and the car pulled like a tractor. Only one pass now separated us from Persia, and four hundred miles from the next poste restante. It was a splendid, cold night and the road – so we were assured – was dry. As we had hardly any Turkish money left, we decided to call in on the army police, rustle up our escort and depart at once.* Stamping our feet in the glacial courtyard of the barracks, we waited while the convoy officer, the interpreter and the jeep driver who had to accompany us as far as Hasankale pulled on uniforms over their pyjamas.

It was a bad road. Thierry had gone on ahead with the officer as passenger. The jeep followed him with difficulty; I sat next to the interpreter. The wind cut across our faces and it was so bumpy that you had to speak through clenched teeth to avoid biting your tongue. Anyway the interpreter – a pale young man lost in an enormous uniform – was not very talkative. He wished we hadn't got him up and avoided my questions by pretending to sleep. After three miles, however, he said:

---

* Erzurum is a military zone. Cameras are forbidden, visits limited to forty-eight hours, and within twenty-five miles of the town foreigners can only drive under escort.

'I learnt French at the Üsküdar *lycée*. I'm a furrier in civilian life…
bankrupt… it was the Greek moneylenders that did it but as long as
I'm in uniform they can't do much… Anyway, the Greeks', he added, as
if in conclusion, 'we'll smash their faces in…' and closed his eyes again.

After fifteen miles my ears were already half-frozen, but I managed
to hear '…in bed we like our women very fat. Haven't you noticed?…
to have an armful, very plump, very white skin – that's Turkish taste…
mine anyway…' The wind carried the rest away.

As we entered Hasankale, I asked whether Erzurum hadn't once
been the Kurdish capital. He laughed in an ugly way, as though to
preface a joke, but only said, 'They won't be back for a long time. We
smashed their faces in… we really smashed their faces in…' (That was
true: in 1921, after the Kurdish rising. In fact the 'minority policy' of
Atatürk seems to have consisted mainly in exterminating one minority
after another.) He continued to mutter away, punching his palm with
his fist. I then noticed his enormous hands, his bearish frame and fists
like logs – and I'd taken him for a runt! It was the outsize uniform,
which even a giant couldn't have filled.

He resumed, 'Every day after work I go Graeco-Roman wrestling.
We have a good team on my street and on Sundays, in the
competitions, we cheat a bit. You should see it – the way we twist and
suffocate… people get hurt every time. What about you? Can you
wrestle?'

At Hasankale the officer got out of the car, wished us good luck and
jumped into the jeep, which turned back. I cautiously shook the
interpreter's hand. We drove on until morning, without passing a
single truck.

East of Erzurum the road is very lonely. Vast distances separate the
villages. For one reason or another we occasionally stopped the car, and
spent the rest of the night outdoors. Warm in big felt jackets and fur
hats with ear-flaps, we listened to the water as it boiled on a primus in
the lee of a wheel. Leaning against a mound, we gazed at the stars, the
ground undulating towards the Caucasus, the phosphorescent eyes of
foxes.

Time passed in brewing tea, the odd remark, cigarettes, then dawn
came up. The widening light caught the plumage of quails and
partridges… and quickly I dropped this wonderful moment to the

bottom of my memory, like a sheet-anchor that one day I could draw up again. You stretch, pace to and fro feeling weightless, and the word 'happiness' seems too thin and limited to describe what has happened.

In the end, the bedrock of existence is not made up of the family, or work, or what others say or think of you, but of moments like this when you are exalted by a transcendent power that is more serene than love. Life dispenses them parsimoniously; our feeble hearts could not stand more.

The Lion and the Sun

WE HAD BEEN driving for an hour and the night was dark when, in the middle of a valley studded with willows, we came across a sort of Empire-style, rather decrepit pavilion in pink roughcast. In the pencil-thin headlight we saw a silhouette caught yawning in the doorway, then it disappeared and a light came on. The Iranian customs…

The acetylene lamp cast its light across the officer's sombre face and deep-set, brilliant eyes. He wore a tunic open over a flannel shirt with speckled stripes, such as our peasants wear. He regarded the car with a smile.

'I am so sorry, my friends,' he said in French, 'you must have a soldier to escort you as far as Maku: that's the law. It's not far – anyway, I'll give you a very small one.'

Where would he get one from? The post was silent and seemed deserted. He disappeared with the lamp, leaving us in the dark, and came back in a moment with a kind of Mongoloid dwarf in puttees, broadly smiling a sweet smile.

'Here he is!' he said, pushing him towards us as though he'd plucked him out of his slipper.

We sat the midget on the bonnet. I drove very slowly over the narrow, treacherous road. Thierry, perched on the passenger seat, lit cigarettes for the soldier who reeked powerfully of mutton and hummed a little tune, his eyes half-closed. On our left, the slopes of Ararat stretched out in the darkness, a wall of over sixteen thousand feet. As we approached the gorge, the air became warmer. Parisian clouds rushed by under a silken moon. The sound of the wheels crushing the sand made a deep, interminable breathing in which the memories of hard Anatolia dissolved, like sugar in tea.

Maku

The inn at Maku was strewn with drowsy greybeards, among whom we discovered the proprietor, prostrate on his prayer rug. He interrupted himself to clear a table on which we could sleep. In the morning, we could just get down and breakfast at it. The other guests had disappeared. Two big coloured pictures, leaning against the wall, represented the Shah and... Jesus at Tiberias. It was a fine day. Through the open door we glimpsed the village, terraced in a horseshoe on the two sides of the defile which separates Persia from the Anatolian plateau: mud houses with gently crumbling roofs, doors painted blue, tiles of vine and curtains of poplars lighter than smoke. A pancake as thin as a newspaper replaced Turkish bread, and a drop of milk the coffee. It was no longer possible to decipher a sign or a milestone; Persian writing goes backwards. So did time: in a night we had moved from the twentieth century AD to the fifteenth century of the Hegira, and changed worlds.

We hung about the police station all morning, waiting for our 'road passes' (every move inside Iran required not only a visa but also special authorisation, the *djavass*), which no one would have dreamed of refusing us, then we left our escort sleeping on a bench, his rifle between his knees. The left shoulder of his ragged tunic sported a marvellously delicate little green lion embroidered against a sun in gold thread.

Tabriz-Azerbaijan

> The beggar's palace is the cloud's shadow
> *Hafiz*

THE LIFE OF A NOMAD is surprising. You cover nine hundred miles in two weeks: the whole of Anatolia in a cloud of dust. One evening, when it's already dark, you reach a town whose slender columned balconies and handful of shivering turkeys somehow appeal to you. In such a town you might drink with two soldiers, a schoolmaster and a stateless doctor who speaks German. Then you yawn, stretch out, fall asleep. In the night the snow falls, covering the roofs, smothering shouts, cutting off roads... and thus you spend six months in Tabriz, Azerbaijan.

To press on eastwards, we would have needed a jeep; to stay, we needed a pass, because Tabriz is in a military zone. And to get a pass, we needed connections. Paulus – the doctor we had met the previous evening – sent us to a police colonel whose tumour he'd removed. He was tightly belted and balding, with the profile of a sparrowhawk, the impression blurred a little by his flushed red cheeks. He had studied in Prussia and interrogated us for a long time in suspicious, very clipped German. In the afternoon we had our reply. His tone had changed; he gazed at us fondly.

'I've asked the general; you may stay here as long as you like.' Then in a very hesitant voice, blushing to the roots of his hair, 'I spent two hours at the mosque and prayed that we would be very, very good friends.'

Doubtless too good for our liking. The following week he was transferred, and we never saw him again. As the poet says, the 'best-laid schemes o' mice an' men...'

What perplexed me most was the guilelessness of the prayer. What a god! You could ask him for anything. But the colonel had kept his word, and our passes were stamped. The next day we rented two

white, low-ceilinged rooms off a small courtyard in the Armenian quarter. We were in Tabriz, and for some time.

Our first evening in the lodgers' kitchen: a widow – a nurse at the hospital – who knew a little English, her elderly mother, and two urchins with jackdaw eyes, scrubbed to the ears, doing their homework under the gas lamp. There were salted cucumbers, sugared green nuts, pancakes and smoky white wine. Neighbours came to sit in the kitchen for a while, to be introduced and to examine these foreign Christians, escaped from an easier world; small shopkeepers encased in dark jerseys, with muffled voices and puffy, anxious faces, who answered all our questions about the town with the proprietorial smiles of those who have known suffering.

Our little street formed the boundary of the Armenian quarter. At the 'bad end' were several Turkish families and a small courtyard through whose closed door the perfidious odour of opium sometimes filtered. *Bad people* said the widow (in English), modestly lowering her eyes. No doubt she would have included old M— in this category. He was a Turkish *arbab* (village-owner), about whom the Armenians told us so many nasty things that we went to visit him out of sheer curiosity. The desire to park our car in the nearby shed he owned was also a draw. He agreed at once and received us courteously, very amused by this overture from 'the enemy'; then he harnessed his barouche and suggested that we accompany him on the Turkey road as far as the hamlet of Sūfian, of which he owned half.

We trotted through the dyers' quarter; on the flat roofs enormous skeins in sumptuous colours were hung out to dry against the pale sky. Then the road gave way to an ocean of red, churned-up earth, interspersed with low walls and leafless trees where crows nested. The countryside still had the bitter scent of trampled leaves and the horses raised clouds of black crickets which leaped across the ruts, chirruping and dying by the thousand. The previous day's snow had almost all melted.

'What about the winter?'

'That was only a shower,' said the old man placidly. 'It'll be here in a matter of days – always soon enough.'

He drove at top speed, asking one question after another in almost perfect French. Like lots of smokers he neglected his clothes, and but for his impeccable manners one would have taken him for the coachman. He amiably explained that, among *arbabs* of his generation, opium was more of a habit than a vice. He never had more than three pipes a day, and could easily give it up. His peasants planted some poppies for him (growing and selling them was forbidden in 1955) in the same way that they provided him with wine, oil and wool. He then asked us a hundred naïve questions about France before admitting that he'd lived there for five years. I was entranced by his discretion; the old sphinx must have known more about everything than he was willing to let on. Anyway he knew his town, and told us about it at some length. When he was a little boy, it was still the biggest city in Iran. Each Friday – the Muslim Sunday – there were wolf fights in the main square, and peasants came from miles around. White wine flowed like water, and there was not a single mullah who raised his voice in protest. The bazaar was famous, not only for the carpets which sometimes fetched fifteen thousand tomans – about seven thousand pounds – per square yard, but also for the best hunting falcons in the Middle East: birds from Tartary which had flown across the Caspian and crashed, exhausted, in the north-west of the province. Tabriz was then wealthier and more populous, and its merchants did good business at the fairs in Leipzig and Nizhni-Novogorod. Then the Bolshevik revolution and the closing of the Russian border plunged the town into a mortal lethargy. The merchant bourgeoisie left for Beirut or Istanbul, and the bazaar's adventurous spirit disappeared. From 1941 to 1945 the Russians occupied the province, and everyone who still had something to lose hastily bundled up their belongings. The occupation was draconian but disciplined. The beggars were swept off the streets and forced to work for a crust of bread. When the Soviets quit the town, they left behind a few asphalted streets, an ultra-modern mill, a university swarming with sympathisers, and stalls loaded with cheap editions of Marx, Lenin and Ehrenburg, specially translated into the Azeri-Turkish dialect. Above all, they left a 'Democratic Republic of Azerbaijan', an improvised republic whose government, overwhelmed, promptly dissolved in anarchy and vodka. At the beginning of 1947 Iranian troops reoccupied the town without firing a shot.

'They issued a postage stamp to mark their reconquest – then they pillaged the countryside,' added the old man, drily. 'I lost a lot of sheep to them.'

We returned to town along Chahanas Street, a broad, melancholy avenue lined with dried mud walls, entirely concealing the houses. The crescent moon shone in a clear sky. It was cold; the air smelt of snow in waiting. Squatting in their doorways, the vendors of wood, charcoal, entrails and boiled rape chatted across the street: shaven heads, high cheekbones, sparse goatees, woollen or fur bonnets.

'You see, the town is neither Turkish nor Russian nor Persian – it's a mixture of all three, of course, but at base it is Central Asian. Our Turkish dialect, which is difficult for someone from Istanbul, is spoken practically as far as Chinese Turkestan. Looking west, Tabriz is the last bastion of Central Asia, and when the old jewellers in the bazaar talked about Samarkand – they used to go there in search of stones – you should have seen the way people listened...' 'Central Asia,' he added, 'since the fall of Byzantium – that's something your historians don't understand any more.'

We went up to his place to drink the last tea of the day. Through the blue-framed windows, I gazed over the town below: an enormous plate of ochre earth, divided in two at the level of the bazaar by the black loop of the river Atchitchâi (the bitter waters). The gentle bulge of two cupolas emerged from a sea of muddy roofs. In the eastern suburbs you could see peasants driving their camels and donkeys, and vans painted in ice-cream colours parked in dark courtyards.

The old Arab geographers recorded that this town – along with Kabul – had one of the best climates in the world. It was so beautiful that the astonished Mongols didn't dare destroy it, and Ghazan Khan, descendant of Genghis Khan, had established there one of the most brilliant courts in Asia. Nothing remains of these ancient splendours today, except the massive fort crumbling beneath the weight of the snow, the labyrinthine bazaar, and a mosque famous throughout the Islamic world, its blue-tiled porch still glowing.

Night had almost fallen, the sky was covered over. As I got up to see whether rain was coming on, old M—, who had taken the art of living calmly to its utmost degree, pulled me back gently by the sleeve.

'If it's raining, the cat will come back inside.'

Tabriz nourishes – or rather, should have nourished then – around two hundred and sixty thousand people, among them Armenians, thirty or so foreigners, and two French members of the order of St Vincent de Paul. Why these priests, when there were scarcely any French people there, or Muslim converts? How had it come about? No one knew any longer, but there they were, and no solitude was more bitter than theirs. I went to see them with the idea that I might borrow some books: I hadn't had a bite of French since Belgrade. The Mission was hidden away behind the French Consulate. Around midday I found the two priests walking there, hands behind their backs, in a bar of sunlight. We quickly introduced ourselves. The Superior, a ruddy, slow, bearded giant from Alsace, had arrived recently. His deputy, Father Hervé, had already been there five years – a lanky Breton in his forties, with a little, bird-like head, feverish eyes and a Quimper accent. He took me into an untidy room: hunting guns, cigarette butts, a pile of detective novels, and student exercises scrawled over in red. Buckshot cartridges were scattered across a darned cassock.

'I have all the vices,' he said with a weary smile. 'It's better that way.'

His hands shook as he lit my cigarette. No doubt he had done brilliantly at his studies in France, and for the love of God or the Mother House spent his nights correcting the wretched essays of university students who mostly – which wasn't their fault – didn't understand even the set subject. He no longer had any illusions about the town.

'Islam here? True Islam? It's absolutely finished – even more so now that fanaticism has re-emerged, with its hysteria and suffering. They come along behind their black banners, smashing up shops here and there, or they go into sacred trances on the anniversary of the Imams' deaths, and mutilate themselves... Not much that's ethical there, and as for doctrine...! I knew some genuine Muslims here, really remarkable people, but they're all dead or have left. And now... Fanaticism, you see,' he continued, 'is the last revolt of the poor, the only one they can't be denied. It makes them noisy on Sundays but quiet for the rest of the week – there are people here who see to that. A lot of things would be better if there were fewer empty stomachs.'

The Superior nodded in silence.

'Our work here is useless,' said the Breton. 'At the last Christmas Mass I was almost the only one in the church – my few parishioners didn't dare to come. It's the end. Anyway, why should they come? Poor things!'

Poor father! I wished that I could open a bottle of Muscadet, put a packet of Gauloise on the table, and make him talk about Brittany, Bernanos, St Thomas, anything – talk and talk, to empty his heart a little of all its unusable knowledge, which was making him bitter.

'As for books,' he resumed, 'go and see the Faculty library; they were sent some batches of old books from France – everything that was thrown out under Jules Ferry – and you might come across some good finds. As for the detective stories,' he added, a bit embarrassed, indicating the heap on his bed, 'I can't lend them to you because they're the Consul's, and he's always re-reading them. What do you expect – he has nothing to do and time hangs heavy on his hands.'

On Fridays, Father Hervé went out hunting by himself, taking out his anger in Christian fashion on the wolves. 'Come with me tomorrow afternoon, if you like. I'll let the chap with the van know.' But he made this suggestion so half-heartedly that I wouldn't have taken him up on it. The Superior accompanied me to the door. He timidly put his hand on my shoulder, as if to apologise for his subordinate's bitterness. He said not a word. He had the air of a patient man, a rock, slow to be moved. The town and exile wouldn't get that one.

Our set-up was perfect: two rooms, or rather, two whitewashed, vaulted passages giving on to a courtyard where a pomegranate tree and a clump of French marigolds were struggling against the first frosts. There were hollowed-out niches for icons, the samovar and gas lamps. In the tiny woodshed separating our rooms lived moon-coloured rats. We each had a table, a chair and a little iron stove corrugated like a waffle. The rent was paid for six months; we were all set. Thierry spread out his canvases; I had bought a ream of white paper from the bazaar and unpacked my typewriter. Work is never so seductive as when one is just about to begin it; so it was left at that stage while we explored the town.

Vast, grimy and neglected, Tabriz bore the marks of its unhappy past. Apart from the main roads, it was a network of little streets bordered by walls of fawn mud bricks, and where they met there were spaces with a central plane tree under which the old people gathered to smoke and chat in the evening. A dull, rough crowd passed through the arteries of the bazaar: ragged cloaks, mournful hats, mud-coloured soldiers, and women enveloped in flowered chadors. Silent fiacres, herds of donkeys, sheep and turkeys went to and fro through the squares. Samovars steamed in shop doorways. Kites hovered over the roofs in a perpetually grey sky. The poplars were shedding their last leaves. It was sinister but spell-binding.

The town is situated fifty-five miles south of the Soviet border. Once a week a train with four coaches leaves Tabriz for Jolfa and then Yerevan, capital of Soviet Armenia. From the foothills of Ararat to the desert beaches of the Caspian, the frontier presents a continuous line of barbed wire twinned with a strip of fine sand on which fugitives' footsteps are immediately detected. Nevertheless, it's not completely sealed; the Soviets allow some small fry to go back and forth, discreetly. In their case, this impressive warning system remains silent. As a local proverb nicely puts it: the sabre does not slice its own scabbard. Thus the Russians are perfectly aware of what happens in the town, and Radio Baku sometimes takes the liberty of interrupting a programme of music from the Caucasus to announce the results of the Tabriz elections – a fortnight before the ballot.

Nearly two hundred miles to the west, Ararat's ice-cap looms above a sea of blue mountains which undulate towards Russia, Turkey and Iran. It was there, in the heart of ancient Armenia, amid the billowing hostile waters, that Noah launched the Ark from which we all came. Its passage left traces, and the first little town on the Russian slopes is called Nakhichevan – in old Armenian, 'the people of the ship'.

Far to the south, beyond the reeds of vast Lake Urmia, the high valleys and ridges of Kurdistan seal the horizon. It is a magnificent region but not much visited, as the Iranian army controls access. The tribes of drovers who live there are known in Tabriz as brigands and plunderers, a reputation as solid as it is unjustified. The Kurds are undeterred by the Tabrizis' hatred and come down from time to time, slung with cartridges, and with devouring smiles gorge themselves on chicken and vodka.

To the east, a dirt road crosses the Chibli Pass at nearly ten thousand feet, and goes off in the direction of Tehran. Beyond Mianeh, you cross the river Qizil Uzan on the banks of which captive Israel 'wept, remembering Zion', and world and language change. You leave the hard country of the Turks for age-old lands, the sunny landscape of the Iranian plateau. Apart from this road, often closed by snow or spring mud, and the almond-green bus which sometimes takes four days to reach Tehran, nothing links the town to the outside world.* In its cradle of poplars, of fawn earth and wind, it has a life of its own; separate.

One can endure an isolated place, without supplies; if necessary, without safety or doctors, but I couldn't stay for long in a place without the post. For years, across snow, sand or mud, the path to the post office was a ritual path. In Tabriz poste-restante letters, having arrived intact, were displayed – like some miraculous fruit – in a window behind a grille to which the sub-postmaster had the key, attached to his watch-chain. So you couldn't retrieve a letter without a visit to this individual and several cups of tea. He was a friendly old chap, threadbare and very ceremonious, who killed time by studying French in an ABC decorated with vignettes showing 'A-rrosoir', 'B-oite' and 'CH-eval', and he relied on us to correct the exercises which the scarcity of mail gave him plenty of time to complete. In exchange, he took personal care of our letters and never lost a one. As for postcards from Europe – especially those featuring women or flowers – he had immediately disowned responsibility; apparently they would make people happy along the way.

When the bus from Tehran wasn't stuck on the road and had brought us something, we carefully took this manna to a cheap restaurant in the bazaar where portions of rice gleamed like snow under cages full of birds made drowsy by pipe-smoke and steaming tea. Only there, with full stomachs and clean hands, did we slowly peruse, syllable by syllable, those messages from another world. I

* Since I wrote this, the asphalt road from Tehran to Qazvin has been extended as far as Tabriz.

would have found these sessions even more agreeable if I hadn't always been the first to finish. Thierry's friend Flo sent him screeds and, to satisfy my hunger, I would vainly try to read them upside down. My attachments were not the kind to write, and it was usually I who, returning from the counter, received a hearty, consoling slap on the back.

After mid-October was the *Muharram*, the anniversary of the murder of Imam Hussein, the Good Friday of the Shi'ite Muslims. (Shi'ites are those who regard Ali as the only legitimate caliph, to the exclusion of other successors of Mohammed recognised by the Sunnis. Most Persians are Shi'ites.) For a day the town resounded to weeping and clamour, seething with fanatical rage against the assassins, dead for thirteen centuries. Vodka and arak ran like water, the crowds were out in force, minds were soon fuddled and the day could easily end in a murder, or the sacking of a few Armenian shops. The police were out in the streets; those Kurds who were Sunnis remained inside, and the few Christians in town were well advised to stay at home.

We were roaming cautiously round the fringes of the Armenian quarter when old M— hailed us from his car and said to hop in. It was the end of the afternoon.

'Come and see how in Persia we weep more over the dead than the living,' he said, laughing.

There was nothing to laugh about; we could already hear the harrowing cries from the cortège of mourners coming down Pahlevi Avenue. Behind triangular black banners filed three groups of penitents. The first were content to beat their breasts and weep; the second group flayed their backs with whips ending in five little iron chains. They proceeded resolutely; their skin was broken and bleeding. The last group, dressed in white tunics, carried heavy cutlasses with which they sliced their shaven heads. The crowds emphasised each gash with cries of admiration. The families and friends surrounding these sacrificial victims watched that they didn't wound themselves too deeply, waving batons above their heads to slow the momentum of the knives. Despite this, one or two fanatics collapse each year, their skulls cut open, and so leave this deceptive world. At the end of the procession, the most euphoric gathered again behind the Post Office for a sort of round dance, keeping time to the onlookers' shouts. From time to time one of the dancers would interrupt himself and with a great yell embed his knife in his skull. It was hard to see the wound because it was almost dark, but twenty yards away the sound of blade cutting bone was unmistakable. Around seven o'clock the frenzy was such that the dancers' weapons had to be wrenched away from them to stop them killing themselves on the spot.

In the villages around Tabriz infant mortality was very high at the time of weaning, then dysentery would take its toll; mothers who had already lost several sons at an early age then promised to Allah those they were expecting. If he reached sixteen, the child would become a mullah, or make the Shi'ite pilgrimage to Karbala (the Iraqi village where Imam Hussein was murdered by the Sunnis), or pay his debt to Heaven by processing at Muharram. Old M—, who had recognised several of his villagers in the cortège, assured us that most of the penitents were in this situation.

That evening, he took us to dinner with one of the rare foreigners in the town: Roberts, a Texan advisory engineer at 'Point IV', an American technical assistance organisation. He had arrived only six weeks ago, had already bravely tackled Azeri-Turkish, produced several phrases, made mistakes, laughed and made us laugh. He was responsible for supervising the construction of dispensaries and schools in the larger surrounding villages. He was still full of optimism, with that American characteristic – so pleasant yet so exotic there – of immediately confiding in one. He believed in his schools, couldn't believe in the Devil, and regarded the procession in silence, occasionally gasping incredulously. The old man, who had practically dragged him to the Muharram, watched his reactions all afternoon with a green, sardonic eye.

There were few foreigners in the town. A stranger is an astonishing thing. Across the garden, over the wall of the small courtyards, from the terrace roofs, our Armenian neighbours observed us – in the nicest way. When we were out, a mysterious broom might sweep our rooms, or invisible hands place a bowl of bitter soup on our table.

A century before, there had been nearly a million Armenians in the province; by then, scarcely fifteen thousand remained clinging to the city. They kept themselves to themselves, packed tight, gathering every evening in the dark kitchens of Armenistan, around the gas lamp, to discuss community affairs or carefully work out their strategy with regard to the bazaar. It was a warm, black-clad little world, hard-working and hidden away, with a devout respect for its glorious past and infinite resistance to misfortune. Sometimes a family 'succeeded', and went to Tehran to try its luck. That was exceptional, and for those in Tabriz life was tough, but with the experience of ancient races they knew how to adapt to it, and how to preserve its savour. During the week, the women – well-guarded behind closed doors – hum while they sweep, beautiful tunes that float up across the roofs; on Sundays in church they naturally sing four-part harmony. Once we got to know them, we learnt that the Arzruni clan provided most of the basses, while the Mangassarians were tenors.

For the most part they are Monophysite Christians and their spiritual leader, the Patriarch at Echmiadzin, lives in Soviet Armenia.* An old man, cut off from the Christian world, his election is the subject of endless discussion. Each Christmas he sent to his brothers in Iran faint but politic encouragement over the air-waves of Radio Baku. Many of them still have family in the Soviet Union, of whom they have very little news, and to whom they send – although they have to watch every penny – parcels of warm clothing. Sometimes they are surprised to receive in return a badly wrapped parcel of sweets and a few cautious lines of commiseration, the propaganda on both sides of the border leading each to believe that the other is the poorer. However our neighbours spoke readily of their miseries, proud of what they had been through and of the suffering still ahead – 'You'll see – it's not over yet...' – with the plaintive vanity of people unjustly and frequently trounced by history, like that of the Jewish diaspora in bygone years. Speaking of the Jews: seven Israeli families, disillusioned by Tel Aviv, had actually arrived in Tabriz and opened a shop in the bazaar. The whole of Armenistan had talked about it with unkind smiles. For once Armenian and Azeri merchants agreed and, hand in hand, prepared to give them a hard time.

---

* After 1959 the diocese of Tabriz came under the jurisdiction of the Patriarch at Antilyas, in Lebanon.

We were not too isolated. At the end of the morning a large grey silhouette sometimes crossed the garden, then a hail of blows rattled the door. It would be Paulus, the doctor thanks to whom we had obtained our residence permits, bringing the news between two house-calls. He plumped down his two hundred pounds in our sturdiest chair, producing from his overcoat a smoked sturgeon wrapped in newspaper and a bottle of vodka, which he opened with a flick of his thumb. After an ironic glance around the room, he would launch – eating all the while – into a sort of running commentary on the locality which almost always began, 'Listen to this – I had to laugh'.

Paulus was Baltic and spoke his improvised French, which he seemed to make up as he went along, with a heavy German accent. After taking part in the Russian campaign, in the *Wehrmacht*, he had fled his invaded country, and as an émigré had been in practice in Tabriz for ten years. He was extremely knowledgeable in his field and a good healer, so he made money, ate enormously and drank even more. His darting wall-eyes lit up a large, pale face, full of shrewdness and intelligence. He had the vitality of a boar, a good measure of cynicism, and a startling belly laugh that would well up and suffuse his face, punctuating even his blackest stories. He was indeed a prodigious storyteller. He had tended the town long enough to understand it, and the whole rough epic of Tabriz passed through him unaltered. He neither judged it nor 'doctored' it, but in his mouth the suspicious deaths and the comical or sordid manoeuvres he'd witnessed at once turned into fables, myths or archetypes, and took on the kind of authority that two thousand years, say, can confer on the ugliest business. (Many characters from Greek mythology would find themselves up in a criminal court today).

One morning he had come back from the Shish-Qilan district, where the police had called him about the body of an old mullah, found half-naked in his small courtyard, beside his nest egg – a sack of crowns – around which he'd been circling all night, apparently, singing in a dreadful raucous voice. The neighbours, terrified by his litanies, had kept well away. When they had heard him fall, then groan, they hadn't gone to his aid because they suspected the old man of black magic, and held him responsible for at least half the miscarriages and venereal diseases in the neighbourhood. The story intrigued us, but wasn't lucky for us. The same afternoon we went to look around Shish-Qilan, a rustic northern suburb at the foot of a hill: muddy cul-de-sacs, stunted almond trees, mud-brick walls and a few shifty old men in mountain gear, who pastured their goats in frost-covered vales or drowsed on the doorsteps of shops covered in pigeon-droppings. At the top of the hill a ruined mosque, spattered with turds and the haunt of prowlers, looked over the outstretched town. The next day Thierry returned there to draw and came back white as a sheet, grazed all over, his clothes torn. As he came back down the hill, a dozen layabouts had surrounded him, knocked him over and relieved him at knife-point of the month's money we had changed that morning at the bazaar.

When we recounted this mishap to Paulus, he had one of those fits of irrepressible laughter that brought us closer together. He himself had only been mugged once, on the road to Urmia… by policemen who had been left on their own a bit too long. A very dangerous man, an armed policeman. He 'had to laugh', he couldn't help it. When he left us, he was overcome again, gasping for breath, his eyes full of tears. We could hear his heavy footsteps dying away between the walls; he had to stop from time to time to catch his breath. It was just before the snow.

November

> The bursting pomegranates bleeding
> beneath a fine, pure layer of snow
> the blue of mosques under the snow
> the trucks slipping under the snow
> the white guinea-fowls whiter still
> the long walls rust the voices lost
> making their way under the snow
> and the whole town, even the great citadel,
> lifted up to the speckled sky
> – it's winter, *Zemestan*.

On the Azerbaijan plateau it comes late but thoroughly. One night the stars in the dark blue sky seem very close, and the people bring out their *korsi* (a sort of foot-warmer which comes up to the waist).

In the night the thermometer falls to -30°; the next day, winter hits town. A cutting wind gusts from the north, stirring the snow and icing the fields. The wolves get bolder and those without jobs in the suburbs gang up to rob the peasants. Beards and moustaches freeze over, samovars smoke, hands stay in pockets. One has only three

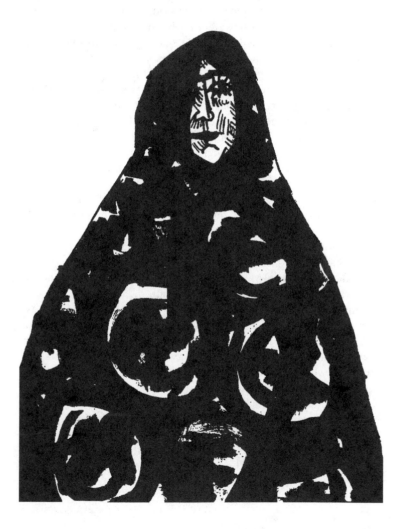

words in mind: tea – charcoal – vodka. On the door to the courtyard
the Armenian kids draw a tall figure with boots and masses of skirts,
with a little sun in the area of her sex. All this is quite poetic as long
as you can keep the stove roaring and pay the wood-merchant.

Ours knew just two words of German: *Guten Tag*, which in his
toothless mouth had become *huda daa*; it didn't matter – it was a
foreign phrase, we were foreigners, we would understand. He was a
slip of an old man, with watery eyes and hands cracked with
chilblains; he watered his logs with a shaking hand to make them
heavier: fig trees, willows, purple-veined jujube – biblical trees,
good for absorbing water. When I surprised him at it, he broke into
guileless laughter and eyed me over his moustache to see whether I
was going to get really angry. The Armenian women in the
neighbourhood used to scold him roundly, saying that his
behaviour was offensive to God, and occasionally tried to make him
ashamed of his wares, but they always ended up buying from him.
Wood was hard to come by; damp or not, it was business.

While Thierry worked on the canvases he counted on selling in
Tehran, I took on pupils for my subsistence. They arrived at dusk,
through the garden, snow up to their hips.

'Ah, monsieur le professeur… dans le Tabriz, elle est bien noire,
notre vie…'

'*A* Tabriz, *à* Tabriz, Monsieur Sepabodhi. You still haven't got it:
one says *à* Tabriz, *à* Paris, *à* Vienne, *en* Italie…'

This was the pharmacist. He knew enough French to discuss
what happened in the town, to explain accurately the three stages of
syphilis which he had wisely studied in the *Larousse médical*, or
slowly savour *Peau d'Ane*, *Le Chat botté* and all the other crystalline
fairy tales which reconcile logic and poetry and in which nothing
more fatal than happiness occurs. It was difficult, though,
explaining fairies to him, because nothing in Persia corresponded to
those fugitive apparitions, with their pointed caps and their sharp
but abstract femininity. The enchantresses of local folklore were a
very different matter: they were either *peris*, the servants of Evil in
the Mazdaist tradition, or the robust female genies of Kurdish tales,
who devoured the travellers they had charmed, having exhausted
them in bed.

Nevertheless it was pleasant. At the end of a chapter the pharmacist would rub his spectacles, murmuring 'I do like Perrault... he's so sweet', then bury his nose in his notebook, red as a peony. While Carabosse or Carabas, syllable by syllable, yielded up their splendours and secrets, night was falling over the town, and then the fleece of snow over the dark streets. My windows would be covered in feathery ice and the first pariah dogs would begin to howl. I snuffed the gas lamp. We had worked well. The pharmacist put on his overcoat, handed me the five tomans which we would soon convert into vodka, and leave me on the doorstep, sighing '*Ah! monsieur le professeur, quel hiver perdu, atroce, ici... dans le Tabriz.*'

We'd convert them into vodka or into tickets for the Passage cinema, always packed because it was warm. It was an odd place: wooden chairs, a low platform, a large, red-hot stove that was sometimes brighter than the screen. And a wonderful audience: stray cats, beggars playing draughts by the light from the washroom, kids grizzling with tiredness, and a policeman responsible for keeping things in order when the national anthem was played with a picture of the Emperor on the screen, often upside down.

Tabriz was no doubt low on the distributors' list, because we saw – besides Iranian films and Westerns supplied by Point IV – the premieres of twenty-five-year-old films. *City Lights, The Kid*, Greta Garbo – you couldn't complain, they were great classics. But like the light from distant stars, actors' reputations reached the town with a generation's delay. Stars long since dead lived on here in secret: the boys were mad about Mae West, the girls about Valentino. Sometimes when the show was too long, the projectionist would speed up the film in order to finish. The story would take on a disturbing pace: caresses looked like slaps, ermine-clad empresses hurtled downstairs. The audience, busy rolling cigarettes or cracking pistachios, didn't see anything amiss.

Going out, the extreme cold took your breath away. With its low walls, white shadows and bare, skeletal trees, the town seemed to be under a spell, settled down and tucked away beneath the snow and the Milky Way. Especially as a wild song rang through the streets, carried on the wind; the police had left on the loudspeakers in the square, and Radio Baku was on the airwaves. One immediately recognised the incomparable voice: it was Bulbul – the nightingale –

the best singer in Turkish in the whole of Central Asia. Once upon a time he had lived in Tabriz, which was accounted one of its glories. But the Russians, who had their reasons, had lured him away with a princely sum. Since then, many Iranian sets had been tuned to Radio Baku to hear him... and heard everything else. His songs were fantastic all the same; there were four different folk traditions in the town, all heartrending, and no one was deprived of music, but nothing rivalled those old Transcaucasian laments for lyricism and cruelty.

We made our way slowly up Chahanas. At the entrance to Armenistan there were a handful of beggars sitting round a fire in an oil drum, as they did every night. They were old, shivering ghosts, eaten away by the pox, but shrewd – and merry. They would roast a few beets they'd dug up from the fields, stretching out their hands to the flames and singing. The Iranians are the most poetic people in the world, and the beggars of Tabriz knew hundreds of stanzas by Hafiz or Nizami, which spoke of love, of mystical wine, of May sunshine through the willows. They chanted, shouted or hummed these as the fancy took them; when the cold pinched, they murmured. One solo would lead to another, and so on until the break of day. May sunshine was a long way off and there was no question of settling down to sleep.

Besides these organised 'families' who pooled their windfalls, there were a few solitary outcasts whose lot was even less enviable. One night, as we were leaving a *tchaïkhane*,* a bald, sick sort of shadow approached us. It was snowing. We gave it what we had left – money for two or three days – and it disappeared as quickly as it had come. Then the snow set in so heavily that we wandered round the labyrinth of our neighbourhood for over an hour before we found our own door. Taking the key out of my pocket, I glimpsed the old man lurking in a corner; he had followed us and waited in the hope of something more. As we took no notice, he quickly stood up; threw his arms round my neck and lurched to embrace me. It was like a nightmare: this skull looming up, covered in melting snow, eyes closed, offering his lips; in a panic I extricated myself from the

---

* Tea-house: the word *ghafekhane* (café) is also common, although they do not serve coffee.

trembling bundle of bones, dashed inside and slammed the door. Thierry laughed till he cried.

'You should have seen yourself, you looked as though you were dancing a tango.'

It would have really surprised the old man to have been scolded for the nature of his proposition; once past a certain degree of poverty, subtle distinctions are abolished to the point he had reached, of having nothing but his carcass to sell. He kept on trying: we had scarcely shaken the snow off our clothes when we heard him return and start banging away, with feeble, monotonous, frustrated blows, as though the whole earth still owed him something. No doubt he was right about that – all the same, we had to go out, take him by the shoulders and push him back into the night from which he had so incautiously emerged.

The Musaddeq trial, which had just opened in Tehran, led to fears of skirmishes in Tabriz.* They didn't take place because that very morning the Governor demonstrated to the town that he was in full control: five armoured cars, several mortars and twenty trucks, carrying troops whose numbers had been increased for the occasion.

The Governor was a wily old man, a cruel jester, oddly esteemed even by opponents of the government he represented. He was forgiven much because everyone knew he had no political convictions and had entirely devoted his rule to building up his personal fortune, with a skill that had won him many admirers. Tabriz had always been a recalcitrant town, but it recognised 'fair play', and well-aimed shots. That unexpected parade, for example, which had the town by the scruff of the neck when it woke up, was absolutely in the style of the man to whom the town referred familiarly by his first name. A despot, of course, whose disappearance would have been welcomed with relief, and who was intently watched in case he should slip up. Meanwhile, informed, bland, pitiless and efficient, he was impressive. The town, familiar with despotism, granted his talent.

---

* Muhammed Musaddeq (1881-1967) became Prime Minister in 1951 and attacked the Anglo-Iranian Oil Co. through his Oil Nationalisation Act of that year. His government was overthrown by a Royalist uprising in 1953; he was imprisoned in 1953 and released in 1956.

Nevertheless, the dawn parade thwarted more than one plan. The majority in Tabriz were still in favour of Musaddeq, and followed the progress of his trial with bitterness interspersed with bursts of laughter when the accused's responses demolished the prosecution. Musaddeq was actually much more popular than the Western press would have us believe. My pupils spoke of him affectionately. Outside tea houses, beggars and porters burst into interminable, hysterical discussions of the matter – and into tears. At the entrance to the bazaar you would occasionally find the carcass of a propitiatory sheep, steaming in the mud, sacrificed by night. For the man in the street, Musaddeq was still the Iranian fox, wilier than the British variety, who had wrested the oil from the West and skilfully defended his country in The Hague. His protean talents, his bravery, his patriotism and his genial duplicity had made him a national hero, and his taking fierce possession of numerous villages made no difference. The fact that after his success production at Abadan fell drastically, for want of technicians, and that the boycott of Iranian oil endangered the country's financial position mattered little to the mass of people, whose situation was slow to improve anyway. If they weren't producing anything, at least the refineries unexpectedly allowed a small trade to flourish: certain light installations were dismantled at night by mysterious prowlers, and taps, flywheels, cables, bolts and pipes were sold at cut-price in the bazaars of Khuzistan.

December

The sky was lowering. Lamps were lit by midday. The sweet smell of oil and the clinking of snow shovels enveloped the days. Sometimes the songs and flutes of an Armenian wedding in a nearby courtyard filtered through the snowflakes. Boiling tea throughout the day kept us warm inside and clear-headed. The more the town settled into the thick of winter, the more we liked it. This idea seemed to worry the widow Chuchanik, our landlady, who often came to see us: it seemed preposterous to her that we should have come so far, and of our own free will, to settle in Tabriz. At the beginning, she thought we must have taken to the road only because someone had chased us from home. She sat in a corner of my room, a plump partridge in a black smock, and in silent reproof observed the camp bed, the bare floor, the window draught-proofed with old newspapers, the easel or the typewriter.

'But what are you doing here then?'

'I have those pupils.'

'But in the morning?'

'You can see what I do – take notes and write.'

'But I write too – Armenian, Persian, English…' she counted them off on her fingers. 'It's not an occupation.'

We would soon abandon this delicate ground for news of the neighbourhood, about which she was very well informed: the newspaper vendor was dead of stomach pains…the grocer's son had just finished a large portrait of the emperor, made out of old postage stamps, which had taken him two years and which he wanted to present himself in Tehran… Sat—, the tanner in Chahanas Avenue, had gambled away thirty thousand tomans the other night without turning a hair. At that I pricked up my ears: it was quite a sum, and Armenistan rumour never lied where figures were involved.

The town still had a few rich people, well concealed, but it no longer saw the colour of their money. For the most part they were great landowners like old M—, hiding the extent of their fortune under a ragged exterior. Fearing betrayal if they invested it locally, they hoarded their money, sending their excess income to foreign banks, or playing behind closed doors for fantastic stakes. Sat— the tanner, who had brazened out his loss, owned at least a hundred villages between Khvoy and Mianeh. A medium-sized village brought in around twenty thousand tomans; thus he could count on an annual rent of two million tomans and his loss was insignificant.

When the bazaar got hold of the story, what on earth did they make of it – the destitute majority who were the town's real face? Not much. They knew that Sat— had a full stomach three times a day, that he slept as the fancy took him with one – or two – women under enough blankets, and drove around in a black car. Beyond that, their imagination ran out; luxury belonged to a world they had no idea of, either from books – since they couldn't read – or from the cinema, which disseminated a foreign mythology. When they penetrated the houses of the rich it was through the servants' quarters, which were scarcely better equipped than their own hovels. They were as unable to grasp the idea of thirty thousand tomans as we are to grasp the idea of a thousand million dollars. Those who have nothing envy nothing beyond what touches the skin and the stomach: to be clothed and fed leaves nothing to envy. But they weren't fed, and hurried barefoot through the snow, and the cold got worse and worse.

Because of this fantastic divide, the rich had lost their place even in the popular imagination. They were so rare or distant that they no longer counted. Even in its dreams the town remained faithful to its privation: everywhere else, fortune-tellers promise love or travelling; in Tabriz, their predictions are more modest, again involving a fine poem (instead of picking a card, the customer pricks with a pin a quatrain in a collection by Hafiz, which the fortune-teller interprets): three pots of rice with mutton, and one night in white sheets.

In a town so well acquainted with hunger, the stomach never forgets its rights and food is a fête. On feast days, the housewives in the neighbourhood rise early to peel, crush, bone, stir, chop, knead, and blow on the coals, and the fine vapour floating from the courtyards betrays the presence of steamed sturgeon, chicken in lemon juice grilled over charcoal, or one of those large balls of mince stuffed with nuts and chopped herbs, bound with egg-yolk and cooked in saffron, which they call *keufteh*.

Turkish cuisine is the heartiest in the world; Iranian has a refined simplicity; Armenistan is unequalled for pickles and sweet-and-sour; for ourselves, we ate a great deal of bread – it was marvellous bread. At daybreak the smell from the ovens drifted across the snow to delight our noses; the smell of the round, red-hot Armenian loaves with sesame seeds; the heady smell of *sandjak* bread; the smell of *lavash* bread in fine wafers dotted with scorch-marks. Only a really old country rises to luxury in such ordinary things; you feel thirty generations and several dynasties lined up behind such bread. With bread, tea, onions, ewe's cheese, a handful of Iranian cigarettes and the leisurely pace of winter, we were set for a good life: life at three hundred tomans a month.*

I now had enough pupils to get by. Indeed two of them, the butcher's sons, sometimes improved our daily fare by bringing some

---

* 150 each – a mill-worker earned about 100.

leftovers swiped from their father's stall. They were red-haired twins, pathologically timid, who knew nothing and learnt nothing but who pleased us greatly when they produced from their satchel a goat's lung, like a large, bloody sponge, or some cheap cuts of buffalo with a few black hairs sticking out. Each Saturday night we went to the Djahan Noma, a restaurant crowded with Kurds and sombre revellers in caps, to eat enough mutton to last us through the week. From time to time Thierry, who was painting in the half-light and thought his eyesight was deteriorating, would shut himself away and cook a couple of pounds of carrots. Apart from this whim, he was no less stringent than I: one day as I scraped around the rim of our cooking-pot he suggested with a gleam in his eye that I could use the scraps to make 'a sort of large croquette'.

'No letters?'

'They're warming themselves along the way,' replied the postman, blowing on his fingers.

There had been no mail for twenty days. It was really like being on the moon. All the same, we felt at home. My pupils still left me time to work. I was trying, painfully, to write.

The departure had been like a rebirth, and my world seemed too new to bend to methodical reflection. I had neither freedom nor flexibility, just desire and panic, pure and simple. I tore up and began the same page twenty times over without being able to get past the critical point. All the same, by dint of stumbling and shoving I sometimes managed the momentary pleasure of saying what I'd thought without being too stiff. Then I would take a break, my head hot, and look out the window at our turkey, Antoine, strutting round the snowy garden – a skinny fowl which we were persuaded could be fattened in time for Christmas.

When work wasn't going well, or when the smell of my shirt began to annoy me, I headed off for the Bain Iran carrying a load of dirty laundry. Ten minutes away, it was a hammam kept by a very clean old trout who smoked gold-tipped cigarettes through her veil. The cockroaches that usually infest humid places had died of cold before autumn. The vermin, too, had perished in the frosts. There was scads of boiling water and gaiety reigned. For one toman you had the right to a cubicle furnished with two taps, a tub, and a ledge of

polished stone on which I began by doing my washing, listening to
the whistling, sighs of relaxation and sounds of brushing that rose
from the neighbouring cubicles. For an extra toman, the washer
would come and look after you. He was a silent, spry old man, as
skeletal as if the steam in which he spent his life had gradually
dissolved his flesh. He began by stretching you out on the stone ledge
and soaping you from head to toe. Then he removed every speck of
dust from your body by working away with a horsehair glove and
sandsoap. Then he sluiced you with warm water. Finally he gave a
lengthy massage, kneading the head, making the vertebrae crack,

pinching the tendons and pressing the joints, sides and biceps with his fists and bare feet. He knew his business and never left a muscle knotted. It never failed: under the hot water and the expert pressure I would feel my nerves relaxing, one by one, hesitations disappearing, and a thousand secret floodgates closed by the cold opening up again. Then I would linger on, stretched out in the dark, having a smoke and meditating, until impatient fists hammering on the door made me give up my place.

I would re-emerge at about six o'clock, light and clean right through to the spirit, and steaming in the cold like a damp dishcloth.

The sky of intense, pure green was reflected in the iced puddles. All along the street, the shopkeepers were prostrated inside their shops, caps turned round with the visor toward the nape, praying hard – among their jars of treacle, turnips, loaves of sugar, sacks of lentils, and flypapers – that Heaven would maintain them in all their possessions. Christmas was coming, and in Armenistan the poultry-vendors were already going from door to door, their backs plumed with numbed and bloody birds still feebly moving their wings. These fluffy old men wore a kind of mitre, had waxen noses and long greatcoats, and criss-crossed the snow like the genies of that enchanted cage in which we were locked up till spring: apparitions of good omen. They put me in mind of the beginning of a Baroque poem which I had unearthed for my pupils:

> *Adoncques Filles de l'air*
> *De cent plumes couvertes*
> *Qui de serf que j'étais*
> *M'ont mis en liberté...*

On such nights, I worked easily and dreamed with my hands in my lap. The stove snored. Antoine the turkey slept at the foot of the bed and his torpor was a pleasure to see. Outside, the sky reigned over darkened houses. The town was quieter than a tomb. The only thing you could hear was the night watchman, further and further away, a sorry old cricket, singing hoarsely to keep up his spirits.

Towards mid-December, the daughter of one of our neighbours poisoned herself for love. She loved a Muslim, and everything got much too complicated. She swallowed *shiré* (the extremely toxic dross or residue of smoked opium) and the boy hanged himself alongside her: Montagues and Capulets. The neighbourhood resounded with the wailing of women. Little notices in black and green were put up on every door announcing the time of the funeral... In the Armenian chapel the girl was laid out with her hands clasped, in an open coffin. She wore a velvet gown, almost new, and gold rings in her ears. At one end of the church the old women formed an extraordinarily noble group: a phalanx of Fates draped in their black shawls, silent, tough, feminine, their eyes blazing. Except for some old gypsy women, I had never seen such sphinx-like dignity, poignant and powerful. They were really the guardians of their race, a hundred times more beautiful than the nubile girls. Once the service was over, the whole congregation filed past the dead girl and then the church doors were opened. In front of the passers-by, two women ostentatiously stripped the body of its jewels and its shoes, then slashed the gown with scissors. It was winter, season of dearth and grave-robbers: it was hoped that by these gestures profanation would be avoided.

The same week, a Kurd died in town without his family there to take him away. Unfortunate man – he would be 'badly buried'. The obdurate anger between the mountain-dwelling Sunnis and the Shi'ite townsfolk was fuelled by a thousand incidents. But the Kurds were famous fighters, and the Tabrizi were too scared to attack them alive; they took their malicious revenge when they died. Kurds who had trespassed into the town ran great risk of being placed on the ground with their faces in the earth instead of being put upright in the grave with their faces towards Mecca, as custom required. Azriel, the Angel of Death, would take offence at their unseemly position and refuse them entrance to Paradise. If a Kurd was in the district hospital and felt his strength going, he would sometimes disappear, steal a horse and ride hell for leather, so as to die in Kurdistan.

One evening, outside the Iran baths in fact, a young Kurd accosted me and asked very insistently for the address of a girl in the neighbourhood. He wore a white silk turban and a belt of new material, sporting a dagger worth at least a thousand tomans. Obviously he was fresh from the washer's hands and intended to go courting. I knew the address, and the girl, whom we had recorded a few days earlier – a young miss, who prided herself on singing beautiful Armenian folksongs as they would be sung 'at the conservatoire', and had made such a fuss that an entire side of tape had been wasted. So I had rather a grudge against her, but not enough to send a suitor with such a determined air to her door. I sent him off in the opposite direction and went on my way.

As you might expect, the Tabrizi spread all sorts of malicious rumours about the Kurds: savages and cutpurses who sold their own daughters cheap and took other men's, etcetera. The Armenians joined in, but it was only lip-service; in fact their relations with the Kurds were better than they wanted one to believe. The wood-sellers of the bazaar dealt with various tribes and had done so for a long time, on an entirely confident footing. Certainly it was said that further away, around Rezaieh, the Kurds still got away with carrying off one of the Armenians they were so partial to, but it was mainly the girls who told such stories to show what extremes their beauty drove men to, and I never had wind of an actual case. However it might be, business never suffered on this account. As the Persians had declared so long ago to Herodotus, 'We think that it is wrong to carry women off: but to be zealous to avenge the rape is foolish: wise men take no account of such things…' (Book I.4).

'For the birth of your Prophet,' explained Mussa, standing in the doorway. He was holding two blood-streaked partridges in his hand, and his eyes smiled above his hunting cape. It was Christmas Eve and he was the first person in town to think of it. Meat was just what we wanted; his timing was perfect. He stayed to eat his birds with us.

Mussa was the only son of a Turkish *arbab* who lived at the end of our street, a likeable, idle young fellow who spent his time hunting, painting miniatures, and endlessly re-reading *Les Misérables* in a Persian translation, which inflamed him with delusions of heroism and egalitarian passions. His head was full of Paris and he wanted to persuade us that he hated Persia, but we didn't believe him for a moment; he was burning for reform, sword in hand. His seventeen years were good for something. His family history, too: under the Qajars, his great-grandfather who disapproved of the Governor had managed to take over the town with some fifty henchmen, and had held power for several months. As a result of this initiative, he had been cut down at a banquet given in his honour. His grandfather, who threatened to re-open the affair, in due course had received a bomb and exploded with it. His uncle had been sprayed with lead by frustrated conspirators whom he had refused to join. As for his father, he had renounced the risks of politics to administer his estates carefully, and had amassed a fortune which left his son at leisure to dream of cuts and bruises, and gallop about in his imagination. Mussa also counted on going to paint in a Montmartre garret. To realise his ambition, he intended to extort several villages' income from his father; 'poverty in Paris' seemed to him so enviable that he imagined it would cost more than a life of luxury in Tabriz.

In the meantime, his father – who loved him – began to admit him into the company of several wily old friends in the evenings, so that he could form opinions, learn how to roll dice neatly, drink without falling over, and speak when he was spoken to. As he also knew his son was a scatterbrain, he attached to him a foundling known in the neighbourhood as *kütchük* (little), to serve both as factotum and Sancho Panza. Very crafty for his eight years, the little one shopped as thriftily as an old Armenian, ran the most delicate errands, and scurried round the bazaar. He was a lucky *kütchük*: his age allowed him to live in the women's quarters, and they stuffed him with sweets and grilled liver. A thick new cardigan, a cap and friendly back-slapping protected this mischievous, merry soul from the cold. Above all, he was fearless – to be fearless and an orphan was some achievement in Tabriz. Anyway it made him someone special and engaging, and the grandmas who encountered him in Chahanas couldn't resist patting him on the head and cooing over him, to which he usually replied with a few well-chosen words so obscene as to stop them in their tracks.

Mussa often came to see us. He had always gone out of his way to be helpful to us, so he had earned the right to trot out on every visit the same stories of Mullah Nasser ed-Din (a comic figure popular throughout the Middle East) and his personal views on painting: 'First learn to paint in the classical manner, then the impressionist, and only then in the modern way...'. He would rattle on, sitting on the camp bed, while I listened with half an ear. I had heard it all at least ten times. On that day I was preoccupied with Christmas, the pivot of the year. So we had reached it already... where would we be next Christmas? What turn would life have taken? I watched the partridges swelling and singing in our battered casserole, with a bunch of mint and a quart of white Armenian wine, that biblical wine found in the bazaar in flasks sealed with a flimsy blob of red wax.

Thin, sacrificial smoke rose over the house, above the scrawls of the well-behaved Armenian students, over the town's roofs, over the frosted, fallow fields around it, over the dormice's holes and the crows' nests, over this sweet, venerable, ancient world.

The few Americans of Point IV, rather on the fringe of town, formed a companionable little group, likeable and isolated. For New Year's Eve they invited us round to one of the patrician houses which, since the departure of the upper-class Armenians, and despite the chintz curtains and record players of the new arrivals, had retained a poignant air of abandonment. We were delighted to see out the year in company: washed, brushed, emotional, we entered the room. The evening was well under way. Dripping with geniality, paper hats on their heads, the Americans shook hands, breaking glasses and singing. A good third of them were drunk and, in their eyes moist with alcohol and goodwill, there were glints of panic: at being so far away, so misunderstood, so different on such a day. Then the uproar would restore them. On the other side of the bar the Iranian guests formed a silent, smiling phalanx. We joined them: that night we felt more akin to them – coming out of our hermitage we were disconcerted by the babble. People were dancing. I invited a tipsy, statuesque young woman. Holding her suddenly seemed such a remarkable thing and so worthy of attention that I forgot the music and stood stock still, clasping her tighter and tighter. After a moment she looked up, gazed at me in astonishment and then in outrage, disengaged herself and disappeared. I drank a great deal, as did Thierry; to things we'd done as well as things still to do, but we had become unaccustomed to alcohol and it soon got the better of us. We staggered out just in time to avoid falling asleep on the spot. The night was hard and splendid, the snow thick, walking difficult. We held each other round the shoulders so as not to fall. We had no desire to go home, and for a long time the kites and dogs of Armenistan could hear us criss-crossing the alleyways, shouting foreign-sounding names.

We wandered and howled for at least an hour – an hour too long. I reached the house with a swollen throat and chattering teeth. There was a hard frost in my room; I lay down on the bed and piled everything I could find on top of me: clothes, rags, wrapping paper, and went to sleep. An unmistakable, light melody woke me well before dawn: through a haze I glimpsed at my bedside an unsteady silhouette, hat over its eyes, looking at me as it whistled Schubert. *Glückswünsche!*... it said, in an ironic tone, holding out the bottle which had bulged in its pocket. It was Paulus. He had spent the evening outdoors, found our door open, and came in to 'offer his greetings'. I took a swig without quite managing to wake up, and asked whether he had ended the year on a good note.

'At the Djahan Noma... a binge, *grausam, grausam Herr Nicolas*! I can't help laughing.'

He didn't like drunks. Although alcohol was his weakness, he was able to keep the upper hand, after his fashion. Even when arak ran like water, he manoeuvred calmly, like an unsinkable barge, more himself and more biting than ever. He sat down, and talked for a moment about the bus to Tehran which, for some reason, he had gone to see off: the baggage tied up with string, the travellers in the snow not knowing when they'd leave, or if they'd ever arrive... *wirklich grausam*. After all, he too was trapped in the town. Then I heard him from a great distance taking my pulse, and much later, the first cockcrow of the year. I woke up the next day with a raging fever and inflammation of the throat. Paulus had already done what was necessary: the widow Chuchanik was in the room busily filling a hypodermic syringe. She had donned her nurse's blouse for the occasion, and looked very pleased with herself...

January

...on the camp-bed in a fragile state of equilibrium, several layers of old newspapers underneath me, between the garden turning grey as night fell and the flickering glow of the stove, I waited for the injection to take effect. Somewhere in the neighbourhood a radio was broadcasting Persian songs, Armenian kids were squabbling in the courtyard, and I could hear Thierry in his room next door, declining *rosa*. He had started the Abbé Moreux's *Latin sans peine* to while away the winter. Amidst all the whiteness, in the echo of those august tongues, in the ancient province of Atropatene which Mark Antony's legions had never been able to conquer, the *regina parthorum* and *pugnare scytham* of the first lessons took on a wider sense, mysteriously boreal, a delectable cradle for my fever. It hadn't subsided. For several days I searched for the weak point of the sickness, the crack, so that I could insert a wedge. It wasn't the arak; it was no longer passing through, and burned my stomach without soothing me. Nor even the Latin primer. I gingerly leaned back against the stone wall, and as I watched the snow falling I made myself cry, methodically, like scouring a chimney or a saucepan: for an hour. That was it. I felt all the barriers of sickness give way and dissolve, and ended up sleeping upright in the heart of winter, as in a soft cocoon.

Looking after me, Thierry came down with the same sort of spasmodic croup, and I got up just in time to look after him. It was easy. When he was sick he was busy, as though about to hatch something or operate on himself. He scarcely replied to questions, not because he was bad tempered but because he was concentrating: the better he was at being ill, the less time he would have to spend on it. In fact he took advantage of the mildest 'flu to give himself a new skin, rapidly recovering and arranging well-spaced treats for his convalescence: a cup of tea beneath the poplars, a fifty-yard walk, a nut, ten minutes thinking of Istanbul or reading old numbers of *Confidences* which one of my pupils lent us, and which he found very satisfying – especially the 'Heart Mail'. He came across gems signed 'a tearful Juliet (Haute-Saone)', or 'Jean-Louis found out (Indre)': 'I have almost never deceived her, however, except for adventures when travelling *which cost hardly anything…*'.

You must have a routine to get through the winter.

Mine involved a corner of the Armenian quarter where the porters ate and drank. Along with the beggars, they were the poorest people in town. That was why they gathered in one tea-house where, apart from the cop drinking tea at the counter, they could be sure of having the place to themselves. The first time I wandered in to it, utter silence fell immediately – as if the ceiling were about to cave in – and lasted so long that I kept my head right down and didn't dare write a line. I thought that I lived frugally, but my shabby hat, my ragged jacket and my boots seemed to shout comfort and a full stomach. I buried my hand in my pocket to stifle some jingling change. I was wrong to be afraid; it was the most peaceful den in town.

Around midday, the porters arrived in twos and threes, stooped and shivering, their ropes slung in coils over their shoulders. They settled down at the wooden tables in a sort of rumble of well-being, steam rising from their tatters. Their ageless faces, so bare and shiny with use that they let the light through, would begin to glow like old cooking-pots. They played draughts, lapping tea from saucers with long-drawn sighs, or sat round a basin of warm water and soaked their sore feet. The better-off puffed away on a nargileh, and between fits of coughing sometimes recited one of those visionary stanzas for which Persia had no equal over a thousand years. The winter sun on the blue walls, the fine scent of tea, the tapping of the draughts on the board – everything had such a peculiar lightness that one wondered whether this bunch of horny-handed old seraphim might lift off in a great flapping of wings, bearing the tea-house away. It was admirable, and very Persian, the way they were able – despite their miserable lives, their worn bronchial tubes and open chilblains – to hack out a little segment of well-being.

By mid-January the cold had intensified and carried off several men whose belongings were auctioned off at one end of the room: a worn blanket, half a loaf of sugar, a bit of rope and even – twice, as I remember – the green sash of the Seied, the privilege of descendants of the Prophet. It was a claim widespread in the town, but especially among the poor and the humble.

Because of their soothing, consolatory habits, most of them hardly realised they were hungry. Apart from their three glasses of tea, they lunched on a bit of Turkish bread and a thin skein of spun sugar. If I were at their table, they would never begin without offering me some first: *Beffarmâid* – it's yours – thus sanctifying their miserable pittance. If I had accepted, their day's meal would be gone. I wondered which commandment enjoined those hollow bellies automatically to offer the little they had? Anyway it was a noble commandment, generous and compelling, with which those famished men were more familiar than we were.

Father Hervé was right: the little library had at least two hundred volumes in French. It was a surprising collection: Babeuf and Bossuet, Arsène Lupin and Elie Faure, René Grousset, the life of Gambetta and the letters of the Maréchal de Soubise, whose graceful style studded with euphemisms – the infantry fought without undue eagerness and yielded to its inclination to withdraw – seemed like a translation from the Persian.

In Grousset's *Empire des Steppes* I found mention of a Chinese princess whose hand in marriage had been demanded by the khan of western Russia. The emissaries having taken fifteen years to get there and back, and reported a favourable response, the matter was finally concluded... in the next generation. I like a leisurely pace; besides, space is a drug, and this story dispensed it without skimping. I told Thierry about it over lunch, and saw his face lengthen. The letters he got from his friend Flo confirmed his ideas about marriage, and he wasn't counting on skipping a generation. In short, my princess was not well received.

A bit later, returning from the Iran baths, I found him on the point of exploding. I went to make tea to give him time to recover, but when I returned he burst out, 'I can't stand this prison, this trap' – and at first, blinded by egoism, I didn't understand that he meant our travels – 'look where we are, after eight whole months! Trapped here.'

He had already seen enough for a lifetime of painting and, above all, absence had matured a relationship that wouldn't be improved by waiting. It brought me up short: better to tackle the question on a full stomach. We set out for the Djahan Noma, and while chewing our kebabs, we concluded that we should separate in the coming summer. Flo would travel to meet him in India; I would join them later for the wedding, somewhere between Delhi and Colombo, then they would go off by themselves.

Fine. I had not really envisaged sickness or love interrupting this adventure, but preferred it to be love. He was pressing on with his life. I wanted to mislay mine, perhaps in a corner of that Central Asia whose proximity was so alluring. Before I went to sleep, I examined the old German map the postman had presented to me: the brown ramifications of the Caucasus, the cold mark of the Caspian Sea, and the olive green of the Kirgiziya Steppe, which was larger than all the territory we had crossed. Those vast expanses made my flesh prickle. And it was so nice the way the great images of nature folded out, with marks, levels and ripples where one could imagine paths and dawns and another even more hermit-like hibernation, flat-nosed women with coloured headscarfs drying fish in a wooden village among bulrushes. (A bit naïve, perhaps, these desires for a virgin landscape, yet not romantic; they arose, rather, from an atavistic instinct urging one to gamble with fate in the hope of achieving something more uplifting and intense.)

All the same, I felt rather nonplussed: we were a perfect team, and I had always imagined our looping the whole loop of our journey together. That had been agreed, I thought, but such an agreement probably had no bearing on the matter. After all, one travels in order for things to happen and change; otherwise you might as well stay at home. And for him something had changed, modifying his plans. We had made no promises; there is something pedantic and petty about promises, anyway, something that denies faith, new forces, the unexpected. In this regard, the town had become an incubator.

Tabriz, so busy in other ways, has rather neglected the fine arts – so old Bagramian, the only painter in the town, was delighted to discover a colleague. Hatted, gloved and wearing spats, like someone out of a silent film, he came to inspect Thierry's work from time to time and let out encouraging shrieks. After vegetating in Leningrad for thirty years, where he taught 'floral design', Bagramian had emigrated, found a handful of pupils and late in life married an Armenian with a good dowry, who kept him in silk cravats and kid gloves. Since striking this bargain he had scarcely painted, and had given himself over to a snug state of bliss. He spent the winter in his dining-room sipping apricot liqueur, munching nougat and cracking pistachios, while spinning a thousand stories to his adoring wife, who shook her head in amazement as she listened. When we visited him, he would detain us with long lectures about the Soviet Union in voluble Russian, which neither of us knew, while she kept filling his glass and tenderly stroking his shoulders, or clapping in applause; she was madly in love with her artist, and her carbuncular eyes shone. Sometimes she would stop him in order to translate: 'He says… don't go there, don't ever… a great, sombre land, you would disappear, you would forget everything… Lethe.'

'Lethe,' Bagramian would repeat emphatically, illustrating his words by dropping bits of orange-peel into his boiling tea.

It was true that he had completely forgotten – so it was said – a first wife from whom he was not divorced, and whom only the second pretended did not exist. Of course the neighbourhood knew all about it and thought that despite his eccentricities, Bagramian had behaved like a wily fox who wanted to grow old in the warm. His coping in this way was perfectly acceptable. Anyway no one would have tried to show him up; people did not begrudge the old man his fun, and in Armenistan life was too hard for unprofitable slander.

His paintings, which he showed us every time, were not as happy as he was. Although they always featured the sun, the gardens were fussy and the paintings were lifeless: patrician ladies with velvet gowns and grim smiles, handkerchief in hand; generals on horseback in the snow with decorations and waxen cheeks. Thierry would grimace and Bagramian, undeterred, would protest every time, justifying his academic style in a frantic argument largely conducted by gestures. He would call out a painter's name, indicating a certain height to show the case he was making. Thierry would reply. They rarely agreed: when Thierry brought Millet down to floor-level, Bagramian, who had put him shoulder high and had copied him for thirty years, fell back into a chair and covered his face. They agreed on the Italian primitives, at about waist level, then gradually lifted a few certain winners – Ingres, da Vinci, Poussin – keeping an eye on each other and their favourite candidate in reserve; in that kind of bidding, each wants the last word. When Thierry, his arm at full stretch, put his favourite beyond the little man's reach, Bagramian clambered on to a stool and got quite carried away, ending up rather clumsily with a totally unknown Russian contender.

'*Shishkin*... an absolute genius,' his wife interpreted. 'Forests of silver birch under the snow.' We were happy with that; in the meantime the table had been set with bottles, soft white cheese and cucumbers, and we were mainly interested in eating – friendship must be nourished. Bagramian was of a like mind.

February

The town had got used to us; we ceased to be suspect. The Armenians, the white Russians, the police colonels, the civil servants dreaming of Swiss finishing schools for their daughters invited us into brightly-lit drawing rooms, where the mirrors, carpets and flounced furnishings were a sure sign of prosperity. They constantly replenished our plates to confirm this impression. They questioned us about our way of life, but circumspectly, because if our hosts were secretly fond of their town, they didn't make the mistake of thinking that we would like it quite as much on a hundred and fifty tomans a month. They hadn't known us for long enough to speak openly about the country and its problems, but they knew that we were sufficiently *au fait* not to swallow the official optimism Persians reserved for tourists. It was embarrassing: prevarications amidst sincere kindness, delicate consideration combined with reticence – conversation would gradually die away, then Thierry would bring out his accordion to set the women dancing. Sometimes, if we insisted, one of the portly bourgeois ladies in black would plant herself in the middle of the room, eyes modestly lowered, and sing in a blood-curdling voice the Armenian ballads of Sayat Nova,* or one of those unearthly Azeri laments – it was as if the windowpanes had been shattered and everything that was powerful, lost and irreplaceable about Tabriz seemed to burst into the room. Eyes moistened, glasses tinkled, the song died away... and heart-warmed, one would drop back like a falling leaf into that amiable, provincial tedium, full of vague desires, which suffuses the plays of Chekhov.

Amidst the foreign voices, the yawns and the meat fritters a confused lethargy would creep over us. '*Allez-y... mangez-y... buvez-y*' our hostesses cried, having lost much of the French they'd learned from the Good Sisters in Tehran. These exhortations reached us through a sort of cotton wool. We would look at each other over our glasses: what were we doing there? How many years had we been in the town, and why? Bagramian's words sounded in my ears: here too was Lethe. We left. It was always snowing; in the cold which nipped our temples we would stare at each other, sated. 'That was fat'; we no longer had any other criterion.

It wasn't surprising. We were exhausted by fever. We had lost weight. We no longer dreamed of eating well but of eating fat. La Nanou was perfect for that. It was a student restaurant, run by two old ladies with mouse-like features and a guilty air, swathed in black shawls and black headscarfs, who cooked up all sorts of greasy messes. The elder, Nanou, had been cook to Pishevari, the ex-defender of the 'Free Republic', who had escaped hanging by a hair's breadth when the Persians returned. Sometimes he came to sit humbly in a corner and sniff the aroma of her stews. I don't know whether he paid, but he was served. I don't know whether he had done her a good turn when he was in power, but they were indissolubly linked by their good or bad deeds. So he lingered, in the

---

* A popular eighteenth-century Armenian bard whose songs have never gone out of fashion.

torpor induced by soup, warmth and a full stomach – which are much more real than the vapours of power – listening to the customers mocking the government, or humming between mouthfuls a few subversive couplets, which the two old cops sitting near the door would stolidly enter in their notebooks.

These gibes referred to an old quarrel between Tabriz and Tehran. The university had been founded under the 'Republic', with Soviet support: it was 'progressive'. When the Iranians returned, they feared democratic agitation and wanted to close down the faculties. But in Tabriz the disturbances had not been sufficient to warrant suppression of teaching. The students, it was said, had taken up arms and won their case, later supported Mussadeq and then regretted it, and gave vent to their feelings in a repertory too vivid to be set down here. Mansur, an habitué of La Nanou who often dined at our table, translated the pick of the bunch for us into Montmartre slang. Son of a teacher from Meshed, Mansur had intrigued to obtain a passport, spent three years in Paris and was now completing his studies in medicine. When the silence of winter weighed too heavily on him, he came to let off steam with us. His communism (*Made in France*) had been overwhelmed by the reality he rediscovered in Tabriz. This harsh and restive town was obviously not susceptible to doctrine. He had counted on the oppressed being models of rebellion and efficiency. It was altogether different: in Tabriz, too many beggars were insultingly carefree, despite the cold, and ironic, despite the pox. They put out their hands to him as dourly as though he were like all the others, and accepted alms with obscene joy, no matter where from.

He was more at ease in our little room; his convictions worked better within a Western dialectic and he could expound his theories to us at length. We put up a sluggish opposition, certainly preferring politics to blow-by-blow descriptions of his French love affairs, full of striking details that made our heads swim. When he was on top form, he even managed to reconcile the two themes that obsessed him and ended up by linking Du Barry's promiscuity with the defects of the profit motive, and Catherine the Great's nymphomania with the development of imperialism. We couldn't imagine Iran transformed into a collective, and we teased him about these rough and ready blueprints, his utopianism, his flimsy evidence – for form's sake, because apart from these fabrications, his confusion and his rebelliousness were entirely legitimate. Many students secretly shared them; under the Zahedi regime such opinions led directly to prison, and an Iranian prison at the wrong end of the stick was no laughing matter. The most prudent thing to do was to stay asleep, because although the town had a heavy hand its sleep was even heavier; alas, youth, with all the encouragement in the world, can't sleep all the time.

Thierry, who had been short of canvas and colours for quite a while, received advice from the post office that the material he had ordered from Switzerland had at last arrived. He rushed to the office, filled in the forms, signed the release slips, paid a tax, went to the customs himself and returned with the parcel, then watched it being unwrapped. Everything was intact – but when he made to take it away, the clerk quickly took it back, explaining that the director – who wanted to give it to Thierry himself – was out for a few minutes. While he waited, they put him in a little room with a heater, tobacco, grapes and tea, and he went to sleep. An hour later he woke up, and went to find our friend the postmaster.

'What on earth am I waiting for?'

'Our director – a charming man.'

'And what time will he be back?'

'*Pharda* (tomorrow)!'

'! (?) !'

'As for your parcel – today you've seen it, and tomorrow you'll take it away. Two pleasures instead of one,' said the old man kindly, and piloted him to the door.

Pharda was always invoked, *pharda* full of promise. *Pharda*, life would be better...

March

Nevertheless, the winter had taught us patience. It still weighed on Tabriz, but in the south it was beginning to let up. Down there, the warm winds crossing the mountains from Syria made the snow melt and swell the streams of Kurdistan. Some evenings, over in that direction, the restless, yellowish edge of the sky presaged the arrival of spring.

I had just discovered in the library a volume of Kurdish tales, collected by the Lescot mission from the region of Diyarbekir. Their freshness was enchanting: a sparrow – obviously Kurdish – fluffed out his feathers and addressed the great king of the Persians who had treated him disrespectfully, chirping 'I piss on your father's grave'; djinns the height of a riding-boot, with donkey's ears, sprang out of the ground with a thunderclap to deliver the most astonishing messages in the dead of night. And there were hand-to-hand fights that would have made Lancelot or Turpin turn pale. Each man struck in turn, and the first blow drove the enemy into the ground up to his shoulder-blades; he then scrambled out, dusted himself down and girded his loins to do likewise – with a scimitar, a club or a pike. The whole land resounded: a hand lopped off here, a nose there, and feelings ran high – along with the pleasure of the exercise.

The clearer patches on the horizon and reading this jaunty literature made us long for a closer look. This involved obtaining a *djavass* because the situation in Kurdistan was tense. The Kurds are pure Iranian by blood and loyal subjects of the Empire, but their unruly behaviour had always disturbed the central powers. Seventeen centuries ago, the Arsacid monarch Artabanus V wrote to his rebellious vassal Ardeshir,* 'You have overstepped the mark, and brought your dreadful fate on yourself, you KURD, raised in the tents of the Kurds...' Ever since this warning, neither the Arabs nor even the Mongols have been able to dislodge the Kurdish shepherds from the high poetic pastures that separate Iraq from Iran. They feel at home there, organising themselves in their own way, and when they are bent on defending their customs or settling a quarrel in their own fashion, it is difficult for the voice of Tehran to be heard over the crack of rifles. Sometimes – when things are rough – they cut off the road and hold traffic to ransom. To discourage such enterprise, the government maintains a heavy military presence in certain border towns, but pays its men so infrequently that they are soon reduced to pillaging the pillagers. Thus balance is restored and authority confirmed, though at the cost of some confusion – which could only be increased by the approach of elections, with their usual train of

---

* Founder of the Sassanian dynasty; quoted by Attheim in *Gesicht vom Abend und Morgen*.

intrigue, pressure and bargaining. This washing of dirty linen was a family affair and it was not the best moment to ask for a pass, but we didn't have another. Neither the administration nor the police were much inclined to grant one, but we were on good terms with the town by then, so each left it to the other to do the dirty work and say no. For two weeks we were shunted from office to office, drinking tea with the top brass who listened politely to anything but the business in hand and kept going back on their promises. We reminded them day after day, straining not to let our impatience show, assuring our interlocutors time and time again that we considered their good faith to be unsullied. We were living on our nerves and learning that ancient game which only the most patient win; and they let us win.

On the evening of our departure, Paulus came to see us. He had just been along the road, which was clear as far as Miandowab and waterlogged but passable beyond. On that section a jeep had been attacked that morning; the driver, smuggling in a consignment from the south, had forced his way through to save his stake, and reached Tabriz with car doors riddled and a perforated lung. Paulus had gone to extract the bullet and get to the bottom of the business. According to him, the attack was launched by Shi'ites from Miandowab or deserters disguised as Kurds.

'Anyone can tie on a turban – anyway, at this time of year the Kurds have other things on their minds; the herds are being let out of their winter grazing, transhumance is about to begin. It's true that they're tough and they fight among themselves, but there would have to be a famine before they would fall on travellers. These stories are circulated to put them in a bad light. Such things can always happen, *insh'Allah*, but they're the exception. Take just enough money to live on, but definitely no weapons. They need those too much. They really love guns, so a dozen or fifteen of them would come to get you... what could you do? You'd have to laugh.'

Paulus was right. There was no sense in going visiting with a pistol. Especially as we didn't really know how to use one. We had set out to see the world, not shoot at it.

Turbans and Willows

THE ROAD WAS SCORED by deep gullies; driving was tricky, and six months of sedentary life had made us less skilful. Several times the car got bogged down as far as the bonnet; we couldn't possibly have got it out by ourselves. The best thing in these cases was to sit back on our heels, look at the scenery and wait for a passing cart. The view was worth it. You could see a long way, despite the humidity. To the north, orchards streaked with snow and planted with spiky trees stretched away towards Tabriz and winter for as far as the eye could see; in the background, Mount Savalan lifted its peaks lightly above the mist. To the west, a desert of marshes separated us from the bitter waters of Lake Urmia. To the south, in the direction of spring, the first foothills of Kurdistan steamed under a shower, beyond a dark plain scattered with poplars. All around us, between patches of snow, the earth was at work – sighing, yielding up like a sponge thousands of droplets which made it sparkle. Indeed, there was too much water. Camels began to cross our path, sodden to their stomachs. The level of the fords rose; we had to strip and find the best way for the car to get through an already strong current.

The Mahabad road

Not a brigand in sight, but groups of six or seven hopeful folk stopped us from time to time. To the Kurdish mind anything with a motor and four wheels had to be a bus, and they set about climbing into the car. We firmly explained that the engine wasn't powerful enough, the springs would give way... they would exclaim, clap us on the back and settle with their parcels on the bonnet, or the running board or the bumper to show they'd be fine, that they didn't mind being uncomfortable, it was only thirty miles after all... When we made them get off – cautiously, because they were all armed – they decided that we must want money and would amiably take a toman from their belts. The question of the car's construction or capacity didn't occur to them; it was a kind of steel donkey made for carrying as much as possible and for dying under blows. We, on the other hand, thought one adult or two children were the most we could manage.

On the outskirts of Mahabad we picked up an old man, spattered with mud up to his bottom, who was ploughing through the melting snow and singing at the top of his voice. Getting into the passenger seat, he reached into his skirts for an old pop gun which he politely handed over to Thierry. It was not considered seemly to hang on to weapons indoors. Then he rolled us a large cigarette each and began to sing away very merrily.

As for me, what impresses me most is gaiety.

Mahabad

Clay and straw houses with blue walls, minarets, steam from samovars, willows on the river bank: in the last days of March, Mahabad was bathed in the golden-yellow of approaching spring. An overcast light filtered through the black bank of cloud on to the flat roofs, where the storks were nesting, clacking their beaks. The main street was just a rut along which walked the Shi'ites in their dark caps, the Zardoshti* in their felt skullcaps, the turbaned, thickset Kurds arguing in husky tirades and staring at strangers with a kind of brazen warmth. Those with nothing more urgent to do walked firmly in our footsteps, a few paces behind, leaning forward slightly with their hands behind their backs – always behind their backs, because their trousers had no pockets.

Thus escorted, we wandered across mud a foot deep, accompanied by intense stares, drinking tea from stalls and breathing in the lively, receptive atmosphere... but two cops with ruined faces were shadowing us, anxious to maintain a semblance of authority and trying to disperse the harmless crowd with a few half-hearted blows.

That was the black side of Mahabad: too many uniforms. There were the royal blue tunics of the Iranian police force, and little groups

---

* Zoroastrians, still numerous around Urmia, their co-religionists are the Parsees of India.

of ragged soldiers everywhere, looking like unpleasant prowlers and trailing around at a loose end. Their officers were not so visible; quite by chance, walking about on our first night, we bumped into a dozen who were chatting at the entrance to a bridge threatened by the river in spate. They broke off for a minute examination of our permits, drily advised us to go back 'before the Kurds rob you', and went on with their debate. Each in turn was shouting in order to make himself heard above the roar of the river, while an orderly jotted down names and numbers in his notebook. It took us a moment to work out that he was taking bets as to whether the bridge would collapse or not. The answer was yes.

There were no Kurdish robbers in Mahabad, only malcontents whom the army was responsible for keeping quiet. But stories of bandits provided a convenient pretext for a large garrison; officials connived at hawking around these rumours and supported them when necessary with arbitrary arrests. The Kurds put up with this occupation in disguise even less willingly in that the army had left a legacy of bad memories. The liquidation of the small 'Kurdish Republic of Mahabad'* in 1948 had been a rough business: the autonomist Kurds, whose claims were modest enough, had been decimated, and their leader, Qazi Mohammed, hanged high despite the most solemn assurances. The people of Mahabad carefully tended his grave and regarded passing troops with a look that boded no good.

The proprietor of the Hotel Ghilan, who was the ex-minister of transport, had fared better than the unlucky Qazi. Condemned to death by the Persians, he had obtained a legal pardon in exchange for several villages; at seventy he retained a thoughtful zest for life and this spirit seemed to light up his inn. It was a building with walls six-foot thick and enormous joists, between which swallows and martins made their nests in the straw. Two iron beds painted sky blue, a kitchen table and a Kurdish carpet in faded colours furnished the room we returned to at night, soaked to the bone. While our drying clobber steamed over the brazier, we wrapped ourselves in blankets and played draughts by the apocalyptic light which rose from the

---

* Contemporaneous with and twin of the 'Democratic Republic of Azerbaijan', which had met the same fate.

flooded street. The proprietor, who brought us dinner, would join us to survey the board, give us a second helping, or to signal by a discreet nudge that we were missing one of the countless tricks which are the salt of this apparently simple game.

A Kurdish storyteller from the bazaar also came to share the meal. He knew lots of legends and pastoral threnodies, and we recorded them. He sang like a maniac, with a sort of decided gaiety that attracted the whole storey. Our neighbours knocked on the door one after the other, and sat down in a row on the beds to listen. They were *arbabs* from the shores of Lake Urmia, corpulent, muscle-bound and sharp as weasels, who had left their estates well guarded and had gathered in Mahabad in order to follow the pre-electoral shenanigans more closely. Apart from a turban of dark cloth with fringes hanging over their eyes, a broad cotton belt and a Kurdish dagger, they wore Western dress: solid, fifteenth-century barons in suits of English worsted, perfectly at ease in that strange room. They examined us and our baggage with the open scrutiny typical of the Kurds, offering us their ornately carved snuffboxes, or smilingly drawing from inside pockets their massive gold turnip-watches, holding them against their ears and making them chime.

'May I come in?'

The smooth-voiced, slant-eyed police captain came in without waiting for a reply, his fangs bared in an ingratiating smile. He put his revolver on the table with his wet cap, greeted the company, and asked how we'd spent the day with a friendliness that barely disguised his annoyance at finding so many Kurds assembled in our room. He was convinced that we only pretended not to understand Persian and were there to intrigue; he resented not having arrived in time to hear more. It should be said that various influences were at work beneath the surface in Mahabad: British, Russian, American, separatist Kurd – not to mention the police and the army, who were not pursuing the same objectives. Each belonged to a faction and it was important to know which one; the captain, newly arrived in town, struggled to keep up to date. The residents of the local prison, by means of complaints and anonymous letters, had succeeded in having the prison governor recalled, and the captain, transferred to Mahabad, half-heartedly assumed his responsibilities as warder and improved conditions for the sake of his reputation. Being at a loose end, he constantly came to visit us – out of friendship or suspicion – and insisted on accompanying us in our wanderings. He even dared to criticise the regime, trying to find out what we thought. Such continual surveillance annoyed us, but he went about his work too skilfully for us to slam the door in his face. Moreover he spoke good English, faithfully retailed to us our guests' most subversive remarks and translated the storyteller verse by verse:

> The rain falls down
> Everything is cloudy and rainy
> What are you waiting for, spring flowers?
> And all this water, falling, falling
> It is the tears from my eyes...

It was an apt song: the inn floated like an ark on the sound of the gutters, and the incessant rain, which swept away one bridge after another, prevented our leaving the town. We were running out of money. The proprietor of the Ghilan had willingly let us have the room and would have trusted our honest faces, but the captain, whose solicitude grew more nervous and his surveillance stricter the longer we stayed, offered us hospitality in the prison. It was a friendly but peremptory proposal: we had no choice.

Mahabad gaol

Daybreak through the bars first touched the copper-buttoned tunic hung against the blue wall, then a poster in Iranian national colours featuring some bemedalled, worthy policemen now defunct; finally, the silhouette of the captain in pyjamas, gargling interminably. Stretched out on the ground in our sleeping bags, we watched morosely as he did a dozen knee-bends, counting as he breathed out, then donned his uniform, smiled at himself in the mirror and patted himself on the back as a man in good trim. Then he would open the windows on the morning downpour, light a stick of incense to purify the air, and sit down in his office, slowly rubbing his hairy hands as though to persuade an invisible, reticent interlocutor.

'Could we go out today?'

He was really afraid not... the town was too restless, the elections... we would be molested and he was responsible... besides,

he particularly wanted us to share his lunch: wild fennel shoots in black butter, a Kurdish speciality which he would get someone to prepare specially. He rang for the duty cop who came at a snail's pace and saluted, concealing in his left hand the knitting with which he whiled away his time, then set off for the bazaar with his shopping-bag.

'Excellent stuff, fennel,' said the captain, breathing in deeply, 'good for the bowels and strengthens the intestines.' A string of dietary admonitions followed. Sound digestion and an understanding of how food worked were the captain's hobby horses. Of course health is a good thing, but to have a daily demonstration! We would turn our faces to the wall and sleep a bit longer; after all, gaols are made for sleeping in and this one provided our first break.

Around nine o'clock the place woke up. We could hear yawning and singing in the cells. The errand-boy from the cheap restaurant next door brought in the sentries' tea on his head; then the barber arrived, his strop over his shoulder, to do his round of the prisoners. The petitioners too, tripping over us to reach the captain's office: pitifully humble relations of the prisoners, professional smugglers, country mullahs who left their donkeys at the door and came in, bowing deeply, to intercede for one of their flock. Eyes half-closed, at ground level, we watched the procession.

One morning, two muddy Turkish slippers grazed my nose and a powerful, heartrending woman's voice woke me with a start. It was a supple, statuesque lady of the night, her face inches thick with make-up. She spoke Azeri and I understood enough by then to grasp that she was complaining to the captain about the soldiers who had enjoyed her but hadn't paid up.

'It's the army,' he replied, 'I can't do anything there. Don't go with soldiers any more, go with my policemen – if they still can – and then come back and complain.'

He offered her a cigarette and had tea served. She sat in the corner on a table, draped in her flowered chador, puffing away, continuing her playful quarrel with the captain. She clearly wasn't a bit afraid of him. You can recognise fear immediately by the lowered voice and eye. She, however, chattered away, swinging a muddy shoe: gibes, grievances, the gossip of the bazaar. Her voice had a harsh vitality; she spun stories, interrupted herself only to break into laughter or to send a few coarsely flirtatious remarks in our direction. Her ankles were caked in dirt, her eyes murderous and magnificent; there were traces of bites around her mouth. She might have been a river in her own right: muddy and deep and strong. She wagged her finger teasingly once more, and disappeared as suddenly as she had come. The captain had a good laugh.

'She wants to go back to the country for a while – she also does the villages, you know, like a pedlar, on foot, with her perfumes in a pouch and an iron-tipped staff.'

Dreadful, humiliating lives – yet so full of strength. I should have scrambled out of my sleeping bag and hugged this virago, except that the guard who kept the door – his hand cupped to his ear so as not to miss a single word – would have been nonplussed.

Our status as guest-prisoners was not precisely defined. In the afternoon we could go out into the town, between two policemen charged with looking after us: two elderly chaperones with café-au-lait moustaches and short breath, who pleaded with us when we forced the pace. We had nothing against them, but their presence was not very helpful; besides, it wasn't particularly civil to be surrounded by policemen among these perfectly well-behaved people. The only way of shaking them off for good was to disappear into the bazaar where, because of a few modest exactions – in accordance with their rank – they wouldn't readily risk themselves. So they would settle in a tea shop on the edge of this dangerous zone, and we would collect them on return to avoid their being reprimanded.

It was a small bazaar, gaily buffeted by the wind. Its stalls opened on to glistening mud and buffaloes with shadows under their eyes wallowing in pools; hangings flapped in the downpours. There were camels, their foreheads covered in blue beads to ward off the evil eye, bundles of carpets, barrels of rice, lentils and gunpowder, and above each awning, there was the white commotion of the storks. In the midst of this bestiary, each Shi'ite shopkeeper calculated at top speed on his ebony abacus; the muleteers shod their beasts in the midst of sparks and the smell of burnt horn, or loaded them up – quite openly – with contraband destined for their cousins in Iraqi Kurdistan. They didn't hang about; seasonal unemployment and the proximity of an uncontrollable border stimulated brisk competition. There were lots of children, too, absorbed in shouting out counting songs or dancing in circles round the spectators – serious, sinister-looking grown-ups. It was thought that you should be inside a circle, not outside it, in order to watch activities properly. There is a Kurdish way of doing everything, and here was a kind of comical, fraternal spirit which pierced me to the heart.

The captain wasn't quite sure of his right to confine us, so in the evenings he invited his upper-crust prisoners for conversation. He treated them gently, partly from genuinely humanitarian motives, partly because he was afraid of being shot by one of their relatives. Both motives are necessary to make a world. Thus we met Hassan Mermokri. His cell blanket over his shoulder, he would come in behind the orderly, salute with supreme nonchalance, and smilingly shake his long mop of hair when the captain said to him each time: 'Hassan, *salmoni tchai dar tchin…* you need a barber.'* He was bare-headed, his tattered trousers were tied at the ankle over those slippers in loud colours that shepherds knit while watching their flocks; his long, slit shirt-cuffs hung over his wrists; and on top he had a dark tunic with a Russian collar, of the kind worn by Kurds on the plains. But his knowledge of Persian** and the pen sticking out of his vest pocket belied his rustic appearance. He was a young *arbab* from the Rezaieh area. When he was sixteen, he had stabbed an uncle who threatened him in the course of an argument. These things happen; there were witnesses in his favour; he hadn't been worried. But four years later, a cousin who coveted the rent from his villages had managed through intrigue and bribery to get him arraigned. Too young at the time to incur the death sentence, Hassan had been sentenced to a hundred years in prison – perpetuity belongs only to God, and doesn't exist in the Iranian penal code. He had been in prison for ten years, and had vowed not to cut his hair until he was released. With every movement of his head, the heavy mane that rippled to his waist flopped over his green eyes. Warming his palms against the glass of tea, he spoke in a subdued voice, slow enough for the captain to translate as he went.

* Literally: you need tea at the barber's, who offers it to his waiting customers.
** The peasants only spoke Kurdish, an Iranian language closely related to the Pahlavi of the Parthian era, and taught at universities in Paris, London and Leningrad.

Hassan belonged to the Kurdish Targuar clan, whose pastures stretched south-west of Rezaieh as far as the mountains on the Turkish border. His family belonged to the gentry and had always served Iran faithfully, but not without taking certain liberties: one of his ancestors had abducted the daughter of a Safavid emperor and perished in the adventure, along with his beloved; another, however, had received from Shah Abbas a fine gold hand weighing three pounds to replace the one he had lost fighting the Ottomans; and there were many more still who had killed for the sake of a few sheep, or three mulberry plants, or a trickle of water (no thicker than your arm) across the rich orchards of Urmia, where apricots, nuts, melons and vines sprang up as if by magic.

'Rezaieh... is Canaan,' added the shrill voice of the captain, who thought we weren't taking any notice of him. 'He isn't lying... anyway he's a good, docile boy, he takes my advice, he likes me – he admires me and I lend him my books. Have you ever seen a gaoler like me?'

I had never seen a prisoner like Hassan: he accepted his misfortunes with fatalistic calm; even the thought of his treacherous cousin didn't disturb that – a bad lot, no more, they are bound to crop up in those large, interwoven Kurdish families. He should have done away with his cousin rather than his uncle. He blamed himself for not being farsighted enough, and thought he was paying for his negligence. His sin, above all, was an anachronistic one, because the folk tradition of the *lex talionis*, the vendetta and family feuds, which had bloodied Kurdistan for so long, was beginning to go out of fashion. Such incidents had become rare, and created a stir. There was still talk about what had happened three years previously in the Bukan valley. The men of two rival families assembled in a house in the village, with their respective mullahs, to sort out a case that had set them at odds for several generations. For a whole afternoon the parties feasted, smoked, and discussed the matter without once raising their voices, but without coming to a solution. So they had banished the priests and everyone under fifteen, bolted the doors and windows, lit an oil lamp in order to see each other's faces, and settled the quarrel with daggers. There were six survivors out of thirty-five guests. The two equally diminished families could no longer watch over their herds, which had promptly been stolen. The lesson had been learned, and the worldly-wise Kurds in the valley had been converted to less radical proceedings.

Night thickened around the gaol. Through the noise of the rain, we could hear the river rising. Hassan, who had begun to show us on a map the whereabouts of the main tribes of his clan, now insistently asked a question which seemed to amuse him a good deal. We didn't understand it.

'It's a riddle,' shouted the captain, who had gone to bed, '*a white castle without doors* – what is it? A white castle…'

I thought this over without success, but we had to wait for the answer as our host had fallen asleep, leaving Hassan to make his own way back to the cell.

It's wrong to say that money flows: it rises. It rises by a natural tendency, like the smoke of sacrificial meat to the nostrils of the powers that be. Iran obviously doesn't have a monopoly on this universal tendency, but in Mahabad gaol it was entirely out in the open. Zeal was not enough to become a policeman; you had to merit the distinction by offering four hundred tomans to the lieutenant of police, which was scarcely profitable for him as he had to offer double that to the colonel for his position. The colonel, in his turn, would have been very foolish to forget all he owed to the provincial commander, who himself had numerous obligations in Tehran. This custom was not officially endorsed: the most punctilious deplored it and the most stoical refrained from it, but low salaries made it inevitable, and the custom was hard to avoid without short-circuiting the whole system and attracting animosity by standing out. Indeed it was generally prevalent. Money gaily made its way upward, and, as everything that goes up must come down, it finished by falling in a benevolent shower on Swiss banks, racecourses and the casinos of the Riviera.

For a humble policeman, four hundred tomans was quite a sum! He could only amass it by getting up to his neck in debt; besides which, he had to pay for his uniform. His salary was subsistence-level, the services he could perform for the prisoners only brought in a pittance and, as he was at the very bottom of the ladder, he could only look to the peasants for reimbursement, wringing protection money out of them or levying fines as his imagination or ingenuity devised. In this respect, his cap and truncheon came in handy. As for the peasants – some of the finest in the world when they were given a little breathing space – they could only take it out on their donkeys, or on Heaven, which never answered back.

Late afternoon. Rain. We were moping. Through the open window we could hear camels squelching through the mud, and the driver singing, squeezing out his voice like a sponge: a phrase, a pause, a savage howl...

'Why is he shouting so loud?'

'In anticipation', laughed the captain. 'Listen to what he says:

"...sainfoin everywhere, wild tulips
it's too much... the sun shines
and the scent of lilac is driving me mad."'

I felt my heart melt with pleasure, just like the viziers in Arab tales. That was the Kurds for you! Such defiance, such restless gaiety, a kind of heavenly yeast working away all the time. They seized any chance of amusement; the people of Mahabad never let one slip, and it had to be admitted that the forthcoming elections provided unbeatable occasions. In a story which was convulsing all the shops in town, a mullah addressed two peasants prostrate in front of a ballot-box.

'Why are you worshipping this box, you scoundrels?'

'Respected mullah, it has wrought a miracle! The whole village put in Qasim and out came Yusef.' And a storm of laughter swept away politics and its corruptions.

The season also had something to do with this tendency to banter. The flood, the drizzle, the squalls promised good pastures soon, and the intoxication of spring bubbling up in the town even reached the gaol.

Puns, snatches of song and dirty jokes flew from cell to cell. After all, under the former director these poor devils had been thrashed, beaten with sticks and tortured in every way: bruises, fractures, acid burns – it was a sorry list. In a black chest painted with rose garlands, where he stored his personal effects, the captain kept a report on the subject so damning to his predecessor that he hesitated to pass it on.

We sometimes saw him take out the wad of paper, pat it thoughtfully, put it back and go off to chat with his lodgers, distributing cigarettes, chick peas and arnica. It was the better part of valour.

This chest also contained, hidden beneath all the forms, a book bound in black which he held out to me one day with some embarrassment: an English bible. He had got it from a condemned man he had known at a little prison he used to run at the other end of the country, an Assyrian Christian* who said on the eve of his execution: 'I have something to do in town this evening. Let me go, and I swear on this book to return tomorrow.'

'Go', the captain had replied, 'but if you're not here to be hanged tomorrow, I'll be hanged in your place.'

This was not strictly true: at worst he risked losing several months' salary; all the same, he hadn't slept a wink. The man returned in time, and left his bible to the captain. At least that was what he told us, with some complacence. Had things really happened that way? Had the captain invented this fable and the shade of this 'perfect being' in order to lend colour to a life that was too solitary? It didn't much matter – it was plausible. The Tehran papers were stuffed with that sort of story. Nothing is impossible in Iran: the spirit has as much room for the best as for the worst, and you have to take into account their constant and fanatical longing for perfection. It can drive the most carefree souls to the rashest of resolves.

The rising waters and the rains had already made two thousand homeless in the town; now they carried away, along with much else, the west wall of the gaol. Several cells were left wide open, and the captain posted guards on the roof to prevent the occupants taking to their heels. We could hear them going to and fro over our heads amongst the storks' nests, yawning and striking flint and steel together to light their pipes. Night had fallen. The captain was fiddling with his radio to pick up Baku; Thierry was drawing under the bare light bulb hanging from its cord; I was quite happy leafing through the Assyrian's bible. In fact the desire to stay dug in here long enough to read the book carefully from cover to cover, and to watch

---

* Descendants of the last communities who, after the fall of the Assyrian empire, had found refuge in north Azerbaijan. They are mostly Monophysite Christians.

the prodigious spring unfold, crossed my mind more than once. The Old Testament especially, with its thunderous prophecies, its bitterness, its lyrical seasons, its quarrels over wells, tents and cattle, its genealogies falling like hail – all this belonged here. As for the Gospels, in this context they regained the dizzying boldness of which they've since been robbed so thoroughly, but it was difficult to find Charity incarnate, and the forgiveness of trespasses remained decently obscure. There was only a supporting cast – centurions, publicans, Magdalenes – and the unavoidable Golgotha. To turn your left cheek to the person who had struck the right was not the custom in Mahabad, where such behaviour could only lead to a pitiful end. If Christ returned there, as in Galilee the old folk would certainly perch in the trees to see him pass, because the Kurds respect courage... then boredom would quickly surge back. Anyway he

would meet the same end anywhere: crucifixion all over again, and fast. Perhaps, in our sensible countries which distrust martyrs as much as prophets, it would only be a matter of locking him up; perhaps his existence would even be tolerated, speaking in parks or with great difficulty getting published, to general indifference, in a twopenny magazine.

Mangur

The water kept rising and the houses along the river collapsed one after the other. The goal was under threat and no one gave us a thought. We took advantage of that to slip away at dawn and climb southwards up the valley, as far as the lands of the Mangur who are the most hard-headed, unkempt and mischievous of all the Kurds. The singer from the Ghilan inn came with us. In order to avoid the military posts he had cut straight across the hills, climbing quickly without pausing. We crossed vast, waterlogged fields which gave way with a squelch under foot. The rising sun lit up the glacier and glistened on the silt-laden expanses round the town behind us. Except for the moving speck of a rider following the ridges straight ahead, the mountain was deserted. The air smelled good and the day promised to be fine.

At the end of the morning, we caught a glimpse of the hamlet of Beitas against the sky: a dozen shacks perched on a spur, round a small dried-mud fort which commanded the valley. From the highest roof in the village, a thickset silhouette was tracking our approach through binoculars. When we reached the foot of the peak, the look-out came down from his perch and rushed along the path to meet us. Twenty yards away he stopped, his elbow shielding his eyes; he hailed us loudly and signalled us to approach. It was the *arbab*, an old man broader than he was tall, dressed in black and spattered in mud up to the eyes. His left hand was missing the index and middle fingers and trachoma had blurred one eye, but the other fixed us, sparkling merrily. Two black greyhounds, mad with excitement, pranced around him.

When you have any dealings with Kurds, always look them in the eye. They need this contact. The look is their way of weighing up a person and finding their way in. They always maintain eye contact when talking and expect you to do the same. Moreover, don't use your left hand to shake with, offer or receive anything: it's the impure hand, which is used for blowing your nose and wiping yourself. Thus we held out our right hands and stared, without saying a word, then the *arbab* tapped us on the shoulder and took us off to lunch.

The dagger is a brother, the gun a cousin, runs a Kurdish proverb. In the one room which constituted his keep, the *arbab* had what looked like a family: in his belt he wore a *brother* at least a cubit long; as for *cousins*, they lined a hollow niche between two loopholes, above the samovar: a rifle with sights, four Brno guns lovingly polished, several *parabellums* with well-worn triggers, and the artillery binoculars he had just replaced. This arsenal was his only luxury; his village was poor, his urchins ragged and his table frugal: a plate of rice sprinkled with clear tea, a bowl of yoghurt visited by flies and a bottle of Rezaieh wine which, as a good Muslim, he refused to touch. But what there was, he offered gracefully – even the wine, as it was within our religion just as it was outside his. The Mangur were so far from being fanatics that they still marked their pancakes with a trefoil cross, in memory of a service the Armenians had rendered them four generations ago.

If the *arbab* thought well of Iranian Christians, he thought less of Musaddeq, whose declarations concerning land ownership had brought about the first peasant uprising in Kurdistan. In the spring of 1953, following a speech which promised 'the land of Iran to the people of Iran', the Kurdish peasants, whose tenure system was semi-feudal, took up their forks and flails and demanded their rights. The landlords took down their rifles and advanced on them, gun in hand. In the region of Bukan, clashes had left about fifty dead. The *arbabs* had even pinned a few leaders by the ear to the gates of their farms – then, having been advised that Tehran would stir up dissent and that the army would seize the opportunity to move in, the next day they delivered a kick up the pants to the troublemakers and had offered them good peace terms, which hadn't been broken since. Convinced that Musaddeq had been playing with them, the Kurds were in favour of General Zahedi's *coup d'état* and had contributed to his success by rounding up several thousand horsemen in south Kurdistan to keep at bay the powerful Qashgai tribe, hostile to the Crown. In principle, then, relations with the monarchy were excellent and the *arbab* wore two decorations on his torn tunic, pinned there by the Shah himself;

at the local level, however, it was quite a different story because of the troops stationed at Mahabad. The *arbab* didn't want any uniforms in his valley, and indeed the soldiers didn't risk going there.

Travellers were another thing; the laws of hospitality shielded them, and they made an interesting change. Given their reputation down on the plain, the people of Beitas didn't often have visitors. The *arbab* grilled us, his mouth full, spraying rice all around him. The singer translated from Kurdish into Persian; although we understood only one word in six, he was an inventive mime and the conversation went swimmingly. When gestures weren't enough, Thierry sketched with a knife-point on the back of his tin plate: our route since Erzurum, the car, the prison bars. The *arbab* was most amused by these graffiti and even clapped to show that he understood. The prison episode specially amused him – 'Prison! Excellent!' He slapped us on the back heartily enough to dislodge our lungs, and had a good time of it.

Just as well, since the valley didn't have much else to offer: an orchard red with shoots, four camels in a prickly enclosure, a herd of buffaloes crossing the sunlit mountainside, a litter of greyhounds, some long-haired goats and a donkey with one eye, like him. Not to mention *hadji lak-lak,** the stork, the bird of good omen who nested each year on the roof of the small fort. Below the village, the stream cascaded between willows, hazel trees and Asian poplars. From where we sat we could see a couple of grey waders in the stream, perfectly still, watching for fish. From time to time the *arbab* tossed a stone to disturb their quiet, letting out a loud belch or a sigh of contentment. It was a mild, quiet day; March catkins, tender shoots and new twigs were out; little copses the colour of wickerwork were coming back to life: a sparse Eden, but Eden nevertheless.

When necessary, the *arbab* supplemented his funds by ransoming the smugglers who passed through his valley to reach the Iraqi bazaars of Kirkuk or Mosul with their consignments of rugs, opium or vodka from the Caspian; they returned with guns, cloth and English cigarettes. It was a good circuit as long as the people of Beitas didn't interfere. They did interfere, however; after all, it was their territory which was being crossed by night, without warning. When

---

* The pilgrim *lak-lak* – the name imitating the sound of its beak

they got the upper hand, the Mangur kept the money, the arms and the worthwhile animals for themselves; as for the opium, which Kurds take in moderation, it was re-sold through middlemen to the garrison at Mahabad, who were only too happy to put themselves to sleep that way. But with armed men on the lookout, these ventures did not always pass off without a hitch: the *arbab* had already lost two fingers and a son, but hadn't allowed such a trifle to stop him maintaining his rights.

They must have been waiting for men to pass through that very night, because on returning from our walk we found several horses tethered at the door, and the small fort crammed with enormous men in high spirits, busy loading their clips and oiling their gun-breeches. Helpful relatives from the nearest village had come to lend a hand. You would have thought that they were getting ready for a wedding, and I would have given a lot to understand the jokes being fired off all round the room. At about four o'clock in the afternoon we left the family to its preparations and set out again. The *arbab* accompanied us as far as the river; we only had to follow its course to reach Mahabad. Halfway down, we stopped to bathe our feet, and watched the night coming down over the snow-streaked slopes, smelling of fennel and anise.

Mahabad

We took leave of the captain, who did not wish to take leave of us. The elections were over, we hadn't robbed anyone; he no longer had any reason to impose his 'hospitality' on us. While on the one hand he was lonely, on the other he was still convinced that we were concealing the real reasons for our travels and he wanted to hold on to us until they came to light. He spun out the farewells, and telephoned in all directions to prove that the road north was not usable. This wasn't easy: on the Rezaieh side the line had been swept away with the bridge; he couldn't get through to Miandowab, cranking the starting handle and cursing the rustic telephone, swearing down the mouthpiece. To us, however, the old-fashioned set with its receiver in the shape of a convolvulus seemed wonderful: we hadn't used a telephone for eight months.

'You see for yourselves,' said the captain, hanging up. 'I can't get hold of them. The bus isn't getting through – you'll never make it. I bet you ten tomans that we'll see you back here tonight.'

Ten tomans – that was quite a bit. We took advantage of the bet to borrow forty, and as he insisted, we shook on it.

The road to Tabriz

The sheet of water barring the road was three feet deep or more, and forty yards wide. In the middle of the current an almond-green bus was lying on its side; another, more fortunate, had made it back to the bank. The jeeps were too heavy to be towed and had to turn back, but the buffaloes, camels and a high-wheeled wagon crossed without difficulty – even a fiacre managed, its brass sidelamps and black hood flapping in the wind giving a tinge of provincial melancholy to all the to-ing and fro-ing. It took us an hour to remove all the luggage, the battery and the seats, to disconnect the electrical fittings and coat the engine with cotton waste, and another hour to find a peasant with a hefty, dappled horse. We harnessed it to the car; then whipping, pushing and pulling our way through the icy water, we slowly made our way back to the Tabriz road and winter.

Tabriz II

THE CAPTAIN HAD GIVEN us an address in Tabriz where we could repay him. It was that of an American missionary, crippled by isolation, a short-sighted, wary man, with those crooked teeth which seem peculiar to certain Anglican sects. He misunderstood the object of our visit and immediately gave us to understand – without even asking us to sit down – that he had enough trouble with Muslims without looking after Christians, whom he only took in at Christmas; anyway, we shouldn't count on him as he hadn't room for another soul. To cut this innkeeper short, we waved the captain's tomans in front of him, and a glint behind his glasses informed us that he knew all about them.

'Wasn't it forty?' he said, counting the notes again.

'It was – but the captain bet us ten, and he lost.'

'Are you sure?' he replied with insulting unctuousness, as though he expected us to burst into tears.

We deserved at least a hundred tomans for never having offered advice to the captain, who had inflicted so much on us. We suggested to the pastor that he take the road to Mahabad and check up in person, and left him standing there – not without noticing in passing some very un-pastoral stains spotting the front of his trousers. We emerged fuming into the snowy alley. 'There's someone who'd jerk off at the sight of a train crash,' said Thierry. I added several jokes in atrocious taste. We had become really gross. Too bad: it was winter again, a time of cold, enforced chastity; we were back in this cruel, overcrowded town. The vulgar slang at least provided an illusion of warmth. We would become more refined in the spring, along with the tender new leaves.

Returning to the widow's that evening, I noticed that someone had visited our rooms while we were away, and had rummaged through our things. The money was still there, but the letters from Europe which I kept in a niche were topsy-turvy, and the stamps had been cut off. I didn't care about the stamps, but in a nomad's life letters can be helpful, and re-read, and as the job had been done with hasty scissors, almost all the lines – the ones at the end – on which you rashly build your illusions, and which are such a pleasure to re-read, had gone by the board. In all the neighbourhood kitchens boys must have stuck these stamps in their albums, jumbled up with those long-awaited words. As the widow wasn't back yet, I went to the grandmother to complain. In Armenistan punishment was always a matter for the elders, since they had the most leisure, the strongest strap, the most equable spirit and were best at measuring out their blows. The old woman put on her old slippers, alerted several shrews of her own calibre who reigned over neighbouring courtyards, and they came down on their brats like lightning. As they confessed, you could hear their sobs coming nearer and nearer, and the little shaven heads rang under hard palms. Within the hour a procession of harpies, their eyes darting fire beneath their black shawls, brought us fistfuls of stamps soaked in tears. They seemed pleased with themselves, and the contrite wailing which filled the night in a diminishing crescendo must have fooled the ears of the Armenian gods. These Christian foreigners were, after all, allies. They paid without haggling. The neighbourhood law, of which the grannies were the guardians, had been infringed, and this law commanded them to be honest, especially in the minor details of daily life and conduct. There was more latitude in larger concerns, which were a matter of fate.

There was still too much snow to drive to Tehran. We whiled away the time by taking the car to be fixed at the Point IV garage, which Roberts, the engineer, had kindly put at our disposal. We saw a lot of him, but he was not the same. He had lost his high spirits. One night I asked him what was the matter.

'Everything... it's this whole country, nothing works.'

He was back from a tour of inspection in a village; work hadn't progressed an inch during a whole month, nor had the peasants made him welcome.

The American Point IV in Iran was like a house with two storeys, on which different kinds of activities took place. On the ground floor, the political level, they were busy fighting the Communist threat by using traditional diplomacy – promises, pressure and propaganda – to keep a contemptible, corrupt but right-wing government in power. On the first floor, the technical level, a large team of specialists were busy trying to improve the living conditions of the Iranian people. Roberts belonged to this group.

Politics didn't interest him at all. What interested him was electronics, the songs of Doris Day and Patachou who he said were *angels*, and building schools. He was a scientist, but also an open, kind-hearted man who took real pleasure in the idea of such useful work: hence his disillusionment.

'Think about it. I go there in to build them a school, and when they see me coming the kids pick up stones.' Smiling, he repeated, 'A school! I ask you!'

I believe that Americans have great respect for school in general, and for primary school in particular as the most democratic kind. I believe that of all the Rights of Man, the one that appeals to them most is the right to education. It's natural in a country which is highly developed in civic terms and where other, more basic rights are taken for granted. School is one of the main ingredients of the American recipe for happiness, and so in the American imagination a country without a school must be the very image of a backward country. But recipes for happiness cannot be exported without adjustments, and in Iran the Americans had failed to adapt theirs to a context which puzzled them. That was the source of their difficulties. Because there are worse things than countries without schools: countries without justice, for instance, or without hope. Thus it was in Tabriz, where Roberts had arrived with full hands and a head buzzing with generous projects, which the reality of the town – each town has its own – frustrated every day.

Let's go back to the matter of his school. This is how Point IV had handled it: they provided land, materials, plans and advice free of charge. In return the villagers, who were all more or less handy as masons, were to provide the manpower and enthusiastically build a local school on the American model, where they would enjoy the privilege of education. Such a system would have worked perfectly in a Finnish or a Japanese community. It didn't work here, because the villagers didn't have an ounce of the civic spirit on which the Americans had counted.

The months passed. The materials mysteriously disappeared. The school wasn't built. They didn't want one. They refused the gift. There was plenty to discourage the donors, and Roberts was discouraged.

What about the villagers? They were poor peasants who had submitted to a tough, feudal farming system for generations. For as far back as anyone could remember, no one had offered them such a gift. It seemed even more suspicious in that among the Iranian countryfolk the West always had a reputation for stupidity and greed. Nothing had prepared them to believe in Father Christmas. They were very much on their guard and scented a trap; they were suspicious of these strangers who wanted everyone to work towards some hidden end. Poverty had made them cunning, and they thought that by sabotaging their instructions, they might thwart the plans they couldn't make out.

Moreover, this school didn't interest them. They didn't see the point of it. They hadn't yet reached that stage. Their preoccupations were getting a bit more to eat, not having to watch out for the police, being able to work a bit less or at least to have a share in the fruits of their labours. The education they were being offered was also a novelty. To understand it, they would have to ponder on it, and it's difficult to think when you have malaria, or dysentery, or that giddiness that comes from a little opium on an empty stomach. If we thought on their behalf, we would see that reading and writing wouldn't get them very far unless their status as serfs was radically changed.

On top of all this, their mullah was against the school. Knowing how to read and write was his privilege, his monopoly. He drew up contracts, wrote down petitioners' requests, deciphered the pharmacist's instructions. He would see to these things in return for half a dozen eggs, or a handful of dried fruit, and had no wish to lose his little income. He was too sensible to criticise the project openly, but in the evenings, on doorsteps, he gave his opinion. And they listened to him.

Lastly, it was a risky business to deposit new materials in a village where everyone needed bricks or mortar to repair those buildings which were obviously useful: the mosque, the hammam, the baker's oven. After several days' hesitation, they helped themselves to the pile and began on their own repairs. Yet the village had a bad conscience, and felt uneasy about the American's return. If only one could explain oneself, it would all become simple... but it's hard to explain oneself. When the foreigner returned, he found neither the school nor the materials, nor the gratitude he had hoped for, just closed faces and sideways glances, as though no one knew what was going on, and boys heaping up stones in his road because they could read their parents' faces.

...It was just a gap to be bridged, but it was a wide gap, because practising charity demands endless tact and humility. It is much easier to rid a village of malcontents than to change its ways, and no doubt it is easier to find Lawrences of Arabia and agitators than technicians who are also good psychologists. Roberts, who was such a man, soon began writing in his reports that it would perhaps be necessary to drop the idea of a school in favour of improving the water supply to the old hammams, which were a source of virulent infection. It was some time before his superiors in America admitted that he was right. But for Point IV to continue, there had to be a steady supply of fresh capital. Thus Roberts's basic problem – a symbolic one – was really the American taxpayer. We know that the Americans are the most generous people in the world. We also know that they are often ill-informed, that they like things to be done in their own way, and that their hearts are warmed by results that appeal to their sentimentality. It is easy to persuade them that Communism can be kept at bay by building schools similar to those of which they have such happy memories. It is not so easy to admit that what works at home mightn't work abroad; that Iran, that old aristocrat who has known all about life – and forgotten much – is allergic to ordinary medicines and calls for special treatment.

Presents are not so easy to give when the children are five thousand years older than Santa Claus.

April

It was a bit less cold, thus one of my pupils unthawed and began to think. (Doubtless the others thought, but judged it advisable not to show that they did.) She was reading *Adrienne Mesurat* – full of backbiting and petty betrayals, a life consumed and smothered by the provinces – where she thought she had come across her own story, I don't know why, and this had got her going. She thought about it even at night. As one thing led to another, she began thinking about anything and everything, dizzy with thought and unable to stop. It was a kind of haemorrhage, a fit of panic. She had to have a stream of new books, extra lessons, and replies to a host of questions: could even a Frenchwoman be so unhappy? Was my beard 'existentialist'? What was 'the absurd'? She had come across these words in a Tehran review.

The beard was simply to make me look a bit older, as half my little class was in its forties. But the absurd? The absurd! I was dumbfounded. In Switzerland I wouldn't have been at a loss for a reply, but how could I explain what was quite beyond the life of Tabriz, a town which couldn't be made to fit any philosophical system. Nothing was absurd here... but everywhere life was on the rampage, pushing up from underneath like a shadowy leviathan, forcing cries out of the depths, driving flies to plague open wounds, pushing out of the earth millions of anemones and wild tulips that within a few weeks would cover the hills with their fleeting beauty. And constantly drawing one in. It was impossible to remain aloof from the world, even if you wanted to be. Winter bellowed at you, spring soaked your heart, summer bombarded you with falling stars, the autumn vibrated in the harp-strings of the poplars, and its music left no one untouched. Faces lit up, dust flew away, blood ran; the sun turned the dark heart of the bazaar to honey, and the sound of the town – a web of secret connivances – would either galvanise or destroy you. But no one could escape it, and in this fatalism lay a sort of happiness.

Since being in the Mahabad gaol, I had been worried by a question myself.

'Please explain to me, a *white-castle-without-doors*: what could it possibly be?'

'An EGG', she said immediately. 'Couldn't you guess? It's easy, even a child knows that.' And she sat back, as though to savour the significance of her answer.

An egg? I didn't see how. De Chirico himself couldn't have worked that one out, yet the least of my pupils could see the association at once. As neither their eggs nor their castles were so very different from ours, it had to be their mentality that was different. And I had accused them of a lack of imagination! No, it was just that they exercised it in a totally different realm.

Mussa and his pal Saidi the swot, and Yunus – the son of a Turcoman mullah – with the *kütchük* always at their heels, carrying the umbrella – what a band! Once the holidays began they were always on our doorstep, frisky as puppies, giggling over nothing, choking on our cigarettes, insisting that we correct their English, begging us to play tangos – but only in minor keys. Saidi even copied them carefully into his music notebook, so that he could sing them in Pahlevi with his eyes closed when women went by – 'ta-ra-ra-raaaa', carried away in a sort of nasal tone. I wondered what he imagined Spain to be like. He wrote out the titles in two colours, with amusing errors: 'Avant de mourir' became 'Avant de mûrir'.

'Ripening is certainly apt,' Thierry told him, 'but that sounds more like pears than passing away.'

Before we left, Saidi passionately wanted us to go round to his place one evening, with our instruments. It was the modest home of needy officials who had killed the fatted calf, rolled out the carpets and left their best room to the band in gratitude for their son's good school reports. There was lemon vodka, white melon, roast mutton and Bulbul's records on an old gramophone. The alcohol went to Saidi's head and he had us play the most lugubrious songs in our repertoire at least ten times. It was a splendid, warm-hearted evening, full of heavy wine and strong food. When we left the room, over-heated by the oil lamps, the *kütchük* was asleep on the carpet, with a coat thrown over him. The others, excited and unbuttoned, their hats askew, were challenging each other to a burping competition.

A little donkey was standing in the corner of the snowy court-yard. As we passed, we saw the mother, a bulky shadow scarce distinguishable from the night, bringing it the melon rinds we had sucked to the skin. We thanked her: it had been a most enjoyable evening and her son was a fine boy. In a husky voice she wished us a good road ahead, and her magnificent eyes expressed her discontent. Then she went up to the room where all hell was breaking loose among Saidi and his friends. The stars were whirling round the sky in the blurred moonlight. Yet we'd not had much to drink. Was it spring at last?

Despite the Tabrizi passion for politics, the elections hadn't aroused a flicker of interest. It must be said that the Governor had dampened their spirits by letting it be known that whatever happened, only his candidate would get in. Although he was a man of his word, a few outsiders chanced their arms all the same. They went so far – like one hospital doctor – as to sleep on a straw mattress in front of the ballot-box already provided through their efforts. All in vain.

On the other hand Old M——, our neighbour, was re-elected in the large village called Gilan where he owned some land – and lawfully elected, as he had too much self-respect to rig the votes. He had even allowed his young opponent – a progressive teacher – to address the peasants gathered in the square first, concerning corruption in Tehran, the rapacity of *arbabs*, and promising them the moon. When his turn came, the old man contented himself with saying:

'What you've heard is all too true… I myself am not a very good man. But you know me: I don't take much and I protect you from people greedier than I am. If this young man is as honest as he says, he won't know how to defend you from the people in the capital. That's obvious. If he isn't, remember he's starting out in life and his coffers are empty; I'm at the end of mine and my coffers are full. Who is the lesser risk for you?'

His words rang true to the peasants, and they voted for him in force.

That sort of crude approach makes sense there. It's not that people are any worse than elsewhere, simply less hypocritical. Whereas the West knows how to make good use of hypocrisy, they much prefer cynicism. They lie to their nearest when they have to, as people do the world over, but without deceiving themselves as to their motives or ends. Thus when they get what they're after, they can rejoice freely among friends. The procedure is more visible, but less tortuous and sugar-coated. Besides, it involves one less lie; they may fool others but they don't try to fool themselves. We've known since Herodotus how much the Persians dislike telling lies. So there are fewer Pharisees in Iran, but a good many smooth-tongued rogues; and the indignation that certain foreigners display on encountering the latter is yet another proof of Western hypocrisy.

I went to find the Old Man to thank him for the garage he'd lent us for the winter, and to congratulate him on his election. Settled in a corner of his gallery with a jeweller's magnifying glass on his fore-head, he was busy sorting into old cigar-boxes his collection of Hellenistic and Safavid intaglios, which he had amassed over thirty years of rifling through Middle Eastern bazaars. There were pendants and bezels of glassy stone, the colour of coral or honey, clearly incised with outlines of Arion and his dolphin, or the mosque of Meshed, Hermes Tristmegistus, or *Allah ou akbar* (God is great) in Kufic script. Both of us took pleasure in seeing our two worlds thus, as neighbours. He showed me at least thirty pieces, one after the other, while chatting away, as serene and sarcastic as ever. When I asked him about the road to Tehran, which was making us anxious, he set aside his stones and began to laugh.

'It's a bit early, but no doubt you'll manage, and if you can't get through, you'll see some amazing things... The last time I did it – ten years ago perhaps – the floods had carried away the bridge over the Qizil Uzan. There was no way of getting across, but as the waters might subside from one day to the next, buses and trucks kept arriving from east and west, and because the banks had been loosened by the rain, many of them had been bogged down at the bridgeheads. I had too. We settled in. The banks were already covered with caravans and herds. Then a tribe of Karachi* on their way south set up their little forges and began to do odd jobs for the truck-drivers, who obviously could not simply jettison their loads. Drivers who were self-employed soon began to sell things on the spot, bartering goods for vegetables from the peasants round about. At the end of the week, there was a village at each end of the bridge, with tents, thousands of animals bleating, mooing and lowing, and camp-fires, poultry, and a few shelters made out of branches and planks to serve as tea-houses. Families rented a place under the canvas of empty trucks, there were tremendous backgammon games, a Dervish or two exorcising the sick – not to mention all the beggars and whores who had rushed in to take advantage of the windfall. Magnificent chaos! And green grass was beginning to shoot up. Only a mosque was missing. What a life!

'When the water went down, everything dissolved like a dream. And all of that because of a bridge that shouldn't have collapsed,

---

* The name given in north Persia to gypsy nomads, musicians and blacksmiths.

because of our disorder and our poor, negligent officials. Ah, believe me,' he said fervently, 'it's well said that Persia is still a land of wonders.'

The word made me ponder. At home what is 'wonderful' tends to be an exception that's arranged; it is useful, or at least edifying. In Persia it might just as well spring from an oversight, or a sin, or a catastrophe which, by breaking the normal run of events, offers life unexpected scope for unfolding its splendours before eyes that are always ready to rejoice in them.

Leaving Tabriz

All the roofs were overflowing. In the gutter, beneath a crust of blackened snow, you could hear a swift, welcome rustling. The sun warmed your cheek, the poplars were stretched to bursting against a sky that was light again. Deep down, slowly, heads, bones and hearts pushed out their shoots. Projects took shape. It was *Bahar*, spring.

In the Armenian restaurant the secret policemen, their tunics unbuttoned, drowsed against a blue wall on which a customer had written with charcoal, in French, *merde au roi*. In the bazaar there was

animated conversation in front of the closed stall belonging to the last surviving Jewish enterprise. Its owner had been more or less crushed by a bale of carpets. The others had already left Tabriz; in less than six months they had been bankrupted, cornered and swept aside. No one had come to their aid: quite the opposite. The town was too tough to hand out any presents – as old as the world itself, and just as captivating. It was a loaf of bread baked a hundred times over. You saw everything there, and getting angry was no use because it wouldn't budge an inch. There is a proverb which runs: 'Kiss the hand you can't bite and pray that it will be broken'. That's what they lived by, and it didn't prevent moments of grace, of ecstasy and of gentleness.

The crows made a great din in the tops of the young branches. In the marvellous light and a mist of golden mud, enormous trucks coming from the west squealed to a halt in front of the bazaar. We drank tea in the street, listening to a clarinet rising from the souk. We recognised it – the Armenian joiner, a careful, sweet man who carried his instrument in a pretty pearwood case.

> Turnips boiled in their juices and cakes scented with lemon
> Caps and clubs
> The fiacre drawn by a horse with a paper carnation behind
>   its ear
> Black window
> Frozen panes inscribed with stars
> Muddy roads leading up to the sky
> Tabriz.

Shahrah

Shahrah: high road... but there
are no roads in Iran, high or otherwise.
Colloquial English-Persian Dictionary
Lieut.-Col. D.C. Philott

The road to Mianeh

TRUST A MILITARY man to make such a statement! Of course there
are roads in Iran, although it must be admitted they could be
better. The one that runs from Tabriz to Mianeh, for example, has
been reduced by large trucks to a sunken path for twelve miles or so.
There are two deep ruts, with a heap of clay and rubble down the
middle. As our wheels couldn't span this, we had to keep our left side
on the central rise and our right in the right-hand rut, and go along
with the car tipped to the point of scraping the edge of the trench.
Besides that, the bonnet pushed along the mass of mud and stones
which built up in front of us, so that we had to stop every fifty yards
to shovel it away. It was a mild day and we sweated as we worked,
watching the hailstorms beating down on the vast slopes all around
us, in high spirits at having resumed our journey eastwards.

We also had to lift the car out of the way so that trucks could get
past. These were mammoth trucks, like forts, in keeping with the scale
of the countryside. They were covered in decorations, blue-bead
amulets and votive inscriptions: *Tavvak'kalto al Allah* (I am the driver
but God is responsible). They travelled at the speed of draught-
horses, sometimes for weeks, heading for some lost bazaar or military
outpost, and certainly towards breakdowns and blow-outs which
immobilised them for even longer. Then a truck would turn into a
house. It would be secured to the spot, fixed up, and the team could
live around the stationary wreck for as long as necessary. Pancakes
could be cooked in ashes, there would be card games and ritual
ablutions. It is a continuation of the caravan. I saw such broken-down

monsters several times, in the middle of villages, with hens sheltering in the shadow of their wheels, and cats having their kittens underneath them.

Mianeh

Every entomologist in the world has heard of Mianeh because of the Mianeh bug, whose bite is fatal. Despite this notoriety, it is an attractive village, ochre with touches of blue, with a mosque whose turquoise cupola sails lightly above the April mists. (But beware of the power-line which is looped across the balcony of the tea-house as innocently as a washing line.)

Mianeh is also the border between two languages: on one side Azeri, in which you count up to five like this – *bir, iki, ütch, dört, bêch*; on the other side Persian – *yek, do, sé, tchâr, penj*. You only have to compare them to understand how pleased the ear is to move from one to the other. Azeri, especially when sung by the formidable old gossips of Tabriz, has its beauty, yet it is a harsh language, made for squalls and snow; the sun doesn't touch it. Whereas Persian is warm, nimble and polite with a tinge of weariness: a language for summer. On the Iranian side faces are also more mobile, shoulders more fragile, the cops less massive – though more menacing – and the innkeeper more resourceful and more inclined to fleece you. We simply ignored the bill he presented to us. It was absurd. He took us for simpletons. Bursting into laughter didn't have any effect; our laughter wasn't genuine. Anger then? While I quibbled over each item, Thierry disappeared in order to work himself into a lather; returning apoplectic with his eyes popping out, he threw a few notes into the innkeeper's lap. He was still mystified and not convinced that we were really furious, but his hesitation was fatal; we had already rounded the corner when he came to and rushed down the steps two at a time, shouting.

The road to Qazvin

At first it followed a valley planted with willows. The mountains were rounded and seemed very close, the river was noisy and the fords bad. Then the valley opened out and became a large, marshy plateau, still spotted with snow. The river was lost to view and our gazes were lost too: the first undulation was thirteen miles away, and the eye could make out a dozen more stretching all the way to the horizon. Sun, space and silence. The flowers were not yet out, but everywhere dormice, voles and marmots were digging away like demons in the fertile land. On our way we also encountered ashy herons, spoonbills, foxes, red pheasants, and occasionally a man whose leisurely pace was that of someone who called his time his own. In a landscape this size it is all a question of scale; even a rider at full tilt gives the impression of dawdling.

Tehran, April-May

The charm of such slow voyages overland – once the exoticism has worn off – is that you become aware of details, and thus of minute shifts in geography. Six months of hibernation had made us into Tabrizi, stunned by the least little thing. At each stage we discovered tiny changes that changed everything – a way of looking, the shape of clouds, the angle at which caps are worn – and, like someone from the Auvergne arriving in Paris, we reached the capital as amazed bumpkins, with recommendations in our pockets of the kind scribbled on a tabletop by a friendly drunk, from which you can only expect misunderstandings and wasted time. This time we had just one: a note to an Azeri Jew whom we immediately set off to find. He looked as though he'd sell his own mother, but he was an excellent chap, full of a confused desire to sort out our affairs for us. No, he didn't think that foreigners like us could stay in an inn in the bazaar... No, he had no contacts on newspapers... but would we like to dine with a chief of police who could work wonders? That sounded fine. It took for ever, under a leaden sun, to eat a sheep's head in yoghurt with an old man who had received us in his pyjamas. Conversation languished. The old man had retired long ago. He had once been chief in a little southern town, but he didn't know anyone at headquarters any more... anyway, he'd forgotten everything. On the other hand, he thought one or two games of chess wouldn't come amiss. He played slowly and nodded off; that took up the day.

At the Phars inn on the edge of the bazaar, the room was so cramped and cluttered that you had to lie on the bed to work. The ceiling was a mosaic of BP petrol drums, which let in the moonlight, and there were several fleas in attendance. The guests were Kurds, Qashgai nomads smelling of mutton, peasants who greeted us with a small, measured smile, and in the room next door an Assyrian merchant who kept counting a very small amount of coins. A wooden gangway linked the rooms to the tea-house, where the radio ceaselessly broadcast the calm scales of arpeggios which make up ancient Iranian music. On the left, beneath the windows, a series of worm-eaten galleries descended to the entrance to the bazaar. Lower down still were clumps of tamarisk, and the mud-brick suburbs whose crumbling, interlocking walls stretched away into the country.

On the right, the old cannons of Tupkan Square, then the neon lights of Lalezar Avenue slope gently upwards towards the best neighbourhoods. At the bottom there are two rowdy taverns where thin little girls in sequined tutus do balancing tricks in the midst of men bellowing and drinking arak. There are peddlars of combs, espadrilles, holy pictures, whistles, condoms and 'Alaviolette' soaps. Then a theatre advertising the Persian adaptation of Molière's *L'Etourdi* and presenting a play adapted from Firdausi's *Shahnameh* (*Book of Kings*), in which the Sassanian Bahram Gur settles incognito in the house of his poorest subjects so as to confound the officers who are harassing them. We went to this one, and it was a camp performance complete with false red beards, anachronistic turbans, fights, tumbling, and the punishment of the wicked. Perfect, in fact. The elegant audience in grey suits and the porters in shirtsleeves applauded vigorously what was in effect a pantomime – not without sniggering from time to time, since the current ruler went nowhere without his police; impromptu inspections were no longer fashionable, nor such dénouements... Next came the newspaper offices and some smart tailors. The lights were softer here, trees more plentiful, voices more subtle. Fabulous cakes shaped like mitres flamed under the coloured lights of the Armenian tea-room. Still higher up, between Shah Reza Avenue and Chemeran Hill, Cadillacs purred past the long, pale walls and blue enamelled porches of aristocrats' houses: there was a sense of space and money. Yellow taxis driven by old, tattered dreamers criss-crossed the night, their floors littered with pistachio shells, and twenty-five miles north of the last gardens, the luxuriant snows of Elburz shone high under the spring sky.

Leaning over the balcony of our inn, we could see the whole of Tehran. We were positioned well below the salt, but we were determined to grab a few morsels. At our age it was still a good thing to tackle a new city from the bottom. The strong smells, the grins, the friendly hunchbacks – it was great. All the same, we had to earn enough to take us to India.

I made some remark or other about Tabriz...

'Listen, listen to him – it's fascinating, all of it!' The speaker made the table shut up, asked me to repeat it; despite his glowing gaze he wasn't paying the slightest attention. Or if by some miracle he were listening, he would have forgotten it before the evening was out.

This was our friend Galeb. He was a new editor on the largest paper in town and very successful. For his article on the H-bomb, for example, he had borrowed a title from the Alsop brothers, and a superb quotation about terror from Rilke. He would have quoted the whole poem because he felt it was so apt, but there hadn't been room. He was prepared to appropriate any number of beautiful things! Still, it was done in the right spirit. He was also a poet, so in a way other people's poetry belonged to him. It was only lack of time that stopped him writing his own.

'*An ocean they call Pacific* – that's good journalism, isn't it? Anyway, my boss was delighted... as for your articles, he's very pleased with them, exactly what we need just now. We're going to take at least four.'

What did this mean: that they'd just take one or that they'd reject the lot? I wasn't on their wavelength yet. We'd have to see. Meanwhile, Galeb had put our photos on the front page with such exaggerated captions that we were amazed to be saluted all over town by unshaven strangers, who swept off their hats theatrically. It was all very entertaining, but we couldn't live on it. So I went regularly to badger Galeb about my articles in a bistro on Yusuf-Abad Avenue, run by a fateful, philosophical Georgian émigré. You went down three steps and when your eyes got used to the dimness, you could make out drinkers seated in front of fresh bottles of Maksus vodka, with a shakily drawn red eagle on the label, munching on cucumbers or smoked fish to ward off a migraine, while the sun lazily washed the avenue, the railings of the imperial palace and the houses of the Armenian merchants, rich and snug behind their insignificant brick walls. Galeb was happy to settle down there when it was hottest, editing his paper or waiting for the girls he pined for, writing on the tablecloth

> ...the day before yesterday: a day
> Yesterday: two days
> Today: three days
> You have not returned
> My heart is burnt...

When I asked if my articles had been burned at the same time, he rubbed his ink-stained hands and replied,

'Not exactly... How shall I put it... They're sleeping. They wouldn't be stuck if only you could give me some *cards*, then I'd take the business in hand.'

These *cards*, which seemed to be absolutely essential for doing anything in Tehran, were notes from influential people recommending us to his director. We had actually sent him one at the beginning – three lines from a senator whose lungs had been healed in Switzerland – but apparently this hadn't carried enough weight. In less than a week it had gone as flat as a bottle of bad bubbly and editorial enthusiasm had given way to total amnesia. The day I went to collect my pieces I couldn't get to speak to the director or his deputy. It was the siesta hour and everyone was off enjoying themselves. Finally I came across an old man in overalls who took an hour to find my manuscripts and who gave them to me saying, 'Here you are, Monsieur, it's a load of rubbish... all the same, tell your typesetters at home that their Iranian colleagues send greetings.' This I've now done.

Nevertheless, this lack of success in no way dampened Galeb's optimism; he continued to promise us favours, cards and wild prospects; to propose interviews or patronage that were out of his hands, out of pure kindness, wanting to cheer us up and give us heart. Where would be the pleasure of promises if they always had to be kept? Cradling our illusions – that was his way of helping us. (Illusions are useful even to the most sceptical of us.) And he did help us. Several times, in order to organise lectures or an exhibition, we visited people whom Galeb rashly flattered himself he knew, using his recommendation. He didn't know them, but false keys can open doors; after a few minutes' embarrassment, the conversation often worked out to our advantage. Galeb went pale when we reported these approaches.

'The rector received you? On my say-so? You know, I've only spoken to him in passing... and it worked? That's fantastic! Between you and me, I tried to meet him two years ago – perhaps you could put in a word for me.'

It was his turn to be disbelieving. We thanked him warmly: we really liked Galeb.

If we were to believe the inhabitants, Tehran was not even a beautiful town. In the course of modernisation, several charming corners of the bazaar had been pulled down, avenues had been straightened and robbed of their mystery, the ancient gates had been knocked down along with an old restaurant decorated with frescoes dating from the Qajar era,* in which you could recognise, amidst the plumed turbans, the Comte de Gobineau in his striped cap against a background of orange trees in pots. You had to go south to the outskirts of the Rei quarter, where the Three Kings had set out from, to gain any real sense of the past. They would also apologise for the very dry climate, the dustclouds, the nimbleness of the thieves, and the magnetic currents which made people glum and irritable. They said: 'Wait till you see Isfahan... or Shiraz.'

* The Qajars were the dynasty ruling Persia 1787 to 1925.

Perhaps.

But in Tehran there were plane trees such as one had only dreamed of, enormous trees, each broad enough to shade a few little cafés where you could happily spend a lifetime. And above all, there was the blue. You have to go that far to discover blue. The eye is already being prepared for it in the Balkans; in Greece, it is not only the main colour but also has an overwhelming effect – it is an aggressive blue, as restless as the sea, but still it encourages a positive outlook, adventurous plans, a sort of intransigence. But here – in shop doorways, on horses' halters, in cheap jewellery – everywhere there is this inimitable Persian blue which lifts the heart, which keeps Iran afloat, which attains a light and patina with age like the palette of a great painter: the lapis-lazuli eyes of Achaemenian statues, the royal blue of Parthian palaces, the lighter enamel of Seljuk pottery, the blue of the Safavid mosques and then the blue that sings and flies away, at ease amidst the ochre of the sand, the gentle, dusty green of the foliage, at peace with the snow, with the night...

To write in an eating-house where the chickens peck between your feet while fifty curious people press against the table isn't conducive to calm. Nor is exhibiting paintings – after a lot of effort – and failing to sell even one. We were tired of running round town from one setback to another, the sun beating down on our backs. But when our courage ran out, we could always go to see the blue Kashan* ware in the ethnographic museum: plates, bowls and ewers which are serenity itself. The midday light imparts a slow pulsation that soon invades the mind of the onlooker. Few vexations can resist such treatment.

Since we couldn't count on newspapers, the Franco-Iranian Institute seemed designed to support our enterprise. Shaved, wearing ties and sweating in our winter suits, we presented ourselves there, determined to wrest some crumb from it. After a great deal of to-ing and fro-ing, the secretary ushered us into the director's office, holding her breath, as if we were going to be devoured.

---

* South-east of Tehran, a town famous for its carpets and pottery, especially in the fourteenth century.

He was a well-built, florid-faced man, busy with an impatient telephone call; at the other end there seemed to be a French tourist in search of cultural information. He looked us over rapidly, saw that we'd come to ask for something and – resolved to discourage us from the outset – suddenly began to roar down the phone: she had been wrong to take the Institute for an information bureau... she wasn't the only one who wanted... advance preparation should be made for a trip to Persia... she would just have to speak to the Persians. At the other end some astonished woman, who obviously would have no idea what had caused this sudden change, was hearing these harsh words delivered in the cutting tone of a man whom it wasn't worth bothering with trifles. He slammed down the receiver and turned his scowl on us, grumbling 'Impossible... a crazy woman... fantastic'. Then, having shown us indirectly what metal he was made of, he indicated that we should sit down, and in a voice that was gentle again, its lower register carefully lubricated: 'Now, what's your business, gentlemen?' On the lapel of his black jacket the rosette gleamed like a little sore eye. In short, he was an experienced diplomat. His manoeuvre had given him the advantage, and for the moment we could only stammer out increasingly modest offers of service. He declined them with inexorable politeness, and as we resorted to new proposals – we would have washed blackboards – he had to retreat behind increasingly slender excuses. We insisted. He persisted in his cordial refusals. The heat was stifling; we had the empty, knotted stomachs of the disappointed. We absolutely had to find an opening before this vaudeville became our downfall. Our nerves were on edge: as he finally came up with the objection that a few light bulbs in the exhibition room were not working, Thierry exploded into laughter and, terrified, I felt it carry me away on a wave. The director looked quite put out and with our eyes full of tears we tried to make him understand by gestures that it wasn't he who had set us off. He had to make a quick choice: even if he hadn't taken the initiative in this outburst, he should at least take the lead – without delay. He began to laugh even harder than us, at first deliberately, in measured bursts, but then for real. When the alarmed secretary knocked on the door, he indicated that she should bring three glasses, and when we got our breath back, everything had changed. A ray of sunshine lit up the carpet. Thierry could have his exhibition there in a fortnight; I could open it with a talk... I could give others, if I so desired. All this now appeared the most natural thing in the world. Would I read my text?

'No, I'd rather like...'

'You're right,' the director cut in jovially, 'I, too, feel I do myself greater justice by speaking merely from notes.' He was back on form.

The opening was well presented: the lighting was excellent and the exhibition looked very appealing. 'The French school', said the director, who was now friendly, paternal and anxious. After all, hadn't he discovered us?

'Princess Chahanas will be coming, *mon cher*. We'll wait for her to arrive, and then you'll say, "Your Highness, Excellencies, ladies and gentlemen..."'

Five minutes later, the rumour went round that she wouldn't be coming; shortly afterwards, that she would be. The orders evolved accordingly.

'As I'll introduce you,' he said finally, 'you'll just have to listen and follow my example.'

He accompanied me on to the stage and for several minutes humorously elaborated on the tricks that travellers in our situation usually got up to, which we hadn't until now; our circumspect behaviour being rewarded by the *exceptional* hospitality accorded us that day. This speech seemed a long way from our motives for painting or speaking, but it was true that without the Institute and its excellent library I wouldn't have been able to get anything done. You don't look a gift horse in the mouth.

I concentrated on my public. At the back were students, a handful of journalists brought along by Galeb, two rows of nuns in wimples – excellent! – two more of senators keen on Anatole France, and retired generals whose ears were certainly more attuned to the sound of the *tar* (a sort of Iranian guitar) than the cannon. In front – with beringed hands and slim ankles – a sparkling phalanx of women of the world and here and there, beneath the layer of attentive hedonism, those anxious, super-sensitive faces which the town could produce. In Tabriz we hadn't been so spoiled.

In the end the princess didn't make an appearance, but a fox terrier escaped from a listener's lap and came to sit on the podium, leaning against my table, and he stayed there until the end. If the Simorg bird – which is born out of its own ashes – had perched on my shoulder, it wouldn't have had such a marvellous effect. Thierry sold a lot. The University asked me to give a paid lecture. The same evening, new friends offered us a rooftop studio in a building in the upper town. A garden of mulberry bushes surrounded the house and as the garden gate didn't have a lock, the factotum put his bed across it. He was an old man in a white tunic whom we had to wake up every time we came in late and who, when we apologised, said 'May your shadow lengthen.'

I didn't forget that it was a fit of laughter that changed the wind for us. Since then, I've always kept something absurd to say to myself when things go wrong: when, for example, the customs officers hunched over your expired passport decide your fate in an incomprehensible language, and after a few ill-received interruptions, you scarcely dare lift your eyes from the ground. Then some silly pun, or the memory of a situation which still seems comic, is enough to give you heart – even to make you laugh out loud, alone in your corner – and it's the turn of the men in uniform not to understand; they look at you in puzzlement, raise an eyebrow, check their fly-buttons and assume an expression… and then the obstacles they'd put in your way are removed, who knows why.

Like Kyoto and Athens, Tehran is a well-read town. Of course no one speaks Persian in Paris; in Tehran, lots of people who will never have the chance or the means to go to Paris speak perfect French. And this is not the result of political influence, nor – like the British in India – of colonial occupation. It is simply Iranian culture, which is curious about everything around it. And when the Persians set out to read, they don't read light fiction or the religiose novels of Paul Bourget. In the Institute's library, the margins of works by Proust, Bergson and Larbaud were covered in notes.

One morning on Lalezar Avenue, passing the open door of a scent-shop, I heard a muffled voice, veiled like that of someone asleep and dreaming out loud:

Tu t'en vas sans moi, ma vie
Tu roules,
Et moi j'attends encore de faire un pas
Tu portes ailleurs la bataille...

I tiptoed in. Slumped against a roll-top desk in the golden light of bottles of Chanel was a large man, perfectly still, a journal open in front of him, reading out Henri Michaux's *La nuit remue*; repeating it as though to help him accept things with which he was only too familiar. An extraordinary expression of acquiescence and pleasure spread over his large, sweat-beaded, Mongol features. He was alone in the shop, and far too absorbed to be aware of me. I wouldn't have interrupted him; poetry is never so well spoken as in this private way. When he finished and noticed me standing two steps away, he showed no surprise and didn't ask me if I wanted anything. He simply held out his hand and introduced himself. Two liquid black eyes, a small walrus moustache, a slightly soft elegance: Sohrab.

Like a mirror, an intelligent face is the same age as what it reflects. At twenty-five, Sohrab sometimes seemed to be sixteen, sometimes forty – more often forty. He had the tone of someone who had already ceased to be surprised by what existence offered. He hadn't always recited Michaux in a perfume-shop: Sohrab had done a lot of odd things, and had started young. At sixteen he was already deep in books, night revels and hashish in the entourage of the poet Hedayat, writer in the line of Lautréamont and Kafka, best known for his novel *The Blind Owl*. Hedayat was dead, he had gassed himself in his Paris attic, but his shade still haunted youthful Iranian literature. He had taken drugs; many people took drugs. He had killed himself; some people killed themselves. He loved funerary flowers, wantonness, abandon, and lived with the sentiments of death and night; his followers did the same. In post-war, police-ridden Tehran, this semi-clandestine bohemia lasted five years. There were attempts at avant-garde activities, a picture gallery, a surrealist magazine that folded after two issues... You slowly draw away from the wolf of reality; you think he's slain for good, and he comes down on you like a ton of bricks. Friends are scattered, the gallery collapses; in order to attract a buyer, you have to organise tea-dances – with pretty girls. Then, when they aren't paid, the girls disappear in their turn, except the oldest one who remains in your arms, who knows why, and whom it takes months and many words to untwine. Then you find yourself alone, barely twenty-one, but already jittery and more nervous than you should be.

Then he'd spent a year as a teacher at the secondary school in Marand, amidst the poplars of Azerbaijan and a class of young, curly-haired provincials – dull, desperate boys, who'd never thought of being able to think. By shaking them up and hacking away at their torpor, he had achieved something like the beginning of an awakening; then tuberculosis forced him to leave. Next he had taken advantage of his illness to study for an engineer's certificate and to join an English oil company in Abadan.

'A good life – very near Kuwait, you know; no need for a passport. Lots of smuggling. We'd go there by sea, taking a little something: Leicas cr-ammed [his voice rose tranquilly] with cocaine. It was a venial sin, after all, and it was only when I wanted to unionise the workers that they showed me the door. You should have heard me though, *mon cher*: I treated them to an a-ma-zing speech.'

An emotional man, moved by his country's distress, he had then joined the Tudeh party*, and adopted the tentative Marxism so widespread among Iranian youth. Although many people were loyal to that creed, their loyalty was not without its reservations. If they thought them craftier than the Americans, the Persians' sympathy for the Russians was only lukewarm. (Slogans, capital letters, marches and the party line had never been their strong points.) There was a certain nostalgia for absolutes, always suppressed but ever present, which *Ogonyok's*** feature, 'Sundays on the collective', for all its briefly optimistic *déjeuners sur l'herbe*, couldn't satisfy. As for doctrine, most of those who really understood it found it summary, simplistic and incapable of maintaining those niceties the world always loses too soon, and to which Iran has contributed so much. But when you don't want a brutal, self-serving conservatism any longer, when you hope for nothing from a West which preaches caution, when you are young and alone and there is no centre party, and fear keeps the liberals quiet, then there is not a great deal of

---

* A populist party with Communist leanings, banned by that time.
** 'Small Flame' – an illustrated Soviet weekly.

choice and you swallow your hesitations. For a while, anyway: once Musaddeq was ousted, Sohrab had given it all up. Now he managed his scent shop, and worked as an expert in a state office which, in fact, he never attended. He had recently stopped taking drugs, and this privation was a terrible strain.

'I try to get out of myself, to be normal; people push me, people encourage me. A woman. It's love, *mon cher*... the season for folly.' But he spoke with such weary detachment that I had the impression he was parroting things which were at least a thousand years old. We were sitting between two gigantic lorries, in a café on the old Shimran road. The storm-lantern lighting the place hissed gently. The sky was full of stars. Sohrab spoke in a slow, subtle voice. Large beads of sweat formed at the roots of his hair and kept falling into his eyes. He could hardly see us. Well behind all his talk he was battling alone with his monsters, his fear, fighting off shipwreck, in this white acetylene light, in his royal blue, double-breasted suit, in his twenty-fifth year.

There are few beggars in Tehran, but at the main intersections rows of young ragamuffins sit around a *djou**, chatting, chewing a flower or playing cards. They're waiting for the red light. As soon as it turns, or there's a traffic jam, they rush up to the cars, clean the front window with a rag and sometimes with spit, and are given a few pence. The policeman, who is not necessarily their enemy, allows them time to finish. Others politely offer to show you the way home, carry a parcel or water the lawn. Each morning a mixed herd of boys, the unemployed, and old men climb up from the bazaar towards the windfalls or odd jobs in the upper town. Sometimes too, for a toman a head, the police rope in this floating and always available crowd to represent 'the Iranian people' and demonstrate in front of the Soviet Embassy, or to stone the villa of someone against whom the authorities have grounds for complaint. When the business is completed, the ruckus continues; they do want their money, but as often as not are dispersed with a fire-hose. The next day, it may well happen that these same 'people' mark their frustration by trooping as students to lay flowers on the steps of the same embassy. The same

* A deep channel which runs along the edges of the streets – the water in it is used for everything.

police arrive at the double, seize the leaders – especially the students – chop off their hair and pack them off to do military service again, or to break stones – there are always plenty of those – in the south. It is a sad merry-go-round, but an admirable method of getting rid of at least fifty unemployed men.

Nevertheless, this method was not enough: it was impossible to park your car without seeing a sort of wave surge towards you, offering to 'guard' it for half a toman. It was better to accept, otherwise your would-be guardian might well let down the tyres in your absence, or disappear with the spare wheel in the direction of the bazaar, where you could go and buy it back. In short, they were offering to protect you from themselves. At first we used to refuse: we were on a tight budget and a toman counted.

And we said to ourselves that the car was too shabby. One day we found it right in the middle of the pavement. It must have taken six of them, with the help of onlookers, laughing away, to get it across the gutter. Until this incident, thieves had been considerate, no doubt because of the lines by Hafiz which we'd had lettered in Persian on the left-hand door:

> Even if your night's shelter is uncertain
> and your goal still far away
> know that there doesn't exist
> a road without an end –
> don't be sad

For months that inscription served as password and safeguard in corners of the country where they had no cause to like strangers. In Iran, poetry that was quite hermetic and over five hundred years old still held popular sway to an extraordinary extent. Shopkeepers squatting in front of their stalls put on their glasses to read it to each other across the pavement. In cheap restaurants in the bazaar, which were full of headstrong types, you sometimes came across a ragged diner whose eyes were closed in pleasure, his face lit up as a friend whispered poetry in his ear. Even in the depths of the country, people knew by heart lots of *ghazals* (up to eighteen couplets) by Omar Khayyam, Saadi or Hafiz. It was as if, in France, manual labourers or the butchers of La Villette had been brought up on Maurice Scève or

Gérard de Nerval. Among students and artists of our own age, this taste often amounted to an intoxication. They knew hundreds of these dazzling stanzas which abolished the world even as they illuminated it, and quietly postulated the ultimate identity of Good and Evil, while they provided the reciter – his fine hands with bitten nails clutching a glass of vodka – with the satisfactions which were otherwise few and far between. They could take turns at reciting for hours, vibrating 'in sympathy' like the low chords of a lute, one breaking off to say that he dreamed of killing himself, the other to order a drink or translate a couplet for our benefit.

Persian is wonderfully musical, and its poetry, nourished on esoteric Sufism, is one of the most sophisticated in the world. Still, in massive doses it has its dangers: it ends up as a substitute for life instead of heightening it; for some, it provides an honourable refuge from a reality which is greatly in need of new blood. Following the example of Omar Khayyam, many young Persians 'grasp this sorry scheme of things entire / and shatter it to bits' – but that's where they stop.

Still dipping into his food, the imam repeated, pausing between words, 'No, the road south is dangerous; better to take the Meshed road. You should see the holy town, and I can give you introductions to everyone.' Imam Djumé is the highest religious authority in the city. He is preacher to the court and nominated by the Shah, who delegates his sacerdotal powers to him. For the rest, he isn't even a mullah but the graduate of a European university, specialist in Koranic law and head of a powerful family that has supported the royal house for several generations. He also has links, it is said, with the British. He is thus a politic prelate, whom several fanatics of various persuasions have already tried to assassinate. It's never certain, when he actually shows himself in public, whether he won't be carried off by a bomb. He is very courageous, much admired by women, and most attentive to his gorgeous wife. At the top end of the table, surrounded by a respectful silence, he eats:

> Compote of iced melon
> Rice with jam
> Grilled chicken with mint
> Curded milk with cucumber and raisins

and reigns over some fifteen nephews, brothers-in-law, aunts or cousins who come and go, bow, eat a little bit, disappear, bow again, return and so forth. He is a sort of affable Montaigne in a white turban, with a full face, a beard along his jaw-line, and intelligent eyes that never leave his interlocutor.

Our proposed itinerary seemed to bother him a great deal. There were two permissable routes from Tehran to Afghanistan: the northern one through Shahrud and Meshed, on which there was a regular bus service; the southern one – which tempted us – was much longer, passing through Isfahan, Yazd and Kerman across the south of the Dasht-e-Lut (the Great Sand Desert), then right along the desert of Baluchistan, and ending up at Quetta, in Pakistan. We knew it wasn't used much – but dangerous?

'– Because of nomads?'

'No,' said the imam, 'no – there's no one at all! That's the trouble – and the sun; there's far too much sun.'

But we'd heard so much about those roads. And here was another person, we said to ourselves, who never left Tehran.

'You've no idea what that sun is like,' he went on, calmly. 'Last year two Austrians wanted to take the same road at this season. They died before reaching the border.'

Then he carefully rinsed his mouth, wiped his beard and took us to sit in the garden while he went to say his prayers.

It was a rose garden, enclosed by high walls, with a rectangular pool in the centre. Amaranth, white, tea and saffron roses, in espaliers and clusters, tumbling over pergolas, drank in the light. A few bushes with nearly black flowers, protected by gauze screens, gave out a stifling fragrance. Two barefoot servants with watering cans sprinkled the sandy paths. It was a paradise of subdued colour; the water was still, and the flowers precisely arranged in a silent circle of tubs. But it was an abstract, imponderable paradise: the reflection of a garden rather than a true one. European gardens are luxuriously rampant, carried away by the greatest possible superabundance of nature. Iranian gardens don't pretend to such oppressive plenty: they rely on shadows and calm. You could hardly discern the outline of the stems between soil and flower. The garden seemed afloat: there, the requisites were the miracle of water, and that light buoyancy.

Once his exhibition was over, Thierry went off to paint for a few days in the province of Gilan. I stayed in Tehran to organise a final lecture and supplement our budget. As the university and the Institute had already shut down, I borrowed the hall from the St Vincent de Paul brothers at the College of St Louis. My unclerical subject, 'Stendhal the Unbeliever', hadn't put them off. They even let me work in a little classroom, smelling of chalk and the holidays, and kept me supplied with cold beer and cigars.

Stendhal hadn't been so welcome at the Institut Jeanne d'Arc, where the Poor Clares educated all Tehran's best bred girls.

'Montaigne, Toulet – they would do at a pinch,' said the Mother Superior, 'but Stendhal! That anti-clerical Jacobin! Why don't you talk about Pascal instead? You're the melancholy type, he'd fit you like a glove and I would guarantee a full hall.'

We were sitting beneath a large silver crucifix, drinking Chianti. She poured herself a glass, adding, 'Of course, I couldn't bring the sisters along – anyway, I've never read him, the infidel. He's on the Index.'

She was a woman of character and spirit, who ran her school in a masterly way, and her caustic manner concealed a very appealing kind of sadness. We understood each other well: she was of Serbian extraction and I love Serbia. She held fast to her origins and was more indulgent towards Yugoslavian revolutionaries than towards writers on the Index. As I was talking to her about music in Belgrade, she went off and came back with a record.

'I'll lend it to you – it's excellent. Be very careful of it, it's very precious to me.' She held out 'The Song of the Partisans', stamped with a large red star.

Out of curiosity, I went to consult the Index at the Internunciature, and saw that only Stendhal's *Journal* was listed – on account of several very lively passages – but on the other hand, it had almost all of Pascal's works. There was a charming monsignor in attendance, from Apulia, and I asked him the reason for this miracle. He replied:

'Stendhal's not really dangerous, and as "Arrigo Beyle" he has an excuse: he loved Italy. But Pascal is a sort of church commissaire. When a Protestant approaches him, it's good news –

he's going to come in; but if a Catholic does, look out – it's because he wants to leave.' They are good at logic in the Trani area.

The eve of departure

Even the tops of the plane trees didn't reach the terrace where we slept. The sky was black and hot. Flights of ducks on their way from the Caspian Sea passed overhead, sounding like oars. Through the branches of Heydayat Avenue, I could see the shopkeepers settling down on the pavement for the night. It was more sociable, and cooler. They laid down pallets, or just unrolled large red and black blankets on the ground. They also carried out their blue enamel teapots, their backgammon sets and their nargilehs; although they couldn't see each other, they carried on conversations across the street. Everywhere there was that feeble, subdued electric light of Asian towns whose grids are overloaded – no harsh light, just enough to cope with the dark without deleting it. Or there was the icy glare of carbide lamps, which lit the dusty foliage from below and turned it green.

This town appeals to me, and as Stendhal is on my mind, let me take the opportunity to say that he would have liked it too. He would have found his world again there: plenty of sensitive minds, a few out-and-out rascals, and in the bazaar, cobblers spouting maxims, whom he could have gossiped with happily. There was the shadow of a court – full of intrigues, bad coffee and dark revels – a little more corrupt than Parma's, which also went in fear of the liberals it imprisoned and where the Fiscal Rassi would have cut the figure of a choirboy. The people had finesse and to spare, commenting on excesses with bitter humour; they were regretful rather than remorseful, and nonchalantly immoral, heavily reliant on divine indulgence. Not to mention the discreet religious circles and the groups of Sufic adepts, concealed in the bazaar, which added an essential dimension to the town and buzzed with the most bewitching speculations about the nature of the soul. Stendhal, who was basically so concerned with his own, wouldn't have remained indifferent.

What struck me most was that the lamentable state of public affairs had so little effect on private virtues – to the extent that I wondered whether they didn't actually foster them. In Tehran, where everything went wrong, we had met with greater hospitality, good-will, delicacy of feeling and helpfulness than two Persian travellers would ever find in my town, where everything works well. We had worked hard, too, and earned enough for at least six months' keep. The next day we'd go and buy dollars in the old bazaar, descending that same Lalezar Avenue which we had found so hard to ascend.

Departure at 7 a.m.

In a café in the lower town, our friends were waiting to wish us *bon voyage*. I hadn't realised we had so many. One last glass of tea, and when the car moved off, ah... ah... with what sighs and glances they saw us melt into the distance. Yet they probably wouldn't miss us at all, and they certainly didn't envy us our destination, because in Tehran they swore that the inhabitants of Isfahan were false friends, those of Kashan all knaves; that the water in Seistan's wells was salty; that Baluchistan was populated by morons. No, what took their fancy was the concept of the Voyage: the surprises, the trials, the mystique of the road. The Voyage was perennially fascinating to the East, and this often worked to our advantage.

The road to Isfahan

'First stage: short stage', say the Persian caravan drivers, who know perfectly well that on the night after leaving everyone will remember that he's left something at home. Usually you don't get further than a *farsang*.* The scatterbrained have to be able to get there and back before sunrise. This allowance for distraction is another thing I like about Persia. I don't think there's a single practical arrangement in the country which fails to allow for man's basic imperfection.

From Tehran to Qum the road is tarmac, but pitted with gaping potholes. From Qum the surface is packed hard and so rugged that you can't go more than twenty-five miles an hour. From time to time, a pale mustard-coloured tarantula zig-zagged across it, or the dark spot of a scorpion going about its business. Grimy vultures perched on the telegraph poles, or else one saw just their tails sticking up from

---

* About four miles – the measure corresponds to the ancient 'parasang' in Xenophon's *Anabasis*.

the carcase of a sheepdog or a camel. We were all the more interested in this bestiary since, during the day, the violent light and the vibration of hot air entirely blotted out the countryside. About five o'clock the sky turned red and, as if holding a torch up to a misty window-pane, you could then see the desert plateau with marvellous clarity; it might have been the one over which the angel led Tobias by the hand. It was yellowish and scattered with pale tufts. Aubergine-coloured mountains surrounded it with strange indentations: they were *distinguished* mountains. That is exactly the word: over thousands of miles the landscapes of Iran spread out with a lean, supreme distinction, as though shaped by a puff of air from the finest ashes; as though bitter, immemorial experience had long ago arranged the incidental features – the water, the mirages, the columns of dust – in such a perfect way that whether it was exulted or discouraged, the country could never disturb it. Even in the desolate south-eastern expanses, where there is nothing but death and sun, the contours remain exquisite.

People were not used to seeing such a small car as ours; it was so full of stuff that they had to come right up to it to make sure that it really was a car. Eyes widened and jaws dropped as we drove past them. One morning, in a suburb of Qum, an old man was so taken aback, and had to turn round so often, that he ended up with his gown twisted round him, falling on his backside with the cry, '*Qi ye Shëitanha!*' ('Who are those devils?') Packs of inquisitive people clustered round when we stopped, and a policeman would laboriously decipher the inscription on the door in case it was something subversive. By the time he reached the second line, the public would join in and the exercise would be transformed into a murmured recital; pockmarked faces would clear and glasses of tea – impossible to obtain till then – would appear as if by magic. There were hours, too, of careful driving towards horizons so wide they scarcely seemed to shift; eyes burnt by the light, siestas in a circle of flies, the evening *abgousht* – mutton, chickpeas, lemons cooked in pepper-water – and nights on the ledges of tea-houses. In short, the lives of travellers on five tomans a day. Right down to anxiety over engine noises, I started to love it.

Isfahan

With the back suspension broken, we slowly crossed the farmland surrounding the town. The sun went down behind tall, solitary plane trees, casting slanted shadows across the mud-brick villages with their worn, gentle ridges. In the fields of mown wheat, the stubble caught the light and shone like bronze. Buffaloes, donkeys, black horses and peasants in bright shirts worked to get in the last of the harvest. We could see the light, bulbous domes of the mosques floating above the outstretched town. Sitting on the bonnet in order to help the sick car, stunned by tiredness, I searched for a word to encapsulate these images, and repeated automatically: *Carabas.* *

A bit later

Friends in Tehran had said to us, 'You must go to our cousins down there, we've told them about you', and gave us an address.

The Persians are very hospitable, of course, but it was late and we had arrived at the wrong time. It was Friday evening, when families get together, and the house was full of children and country cousins to-ing and fro-ing in their pyjamas, munching dried apricots, playing backgammon, bringing in blankets, lamps, mosquito nets. Too exhausted to sleep, I busied myself sorting out our medicine-chest on the dining-room table. The men passing through the room greeted me affably; some sat down and watched me in silence. One large, jovial stranger thus kept me company throughout. After a moment, he asked whether he might use the thermometer, put it in his mouth, and continued to watch me. He had eaten too much in breaking the Ramadan fast, and feared that he might have a fever. No: his temperature was 37.5°. That's all I ever knew about him.

The radio was broadcasting the beautiful, ancient Persian music of the *tar*. It was like a completely detached Segovia, or a piece of broken glass slowly falling to the ground. But our host soon turned it off, saying that such music prevented thoughts of God. He was a merchant in the bazaar – courteous, very pious and blessed in his business. He told me how strictly he was bringing up his sons, who were already so polite that they were almost invisible. I found it very difficult to listen. The tiredness from Tehran had caught up with us in this welcoming house, and now it had arrived it cut me off from everything else. What we needed to do was to sleep for a week.

* The Marquis de Carabas in Perrault's tale, *Puss-in-Boots*. –Trs.

You could easily fit about a hundred buses in the courtyard of the Royal Mosque – the Masjid-e-Shah – and perhaps Notre-Dame as well. It forms one small side of a piazza or maidan measuring about 1,700 feet by 550. In the old days there used to be tremendous polo tournaments here, and the riders passing the imperial box at the gallop would look smaller than a capital O well before they reached the end of the maidan. Under the thirty arches of the bridge which crosses the Zaindeh Rud, you can see ants busy tugging what look like postage-stamps in the direction of the piers; these are men going to wash rugs that are over thirty yards long.

In the seventeenth century Isfahan, with six hundred thousand inhabitants, was the capital of an empire and one of the most crowded cities in the world. Today it has no more than two hundred thousand. It has become provincial, it has shrunk, and the vast, graceful Safavid monuments float above it like clothes that have become too big. It is also run down and crumbling away, because Shah Abbas was in a hurry to impress and didn't take the time to build soundly. It is precisely because of this very human vulnerability to time, which is their only imperfection, that these buildings seem so accessible and moving. 'To defy time': I am quite sure that, since the Achaemenians, no Iranian architect has succumbed to that inane ambition.

The Royal Mosque, for example: not a storm passes without its losing a heap of irreplaceable earthenware tiles – a few dozen out of more than a million – but the whole thing is so vast it would take a fifty-year storm before the loss was noticed. Nevertheless, they fall in the slightest wind; from a great distance they bounce down and then break into dust without your hearing more than a faint sound of falling leaves. They are a famous blue – I'm back to blue. This time it is combined with a little turquoise, yellow and black which makes it vibrate and gives it that power of levitation which we usually associate with sanctity. The enormous cupola, covered in blue, lifts into the sky like a captive balloon. Beneath the dome and in front of the palaces forming the maidan, the Isfahanis go to and fro, out of scale, affable but not particularly trustworthy, with that air common to inhabitants of towns that are works of art: they seem to be the jury in a competition which the foreigner, no matter what he does, will never understand.

That said, Isfahan was exactly the marvel we'd been promised. It alone was worth the trip.

Last night we went for a walk by the river. Is it really a river? Even where the waters are highest they get lost in the sand, scarcely sixty miles out of town. It had almost dried up, forming a wide delta of sluggish, luminous rivulets. Old men in turbans crossed it on donkeys in a cloud of flies. For two hours we followed a hot and dusty path bordered by croaking frogs. Through the gaps between willow and eucalyptus, we could already make out the whiteness of the desert and the mauve Zagros Mountains; their jagged outline reminded us of Provence, and there was exactly that warm, dangerous intimacy with nature that one finds sometimes on summer nights near Arles or Avignon. But it was Provence without wine, boastfulness or women's voices; in short, with none of the obstacles or the uproar that usually separates us from death. I had no sooner said this to myself than I began to sense it everywhere: death in the glances we exchanged, in a herd of buffalo, in the lighted rooms open to the river, in the tall spirals of mosquitoes. It came at me, full tilt. And what about this trip? A mess… a failure. You travelled, you were free, you were heading for India… what then? I could repeat 'Isfahan' to myself as much as I liked: Isfahan meant nothing. This impalpable town, this river which didn't flow anywhere – these were not the right things to provide an anchoring sense of reality. Everything spoke of dissolution, refusal and absence. At the bend of the riverbank, the uneasiness became so strong that I had to turn back. Thierry's heart was also in his boots; he shared my feelings although I hadn't said a word to him. We returned at a run.

It's odd how the world suddenly goes bad, turns rotten. Perhaps it was lack of sleep? Or the effect of the vaccinations we'd renewed the previous night? Or the Djinns who, it is said, attack at night if you walk beside water without mentioning the name of Allah? No, I believe that there are landscapes that are out to get you, and that you must leave them immediately otherwise the consequences are incalculable. There are not many of them, but they certainly exist: five or six on this earth for each of us.

The road to Shiraz

The village isn't marked on the map. It was planted on a cliff overlooking a dried-up river. It wasn't exactly a village, more of a formidable, crenellated ants' nest, its walls cracking and crumbling under the unimaginable reverberation of the midday sun. It was abandoned except for the tea-house, where about fifteen Qashgai shepherds were resting while their flocks cropped the nearby mountains. They were magnificent brutes, their sharp faces blackened by the sun, and they wore those mitres of light felt which go back to the Achaemenians and are the mark of their tribe. They were sitting in a row along the ledge, or squatting in corners, rifles across their knees. Several held a distaff of dark wool in their left hands, and sang as they spun. A grunt followed by a heavy silence answered our greetings. They didn't utter a word, looking from us to the car at the door and back again. Passing around cigarettes eased the atmosphere a bit. As the owner didn't seem in a hurry to serve us, we began a game of cards to keep up a bold face, then Thierry fell asleep, and I began to clean the grazes I'd got when tinkering with the engine. When they saw the first-aid box, the Qashgai drew nearer, murmuring *davak* (medicine), and I had to bandage a whitlow and a sprain, and dab a few ulcers they had coated with dung or sump-oil. The healthy ones, despite derisive booing, also asserted their right to treatment: a giant had been pricked – like Sleeping Beauty – by his distaff; another was suffering from an invisible thorn in his foot; and a third, even more sinister-looking, from palpitations and vapours.

About three o'clock we took to the road again. Outside the door a few chickens pecked at the burning ground to dig up the scorpions to which they are so partial. The Qashgai accompanied us to the car. It wouldn't start: the battery was dead, worn out by the sun. We put it into third and pushed it towards the steep slope which began at the end of the village. The Qashgai were lending a hand, and it took us a moment to register that their eyes had lit up, and that while they were pushing a bit, they were pulling even harder. Yes, they'd found us sympathetic but our luggage was a very beguiling sight, and we had difficulty in disengaging the large hands now reaching for it, pretending to laugh – a hollow laugh – knowing that only the pretence of farce would stop our coming to blows. At the same time we were pushing like galley slaves, and as the slope was steep and the car was laden, it soon got up enough speed for us to leap inside. A few zigzags on the level of the earthen walls left behind even the most zealous of our helpers.

With this impetus, the car crossed the dried riverbed at the foot of the cliff, then came to a halt, even deader than before. For two hours we worked on the engine and under the car, but in vain, trying to find a short-circuit under the encrusted dust, with the sweat blinding us… The next village worthy of the name was over sixty miles away. The sun was beginning to sink and we had no desire to spend the night in the shadow of that accursed castle of baked earth. Fortunately, as it grew cooler there was a little traffic. First of all an elderly NCO, who came on foot from a nearby lookout post, and contented himself with saying that Allah was great but the motor was *sukhté* (burnt out), and sat down on a rock. Then came a jeep on its way up to Isfahan, with two veiled passengers. The driver kindly picked up our tools, did what we had just done, with as little success and, unnerved by his impatient clients who began to call out and peep the horn, he broke the distributor head in trying to force it, apologised, dumped us and drove off in a cloud of dust.

Evening fell. The soldier hadn't stirred from his rock and we were beginning to get worried when Fortune sent a small truck, which stopped alongside us. It was newly repainted, it was empty, and its deck was large enough for our car. It was going down to Shiraz, like us, driven by three Goupil fellows. Of all the Iranians, the people of Shiraz are reputed to be the friendliest and happiest, and these were pure Shirazi: fairly cunning, shrewd, unshockable and moderately grasping. They agreed to take us – and our car – to the town of Abadeh. The oldest of the three took the wheel, drove his truck to the bend in the river at the risk of breaking his neck, and reversed so that the deck was level with the road; we put the car on to it, ourselves into the car, and thus established we set off southwards at a sedate pace, as the first handful of stars rose from the edge of the desert.

It was night when we reached Abadeh, where everything was already asleep. It was a dump anyway, and we couldn't have got the car repaired. We were lucky to find something to eat. Dipping my pancake in a bowl of sour milk, I watched our truck-drivers: the owner, the mechanic, the boss-driver – the usual trinity of tramp-trucks. They had just had a successful trip to Tehran and talked endlessly about the packet they were going to make in Shiraz. I listened with that feeling of long familiarity and habit that perhaps arose from tiredness. The boss in particular had something ungainly about him that seemed inexplicably familiar. When the meal was finished, they proposed that we should go on with them to Shiraz, which they wanted to reach before dawn. As they were travelling empty anyway, and as we were *saya* (travellers), they would carry us for free. We spent a good hour securing the car with ropes before climbing back into our perch; there were nearly two hundred miles and the road promised to be bad. It began by rising above six and a half thousand feet, then cut through the middle of a desert edged by black, jagged mountains. Above the noise of the engine we could hear the bells of invisible camels. The sky, dizzyingly pure at this height, covered us like a bowl. When it wasn't bumpy and we didn't have to watch the ropes, we let ourselves loll gently, our heads in the cool air bathed by stars.

Two-thirds of the way along, a lantern held at arm's length and logs across the road forced us to stop. I heard the boss talking to a trooper, then he turned off the engine. Beyond the logs we could make out the dark shape of a military post, and a truck with its lights out. It was carrying sugar from Shiraz, and had just been attacked four miles away by a tribe of Kaoli* migrating south. Despite a bullet in the jaw, the driver had managed to get through and to reach the post; now the military were stopping traffic until sunrise. The cold was biting. We spent the remainder of the night with the team on the ledge in the fort, surrounded by the stink of opium, between the dozing, wounded man and three ghostly soldiers, their lips blackened with opium, passing the bamboo around. As the boss went to blow out the lamp, I saw his face clearly illuminated for the first time and understood why it had intrigued me: he was my father's twin – a bit older, darker, more battered, but my father all the same. It was so startling that I suddenly recalled the sound of his voice, which I had long forgotten. (I'd heard so many others in the course of the year.) I heard then, word for word, his parting sentence to me: an embarrassed warning about certain women who... in the ports.

Not much opportunity for that. I was pleased, though, to have recaptured his voice: luggage like that doesn't take up much room.

We left at dawn. The moon was growing pale. An arm's breadth stream, edged with a streak of dark, damp grass, flowed in front of

---

* The only real Persian nomads, the Kaoli had come from the East a long time ago and belong to the same group as our gypsies.

the fort and twisted its way toward the desert. To the south, blue mountains closed off the horizon. Twice the team stopped and, tools in hand, disappeared under the chassis. The second time we went to see what was going on. The mechanic was fixing a broken back suspension spring with wire; the boss had taken out the battery and was pissing on it in small spurts, to liven it temporarily; the owner was cautiously adding a little water to the brake fluid. These are expedients you use only in the last resort. The new paint had fooled us. The truck was worn out, and it was in this old banger that they proposed to cross the mountain.

Round the first bends of the pass, we overtook the previous night's attackers. Beasts of burden covered the road as far as one could see; herds cut right across the slopes. Bells, baying, bleating and guttural voices resounded in the half-light. The women were dirty and splendid, covered in silver jewellery. The youngest, mounted on ponies, were breast-feeding dust-covered babies; the old women, stiff as pokers on top of their camels, amidst bundles of rugs, with rifles slung across their shoulders, were spinning from distaffs. The men, on foot, were yelling and brandishing their crooks to urge on the flocks. We could see boys asleep, slung across saddles like parcels, and ruffled cocks hung from pack-saddles between teapots and tambourines.

Unlike the Turkish-speaking tribes of Bactria and the Qashgai, who have been integrated into Iranian life, the Kaoli live on its fringe. They are scattered almost everywhere throughout the country, but most of them still come down each year from Seistan to the region of Bushire and north-east Iraq. On the way, they graze their lean herds, bleed horses, tell the future and mend cooking-pots. Sedentary folk, who do not regard them as 'believers', hate and fear them, and even accuse them of stealing children. Stealers or stolen, they were out in force anyway, and their herd was large enough to cover both sides of the pass.

It was on the first part of the descent that we heard the brakes popping. (That's what you get for putting water in them.) We were going too fast to jump out, and up in our perch the backdraught was cutting across our faces. Several oaths rose up from the cabin, soon followed by a grinding of the gearwheel in third as it gave way, then a sharp click of the handbrake, doing the same. The mechanic leaned on the horn and hung out of the window, shouting to clear the way. In front of us, two groups of Kaoli burst apart like overripe pomegranates. We went by at top speed, without hitting a soul, and got round the first bend by the skin of our teeth. Another slope was more or less clear and a second bend was concealed by the mountain. The truck continued to accelerate. I said to myself, 'Behind this one, there must be the plain…' I refused to believe our trip could end like this. It wasn't the plain and thirty yards ahead the road was black with animals, women and children. There ensued a whirlwind of rags and curses, falling and yelling, bells pealing, panic-stricken camels galloping off, an explosion of hens. Colours dashed to the side of the road – but not fast enough. The mechanic shrugged at us helplessly and retreated behind the door. Convinced that this was the end of our journey, we shook hands and pulled down our caps to protect our faces; the driver, with a mighty effort, wrenched the truck off the road into the mountainside. The shock was followed by silence, broken by the sobs of a stray girl who'd lost her nerve.

When I'd gathered my wits again, the dust had settled. Well ahead of us, the Kaoli had regrouped and were proceeding downhill. There was blood all over us, the windscreen and the luggage. We weren't badly wounded, but blood was spattered everywhere. We looked for the team: leaning against a rock, half in shadow, the three cabin-mates were peeling and salting a small cucumber. Of course there were a few broken teeth and bruises, but as it had been written that they were not to die this time, they set about restoring themselves as quickly as possible. They were slowly munching, faces creased with pleasure, and were talking – for a change – about the wild time they were going to have in Shiraz. There was no mention of any accident.

For four hours we watched the file-past of Kaoli whom we had overtaken on the way up, their heads held high in the fiery sunshine. And when the road was finally free, the truckers stretched, reckoned up the damages, and calmly set about putting their scrap iron to rights – banging it with stones, with a roadmender's sledgehammer, with an enormous awl – for the burst tyres – as if fixing up a cart. I took a leaf out of their book: one has too much respect for mechanical things, as, indeed, for so much else. By five o'clock the engine was working. Trailing a rock weighing at least half a ton as our brake, we rolled down on to the plain.

Shiraz: the same evening

Sitting between the bay trees in the courtyard of the Zend inn, we looked in disbelief at our shirts covered in dried blood, the corncob and the bottle the boy had just brought us, and our two knives stuck in the table. Tehran already seemed years away. What would it seem from Kabul? We had only done a quarter of our journey, but we tried to persuade ourselves that it was the hardest. I saw us again on top of that crazy truck, hurtling at murderous speed, with the astounded gypsies scattering like tufts of wool, during those ten interminable seconds which we had thought were our last – and then, this exquisite, quiet town, smelling of lemon, where the best Persian in Persia is spoken; where all night long you can hear the murmur of running water, and the wine is like a light Chablis purified by a long sojourn underground. Shooting stars rained down on the courtyard, but however hard I searched, I couldn't find anything more to wish for than I had. As for Thierry, he was convinced that this gift from fate was the forerunner of others. He was already wondering what they would be. It was part of his nature to think of invisible cogs in vast celestial mechanisms working day and night in his favour.

The hammam was still open, and our beds made up on the terrace. But weariness nailed us to our chairs, and also the pleasure of calmly chewing away in the dark, between the lordly shadow of death and the life of the lords that the summer had turned us into.

Hotel Zend

In the courtyard of the inn, a peasant family sit on bundles, surrounding and joking with an old man in a daze of happiness. A woman, laughing, tugs a clean shirt over his rags. Children pat him, as if he were a horse. A cigarette makes the rounds from one mouth to the next. Each person drags on it carefully, eyes closed so as to lose nothing. The whole group exudes such intense rejoicing that one is almost forced to pause. Not a single common face among them, and here, too, that ability to seize on the smallest crumb of enjoyment. They explain to me graciously that they are celebrating their grandfather's release from prison. Prison? With that head? What else could they take away from such a man?

Shiraz is, nevertheless, a town whose gentle art of living affects even the police; but not a day goes by in that country without your encountering some disgusting injustice, and without your being moved by some quintessential quality of Persia, slowly distilled and wise. Despite the poverty on the one hand and the baseness on the other, it remains the most consistently refined nation in the world, and also the most resigned. Why would a peasant, deprived of everything, have a taste for traditional poetry, which is not at all a rustic form of expression, invariably re-paint his door in the rarest shades, or make *ghivé* – espadrilles – out of old tyres with an austere and thoroughbred precision which immediately suggests the country's five-thousand-year-old culture?

For me, nothing is more heavenly than certain tea-houses along the road, with the glowing light of their worn rugs.

From this courtyard, one could see a dark, cool cave down a few steps, scattered with cockroaches, or with housewives in their flowered chadors, squatting over the preparation of their stew.

Squeals, quarrels, strong odours: it was the women's room. But I had something better: the terrace where I unrolled my bed gave on to a room occupied by a family from Bahrain, on pilgrimage to Meshed, with their young gypsy servant – the handsomest thing I'd seen in a long while. She wore a green kerchief on her head, a loose red blouse to cover her arms and breasts, and full trousers of the same green silk as her kerchief, drawn in at the ankles with two silver bands. At night she came silently to drink from a leather goat-skin left to cool outside the door. I had never seen anyone move so lightly! When she had drunk, she remained sitting on her heels, looking at the sky. She thought I was asleep. I would open one eye, not moving, looking at her: at her bare feet, and the dark branching of her thighs, the tender line of her neck and her cheekbones gleaming in the moonlight. It was because she thought herself alone that she was so touching and so uninhibited. At my slightest gesture she would have flown away. I lay as if dead, and I too quenched my thirst, with this supply of grace. It was very necessary there, where the young and desirable are veiled, robed and silent.

As for the women of easy virtue, who sometimes tossed us a word or even a whole sentence, they weren't all ugly, but you knew they would end up with those ogreish voices that go with their trade.

Even the best maps of Iran aren't exact. They indicate large villages which have since shrunk to a single abandoned fort, water long since dried up, and tracks covered by sand. Thus the one supposed to connect Shiraz to Kerman directly, via Saidabad, simply doesn't exist any more. We had to go back along the Isfahan road as far as Jusak and then turn off eastwards.

What remains of the royal town occupies a rectangular terrace backing on to the mountain and looking west over the Marvdasht plain. At the time (c.600–500BC) when the King of Kings came to inspect the work on the future capital of the dynasty, this plain would still have been covered in crops. The irrigation system declined along with the site, and today what you mainly see from the ruins is arid, dry land or the dusty trail left by a truck, or those dust spirals rising to the sky which, at the beginning of summer, move slowly in twos or fours between the retaining wall of the esplanade and the violet mountains on the western border of the plain. As for the town, it still wasn't completed when the Greeks put it to the torch. With the exception of the monumental flight of stairs leading to the terrace, the lower walls of a staircase covered in bas-reliefs, and two immense columned rooms whose orientation has become difficult to work out, it is a building site with enormous stones, sacked twenty-four centuries ago. Beside the columns shattered by the heat of the fire, there are colossal bulls' heads, still waiting for their ears – they must have been sculpted separately then added on. The proximity of what is unfinished to what has been demolished gives the ruins a sort of ambiguous bitterness: the unhappiness of having been destroyed before it had really lived. (The Achaemenians used it mainly as a necropolis, preferring to live at Susa.)

Passing travellers can stay in a room fitted out in the apartments of Queen Semiramis, the wife of Xerxes. It contains two iron bedsteads, a pretty Qashgai rug, and a Second Empire bath patterned in black and yellow. The man who looks after the ruins – a minor official – will settle you in without enthusiasm, since your presence will involve him in a bit of work, and also because he doesn't like Westerners, especially Greeks. He considers Alexander's conquests to be the work of drunken shepherds on the razzle, fit only to destroy and pillage, and the Battle of Arbela like the Catalaunian Plains* gone wrong. It's merely disgruntled nationalism, but so ancient as to have become respectable. And then we weren't objective ourselves, only our bias was more recent. Alexander, a sensible coloniser, brought Aristotle to the barbarians; thus the widespread mania for believing that the Graeco-Romans invented the world; and thus the contempt – in secondary education – for things Eastern (just a bit of Egypt, Luxor and the pyramids, so that children can learn to draw shadows). The Graeco-Romans themselves – see Herodotus, or the *Cyropaedia* – were not so chauvinistic. They greatly respected Iran, to which they owed much: astrology, the horse, the postal system, many gods, a few good manners, and no doubt also that *carpe diem* of which the Iranians are such past masters.

All the same, the caretaker wasn't as well-informed as I was. He absolutely refused to admit that there had been Greeks at the sixth-century court of Darius I.

'No, monsieur, no... they didn't exist until much later. They spoiled everything.'

So many centuries and keeping watch over such famous ruins had turned his head. As he didn't like the idea of our walking round when he wasn't present, he spent a long time warning us against the porcupines that lodged and made love in King Xerxes' irrigation channels. He claimed that they let off their quills like arrows, and demonstrated this with his fountain pen.** Moreover, he had the dark lips and feverish eye of a smoker disturbed at a bad moment. He stammered, apologised and left me in mid-sentence, dragging his pretty little daughter by the hand, back to his pipes, his fantastic chronologies, and his porcupine archers.

Persepolis, July 7th

We rose at dawn. We had packed and were full of plans. Each of us secretly wanted to drive, heading for India, with its trees and water, and its different faces. Thierry took the wheel, pulled the starter and got out, panting with disappointment.

---

* When the Huns under Atilla were stopped by the Romans near Châlons-sur-Marne, in 451. – Trs
** As a matter of fact, they do.

When a truck-driver called for advice lifted his head and murmured *automat sukhté*, it didn't necessarily mean that the coil was burnt out. But it certainly meant that somewhere under the car, or inside the car, in some inaccessible corner, in an invisible coil, one wire – one out of twenty – had lost its insulator, or that a little platinum contact had dissolved in the centre of a well-sealed device, of the kind that would never be opened in a European garage, and it meant that all our plans would have to be shelved, our itinerary postponed – and for how long?

It meant: unpacking all the luggage, taking out the battery, working under a horrible sun because there was no way of getting into the shade, and looking for short-circuits concealed under grease; or in the blinding light handling screws the size of nail-parings, which slipped from our fingers and fell on the burning sand or into clumps of mint, which we searched for on all fours because you could only find replacements in Shiraz, and we couldn't go back there because our *djavass* had expired.

Which meant: pushing the car as far as the village at the foot of the terrace, stopping the first truck and keeping it with a thousand inducements until a second one arrived, connecting up both their batteries in an effort to get the engine started, because we operated on twelve volts and the trucks on six; after vain attempts to get the car in motion, it meant getting a tow right across the plain, as far as the bas-relief of 'The Triumph of Shapur', where we scarcely noticed the Emperor Valerian on bended knee to his Sassanian conqueror, our stomachs were so knotted over the mysteries of the magneto.

It meant: messing about, refusing to give up, surrounded by white-hot metal until the time when one after another, in the acetylene light, around the dismembered car, the cunning old mechanics whom we had gone in search of at the neighbouring tea-house tried their repair tricks on an area that might have been past repair, shaking their heads, leaning over the distributor, the coil, the starter motor, the dynamo, like haruspicators bending over organs of ill-omen – a rich area for folklore – and finally diagnosing a faintly scorched smell, a black spot on a platinum screw... perhaps... perhaps, but it was all very unsure...

Which meant: sending an unknown truck-driver to Shiraz with money, the battery, the suspect parts; waiting for hours, and, on his return, hope alternating with despair as it became obvious that whatever was wrong, it wasn't that; putting the battery in, taking it out, scratching our heads, puzzling our overheated heads for some idea that we hadn't yet had...

Thus it went from six a.m. and for thirty hours on end until the evening of the next day. Suddenly, Iran seemed to turn very sour under its weight of sun. I weighed up the stolid patience it would take to get our permits extended. Thierry despaired of being in time for his rendezvous in Ceylon and when an egg he'd pinched from one of the caretaker's hens the previous evening, and had since forgotten, broke in his pocket, I thought he was going to burst into tears.

The sun was turning red when one of our helpers, who had fallen asleep for a moment in the sand, stretched out with a half-smile, wrenched the connections from the dashboard, made them into a sort of plait and got the engine to work. So we got across the Kerman desert on a jumbled ball of wires, driving through the night to make up time.

Mechanics, progress – they're all very well and good! But you don't realise how dependent you are, and when they let you down, you are in worse straits than those who believe in the White Lady or Friar Rush, or have to rely on the most recalcitrant genies for their rewards. At least they can reprimand them, like the Hittites; or let off arrows aimed at the sky, like the Massagetae; or punish the lazy ones by removing the ritual food from their altars for a while. But how can you revenge yourself on electricity?

We had never found any alcohol in a tea-house, but that evening a bottle of wine was waiting for us in the village. A passing truck had left it with the proprietor expressly for us. Another driver had left for our attention a block of ice and a tow-rope. In this mobile milieu, news travelled fast and all the truck-drivers going up to Shiraz already knew about our difficulties. We recovered, drinking slowly, seated on the red and white rug that covered the ledge: cucumbers, onions, dark wine and friendship – a precious thing in such circumstances. Outside, the wind began to blow up a storm, while we became absorbed in the game of backgammon we'd been playing since Tabriz.

Going up to sleep in the ruins of Persepolis had been well worth all the bother. They were especially beautiful at night: a saffron moon, the dusty, swirling sky, velvety grey clouds. Owls perched on the truncated columns and on the head-dress of the sphinx who guarded the entrance; crickets sang in the dark crevices of the walls. It was a funereal Poussin. One couldn't blame Alexander too much: this way the city was still redolent of him; its destruction brought it closer. The stone was not of our era; it belonged to other interlocutors, a different cycle. If you worked at it, you could make it speak our language, but only for a while. Then it lapsed back into its own, which signifies disconnection, abandonment, indifference and forgetfulness.

The Surmaq tea-house

Although there was nothing but this shack, the police station opposite and the moon over salmon-coloured sand, stretching out as far as the eye could see, it looked as though Iran's entire fleet of trucks had docked there.

Wasted faces, grizzled hair beneath American army-surplus woollen hats, black Azeri caps, even a few Kurdish or Baluch turbans: thin genies with the hands of pianists – despite crank handles and oil – who came through the doorway like blind men, still full of the sound of the engine and the vast nocturnal landscape, hurrying to join the taskforce round the brazier where the opium pipes were heating. In the night that had suddenly turned glacial, the mastodons – twenty to twenty-five tons, which trundled from post to post at ten miles an hour – formed a black rampart around the mud hut. Inside, once they'd got used to the harsh carbide light, the dead-tired nomads greeted and recognised each other, and asked where each was headed. The replies were murmured, with discreet gestures of the fingers: they were going from the Persian Gulf to Khorasan, or to Erzurum in Anatolia looking for walnuts, or *ins'h Allah* going down to the Straits of Hormuz on the cursed Bandar Abbas road. On the wall above the samovar, you could see pictures: the death of Immam Reza, the Empress in three colours, and old starlets with pale breasts, ripped out of pre-war Italian magazines. There were few words; opium clouds expanded the space around disembodied forms. The meat for the next day, hanging from the ceiling, wrapped in a flowered cloth, swayed in its bodyguard of flies.

Occasionally an imperious Cadillac drew up between the trucks and by tooting its horn turned everything in the tea-house upside down. It would be a governor returning to his post, or an *arbab* nearing the end of his life, hastening towards hospital. Amidst agitation and a confusion of multi-coloured coverlets, a bent and moribund old man would be unloaded, his arms hanging down, heavy with bracelets and a fine gold watch. Wives in chadors would stand round, uselessly fanning him, while the impassive driver and his assistant would gulp a helping of rice and cherries.

Occasionally, too, through the half-open door, you could see by starlight a cop armed with a long stick with which – as in the good old days of the tolls – he sounded out the trucks' freight with absurd, resounding blows. 'He's looking for God...' breathed one of the smokers, and a thin smile went round the group.

But Surmaq was still on the highway. We then left it to branch eastwards. As we advanced, life became sparser, trucks less frequent, the inhabitants more scattered, and the sun hotter.

The Yazd road, July 10th–12th
Leaving Surmaq, you first of all cross tracts of red and black scattered with patches of salt. After sixty miles, the salt wins and woe to those who haven't got something to protect their eyes. We drove from four p.m. to seven p.m. over the excellent dirt road without meeting a living soul. Because the air is so dry, you can see ahead for incredible distances: that construction over there, under a solitary tree, how many miles away was it? Thierry said eight and a half; I guessed ten and a half. We made a bet, drove on, and evening fell before either of us won: it was thirty miles as the crow flew. Suddenly, we also saw high mountains that were several days away. We could make out the snow-line perfectly clearly – in that oven! – and the rock. Some of those mountains south-east of Yazd are over twelve thousand feet high. As the earth's curve hid their foothills, only the tops appeared: fingers, teeth, bayonets, breasts; an archipelago flung far and wide, floating on a cushion of mist within the confines of the desert. As we advanced, more of those jagged silhouettes surged up from an horizon as vast as the sea and beckoned to us.

Abarquh

The architecture here was large-scale and fantastic: yellow earth, high, crumbling walls, square minarets bristling with what looked like long stalactites, deep alleyways. Only confident, haughty, perhaps rather precious people would have built like this. The old geography books said, Abarquh: eighteen thousand inhabitants. The town must have been important under the Qajars. And then?...

Was this crumbling, deserted, silent labyrinth still a town? Wherever you ended up, you could hear the same millstone grinding in the depths of the same house; wherever you went, you encountered the same barefoot donkey-driver in his black jacket, who seemed to have lost his tongue. After an hour's search, we managed to locate four eggs which we swallowed whole, opposite a half-collapsing mosque topped by a vertiginous wooden cage which the muezzin had just entered. We could see him, small and distant, moving about between the bars like a sacrificial victim, like an excited cricket; then he began to shout and chant in a warm, Negro voice, high above the town where silence reigned like a Great Plague. It seemed less like prayer than furious recrimination and terrible grievances.

We slept badly beside the car, and set out at dawn.

??

We had wondered a great deal about the cake made of earth, standing alongside the track in the distance: it looked something like an upside-down dice cup, or an upended egg. But it was a square, blind fortress, its crenellated top rising a hundred feet above the salt desert. There was absolute silence; the sun was vertically overhead. A stream crossing the track ran into the fort, passing beneath a gateway scarcely wide enough for a donkey with a pack-saddle. We followed it, and beyond there was a skinned sheep hanging from the vault, children's cries, little streets lined with many-storeyed houses, a large expanse of turquoise water surrounded by walnut trees and maize, and little terraced fields rising to the level of the walls. In fact, a whole town was living off that thread of water. Looking up, you could see narrow flights of steps zigzagging up to the crenellations and the sunshine, as though from the bottom of a well. The few inhabitants of this steep square turned round in surprise on seeing us, and the boldest of them offered us tea at his house. Some hundred people still cling to this place, which is called Fakhrabad, and live off the small herds they pasture in the mountains, two days' walk away. Sometimes a grocer's truck coming from Yazd stops outside the gate; and sometimes a whole week goes by without their seeing anything passing below the walls.

Even the wind doesn't get in. Several years' dead leaves carpeted the roofs, the terraces, and the acrobatic steps, crackling under foot.

Yazd

In Yazd, most things arrive by truck from the west. Life is dear and the Yazdis – who are said to be the greatest cowards,* the best gardeners and the finest businessmen in Iran – endeavour to make it dearer still. But at the beginning of July the heat is free, along with the thirst and the flies. A hat and dark glasses are not enough protection for the Yazd desert; you need to be muffled up like the Bedouins. But we drove bare-armed, our shirts unbuttoned, and in the course of the day the sun and wind relieved us of several litres of water. We thought we could re-establish the balance by drinking about twenty cups of mild tea at night – which were soon sweated off – and then we threw ourselves on to steamy beds in the hope of sleeping. As we slept, however, dryness was at work; it smouldered like a bush-fire; one's whole maddened organism cried out, and we found ourselves on our feet and panting, noses stuffed with hay, fingers like parchment, rooting round in the dark for any scrap of moisture – a drop of water, even old melon rinds to plunge our faces into. Three or four times a night this panic would hurl us out of bed, and when sleep finally came it was dawn, the flies were humming, and old men in pyjamas shouted to one another across the courtyard of the inn as they lit the first cigarettes of the day. Then the sun came up and began to pump us out again...

It was also too hot to keep our hair. At the exit from the town, in a smoky, ramshackle quarter, a barber working in the shade of a plane tree shaved our heads. While he dealt with my chin, I looked at

---

* A Yazd infantry regiment under Nadir Shah, returning from the conquest of India with arms and baggage, requested an escort for crossing rebellious Baluchistan – see Sykes, *The Glory of the Shia*.

the 'towers of silence' in which the Zoroastrians – of whom there are many in the town – used to expose their dead.* I also gazed at the plane tree: remember it! Travelling east, there won't be another for a long time.

The road to Kerman

For two hours we had kept our eyes on a tea-house set like some absurd object in the middle of the iron-grey desert. When a gust of sand hid it from sight, we slowed down until it came back into view and we had our lodestar for the leagues ahead. However slowly we drove, we had reached it by eleven a.m.: a cupola of dried earth, a shapely curve, whose interior, black with smoke, caught a little light through a hole pierced through the top.

Although many things are permitted in Persia, it is forbidden to fart, even in the middle of the desert. When Thierry, who had fallen into an exhausted asleep on the ledge, infringed this rule, the proprietress turned on him like a snake, wagging her finger. She was a dirty old hussy who went to and fro in her hovel with two enormous tomcats at her heels, singing in a hoarse voice as she poked the charcoal in the samovar. Once tea was served she lay down and began to snore. As for her man, he slept against the door under a sheet crawling with flies, pickled in the reek of opium.

Once your eyes were accustomed to the half-night, you saw a single stream coming out of the ground in the centre of the room, filling a small round basin and then, two steps further on, trickling away into the earth. A few pale fish, risen from this underground vein of water, lazily paddled round the basin, or nibbled at the rind of a melon cooling in the water. A muslin bag of curdled milk dripped beside the water with a drowsy slowness. It must have been past midday. Outside, the sand continued to blow and the sun to beat down. We had to wait: we couldn't drive before five p.m. without the risk of our tyres bursting. From time to time, one of the fish leapt up to swallow a fly, with a miraculous, watery 'plop' which sent our memories curling back.

---

* In order not to stain them with earth or fire, they exposed their dead for the vultures to devour.

Military post: Kham, 7 p.m.
A squat little fort with crumbling ridges: the storm had begun to batter it like a reef. A woman appeared on the threshold and made a sign to us to pull over and come in. She wore golden rings in her ears and the straight black trousers of eastern Iran; she held a copper cooking-pot, which the gusts of sand set ringing like a gong. We took refuge in the fort, sick with thirst and wind. In the shelter of the high mud walls we found an almond tree, a peach tree, a vegetable plot and three hoary soldiers sitting cross-legged, learning to read from an ABC with letters the size of their hands. Elderly schoolboys, tinged with trachoma, who laboured all the harder over their syllables because the head of the outpost took advantage of our presence to inflict a dictation on them: 'Bagh-dad.... She-her-ezade...' – no doubt it was a pretty story, but at that distorted pace the result wasn't too good. The eldest made six mistakes in two lines... but mistakes are at least a sign of life: there was laughter, confusion and charming hospitality. They unrolled a little lavender-blue rug for us and made tea. The large woman, who was the companion of these gentlemen, dandled an infant whom they coaxed or tickled with a blade of grass to make it smile; then each one was proudly photographed with the baby in his arms. A whole flock of partridges, blinded by sand, came crashing down like hail on the garden, and chirruped amongst the vegetables.

Anar, 11 p.m.
The headlights lit up less than ten yards ahead, and eddies of dust hid the stars. We drove very slowly until a blank wall running beside the track for two hundred yards showed us the town we'd been waiting for. The postern was tiny, and, as at Fakhrabad, a whole village rested behind the iron-barred door. I knocked with my fist. Silence. I picked up a stone from the ditch, and beat on the door for a long time. We heard the noise of footsteps approaching, receding, then returning, and a husky voice: '*Qi ye...*'. We explained. There was an interminable commotion as the bolts were chivvied, then the gate opened on an unshaven peasant with a lantern in one hand and a club in the other. He declared that one could neither eat nor sleep there. He waved a hand towards a light floating in the night two *farsang* away, and quickly closed the door-flap on sleep and security.

There was a little tea-house, so we lay down for a few hours in the dark, unable to close our eyes. There was only one truck from the east parked in front of the shack, and on the ledge there was a bearded driver with a pink turban and liquid eyes, who seemed even more foreign to the place than we were, and soliloquised in an incomprehensible dialect. We thought we understood that he was on his way from Quetta, doing our trip in reverse. We could get no more out of him. It was the first time we'd had a sign from the Indian world.

We left before dawn.

Rafsanjan, 6 a.m.

The town seemed even more matutinal in that we hadn't slept a wink. Between two heaps of pistachios, the touch of the barber's chipped razor half-woke us up. The hammam did the rest. It was a tumbledown place, deliciously cool, built around a well of stagnant green water. Stretched out on the damp tiling, we abandoned ourselves to the bath attendant who worked over our bodies with sand-soap, wringing out his cloth that had swollen like a bladder with great gobs of lather, and kneaded our joints with his feet and hands. Through half-open eyes, you could see his thin, preoccupied face and, beneath the cloth wound round his waist, a happily dangling pair of testicles gilded by the sun, which was already making the pools of water gleam. Half-drowned cockroaches swept past our faces. With groans of pleasure we felt the weariness loosening its grip and night leaving us; we were coming back to ineffable life.

Kerman

When we finally reached Kerman, we saw that the hardest part was yet to come: over four hundred miles of blazing heat and mountainous desert all the way to the border, and as far again across the Baluch desert to reach Quetta. For the first one hundred and twenty-five miles, as far as the ancient fortress of Bam, the road is still in use. Beyond that, it runs into sand, traffic dries up, life wears out and the country stretches on as though it didn't have the energy to stop. Don't even mention the sun! As for shelter and encounters: they were as frequent as rice grains scattered in a storm.

For five hundred years, Kerman was famous for shawls and blind men, as the first Qajar emperor had blinded twenty thousand of its inhabitants. Today it is famous for gardens and carpets with their pink and blue leaf designs. We spent our two days there in the cool depths of Point IV, underneath the car, tools in hand. It wasn't so bad, being there; after so much desert a little shade and a small, enclosed space were all we wanted. The second day – a Friday – we even had company. The whole town had heard that two *firangi* (strangers) were spending God's day working on their car, and a number of truck-drivers in their Sunday best came along and turned the garage into a

salon: Armenians, Zoroastrians, Muslims; with polished shoes, new turbans, stiff collars, and white tunics or braces. Those who thought of something useful carefully rolled up their clean sleeves before gripping the monkey-wrench or screwdriver; some of them even went off to get their own tools; others disappeared, to return laden with cakes and vodka. It was all very merry, the only thing missing was music.

We scarcely saw Kerman by day, just enough to glimpse that atmosphere of pillage and demolition – as though Tamburlaine had just passed through – which the implacable midday light gives to all the towns of eastern Iran. But we did see it by night. Once we were washed and refreshed we would promenade, accompanied by a few young cyclists who would bike past, return, then pedal on the spot in order to fling us the same English phrase over and over. And at night, Kerman became beautiful; its burning, grimy, broken aspect gave way to the sweetness of the widest sky in the world, and of some greenery, and the ripple of water, and cupolas swelling against luminous grey space. At the end of the town, our escort left us: three enormous trees, a wall of dried mud, then a sandy plateau wider than the sea. Stretched out on the cooling desert, we smoked in silence and wondered whether we'd ever see the end of it. Broken fingernails, the quick flair of matches, the graceful, weary arc of discarded fag ends which sizzled out in the sand, stars, stars – stars clear enough to outline the mountains barring the horizon in the east... and gradually, peace.

Leaving Kerman, July 17th

After two and a half days, the fault was located and repaired. The people who helped us – some of them for a whole night long – didn't want money; they would have liked a bit of music, but the accordion was full of sand. At sundown, they squeezed into an old rattletrap stuffed with provisions to come with us as far as the pass overlooking the town. There was a stream scarcely a cubit wide which, out of some kind of superstition, they were afraid to cross. So they sat on the west bank with their feet in the clear water, and we sat on the other side, and we stayed there a long time, feasting and watching the full moon rise over the limitless landscape. Then the Armenians shook hands with us, the others embraced us in the Muslim way and they got back in their car, yelling songs, and headed back to Kerman.

We set off east again, the car heavy with its ballast of drinking water, petrol, melons and a bottle of cognac – essential for such crossings – and several flasks of Kerman wine, the colour of dried blood and strong enough to raise the dead.* The track was good and sloped gently upwards. The moon was bright enough for us to turn off the headlights and save the battery. It was a delight to have all the lights out and at ten miles an hour, to eat our way through those vast, solitary, coral-tinged undulations.

The same night

After about sixty miles, we reached a tea-house run by three little girls who were fast asleep, and served us tea almost without removing

* At least 15%. In the gardens surrounding the town, the vines are planted in ditches several yards deep so that it's easier to water them.

their fists from their eyes. The two drivers smoking on the ledge seemed hardly more alert. (The few ghostly figures we met that night seemed not to have slept for a hundred years.) As for us...

How could we sleep, in that fug? People took a lot of opium in eastern Iran, especially the long-distance drivers, with their exhausting lives. When you mentioned opium to a Persian, he protested. If you persisted, he would explain that it was the English who had introduced it into the country and encouraged its sale... etcetera. (It must be said that hail couldn't fall on the rice-fields nor a bus down a gully without England at once being blamed.) Perhaps there was some truth in the story; the English had certainly gone to war in China over opium. Anyway the habit had taken, and on the road from Surmaq to Bam we had found it in every second tea-house. I like smoking; I had a hundred opportunities to try it. But the smell! While the smell of hashish is pleasant and liturgical, opium smells of scorching, of burnt fuses; it immediately suggests despair, silk-paper lungs, purple velvet entrails, and fools' bargains. It doesn't even keep the flies away.

The opium-addict insists that after two or three pipes he thinks faster and better and arranges his images more harmoniously. But he mostly keeps them to himself, and his neighbour rarely profits. On the contrary, everyone suffers: his gestures become clumsy and blunted – with what unbearable slowness he knocks his bowl of tea over your knees! But you have to smoke it yourself to understand the opium-addict and his pace, and even curiosity didn't tempt me to do that. So, we rarely lingered in tea-houses.

At two o'clock we first saw the headlights of a truck that we passed at four. At five, the palm groves and astounding crenellations of Bam rose against the green band of dawn. Files of camels and the first herd of goats passed by, steaming, in the deep lanes. Enormous mud walls with twisting posterns protected all the houses. It had a sort of imperiously African look, with the added dimension conferred by a thousand years of written history.

For centuries, Bam had served as an outpost and citadel, confronting Baluchi incursions and the Afghan peril. It always sheltered a general and a garrison, and sometimes launched a punitive expedition eastwards, whose departure – it is said – occasioned floods of tears as the soldiers feared it very unlikely that they would return. Today Baluchistan is tranquil, these sorrows have disappeared along with the general, and Bam is chiefly a mosaic of gardens surrounding the strong forts which are now agreeable properties for the *arbabs* of Kerman.

Bam
In a garden, 18 July

'And it shall come to pass in that day, that the Lord shall hiss for
the fly that is in the uttermost part of the rivers of Egypt...'

(Isaiah 7:18)

He should hiss for them here. I have to have my say about the flies of Asia. You can have shade, the sound of a fountain, soft rugs, weariness – everything is set fair for a welcome sleep. But if there is a single fly about, the plan has to be shelved. At least, I have to shelve it, and as we were running four or five nights behind, I couldn't have felt more frustrated. (Thierry, however, slept like a log and the sight of him sleeping filled me with genuine dislike.) There was no other resort than to keep working in the hope of getting completely worn out: clean the contact points, the spark-plugs, grease the springs. Repack the luggage, fill the bottle with drinking water, put a handle on our shovel. Bargain for some supplies in the bazaar, noting that the women in blue and black rags who idled along in the shade, rushed when crossing patches of sunlight so as not to burn their feet, which gave the street an absurdly broken rhythm.

I went to a garage to recharge the battery. There was just one, run by a Greek, the only shipowner in this sandy port, who sometimes sent his trucks into the sun-swell towards Zahedan. He hadn't done so for two weeks, however, because a dune was covering the track after the post at Shurgaz, though he assured me that it could be passed all the same. He didn't know anything about the Point IV jeep which was supposed to be on the road about then. Yet we had left before it precisely because we had wanted it to be able to follow in our tracks.

Fahraj, the same evening

East of Bam, the track crosses a sandy yellow hollow from which the tomb of a Mongolian chief rises up like a single finger. As we reached the top, a group of nomads travelling beside the road stopped us in order to hand over a scrap of torn paper. It was a note from the Point IV driver. The jeep had already been past and would wait for us at Fahraj as long as possible. 'Possible' meant until about ten p.m, as they had to cross the Shurgaz dune before dawn, at a time when dew and cold made the sand a bit firmer. We stepped on the gas. Around nine p.m, less than twenty miles from Fahraj, the cog wheel in third – our cruising speed – snapped. We had to drive in second at five miles an hour, taking advantage of the slightest slope to put pressure on the engine, picking up speed and shifting into a higher gear, praying that it would hold. We didn't get on very fast. When we reached Fahraj at eleven p.m, the jeep had just left.

Fahraj: a place where someone was waiting for us! You'd expect a village. It was an isolated telegraph outpost, with one shaky tamarisk, and one carbide lamp under which three silent nomads sat round a sleeping policeman. We woke him up and asked him to telegraph the station at Shurgaz to stop the jeep and send it back. If the message got through, it would arrive at about two a.m. There was no question of getting any sleep. We waited and couldn't see anything coming, drinking cognac and cursing the telegraph. (Waiting in a trance, dizzy with the desert; one of the nomads slowly crushing a scorpion under his slipper...)

At the beginning of the century, under the last Qajars, the newly-installed telegraph wires hummed with reports transmitted to the Court from the depths of the provinces, all of them beginning in roughly the same way: 'King of Kings, Pivot of the World, Most Serene Pastor' and then came the stories of revolt, famine and big financial deals. All that pomp! And now a modest SOS, on which we depended so much, which it couldn't be bothered to pass on...

At two a.m. there was still nothing, but alcohol had given us courage and we set out for Shurgaz in our moribund car. If the jeep had turned back, we couldn't miss it: there weren't a lot of people about in that part of the planet.

Later

I drove until dawn, trying to cut the knot that was preventing me from sleeping. The desert had taken on a malign, ashen colour. The moon lit up the horizon and the gigantic sort of cairn which served as a marker for truck-drivers along this stretch when sandstorms wiped out the track. It was the southern extremity of the Lut desert where year in, year out, half a dozen drivers turn to dust because of a broken axle or a battery dried out by the sun. The Lut was infamous anyway: Lot – from whom it took its name – saw his wife transformed into a pillar of salt there; numerous genies and ghouls prowled round it, and the Persians placed one of the Devil's dwellings there. If hell is an anti-world, its malevolent silence only troubled by the buzzing of flies, then they are right.

Having threatened us for six hundred miles – we had been warned about it as far back as Tehran – the Shurgaz dune turned out to be not so bad. The track had disappeared for about three hundred yards, and where it branched off the blackened carcass of a wrecked truck showed us at least where we shouldn't attempt to go. The sky was already turning green. We had let down the tyres completely, in order to increase their grip, and three children who had been sleeping beside the wreck – where had they fallen from? – helped to push. In an hour, we were through.

5 a.m.–7 a.m.

There was one last military post.

I respected the soldiers who ended up living in this Gehenna: two solitudes, two riding-camels, two mess-tins, one sack of broad beans or flour, and two revolvers. Or rather, two holsters; very often they were no longer armed. An armed man left to his own devices like this is dangerous: he could get too much sun and then shoot in all directions; or, who knows? at himself. And a weapon arouses envy. What if prowlers knocked him out in order to get hold of it? No, much better to take the initiative and sell the revolver, perhaps even to the very people he was supposed to keep under surveillance. Thus no one mistrusts him and he can sleep in peace. With the money, he buys a bit of food or opium to pass the time while waiting to be relieved. It is the best way of lasting out, and as unpleasant as the life may be, the view always has its attraction.

We wanted to ask about the state of the track. Thierry got out of the car and went towards the post. I got out of the driving-seat to follow him and after two steps, fell face down in the sand – it was not burning yet – and went to sleep. Thierry came back, lugged me to the door and shoved me into the passenger seat without managing to wake me. The sun soon stoked up. At seven a.m. it rose like a clenched fist and the metal began to heat up. I had often thought about the sun, but never as a killer. When I came round, I heard Thierry muttering to himself: 'Got to get the hell out of here... get the hell out of here...'. He also told me that according to the police, there was more sand to pass before Nosratabad.

10 a.m.

For thirty yards the sand was almost liquified. We unloaded the car to lighten it; shovelled sand to even it out; collected sticks and stones to lay on the track, then covered them with all our clothing; let down the tyres and pushed the car along, shouting to get some air into our lungs; blew up the tyres and repacked the luggage.

The sun eventually made you see everything in black. All the same, we noticed that our arms and faces and chests were covered in a thick crust of salt.

Noon

We pretended not to have seen it, but it definitely was a mountain, and the track went across it at an impossible gradient. It was the little Gaoulakh pass, a name that I only found out two years later on an old German map. Certainly it isn't very imposing: a jumble of smoky black rocks, three skeletal tamarisks bearded with melancholy, a few savage bends in the road. Not very high, either, but located exactly where the life has gone out of you, where courage flags, where water leaks from the body as from a cracked jug. And at that season, at that hour! We had to climb it four times in order to lug the baggage to the top. Then we grabbed hold of the car, our hands wrapped in rags as the metal was too hot to touch. First let in the clutch, leap out, push... until the point where everything went dark. At the top of the pass, the pistons snapped with a terrible sound, and tears trickled down our cheeks. I put Thierry, sobbing, in the shade under the car. It was high time we arrived somewhere.

Two hours later, the sleepers in the Nosratabad tea-house thought they must be dreaming, hearing an engine at that forbidden hour. In the south Lut, in July, no one drove after sunrise.

Nosratabad tea-house, 2 p.m.–4 p.m.

Slumped against the ledge, too strung out with exhaustion to sleep, we gazed at the earthenware jar of drinking water, sweating its large drops. It was placed on a sort of altar, like a god, surrounded by brambles. We could also see the white tunics of the tea-drinkers emerging from the shadows in successive waves of light during the day. We realised that the cursed little pass had made a difference to the world, and that the faces no longer looked like any of those we knew: with their white turbans, their black hair and fringes, their scorched features like the knave in a pack of cards, and the impression they gave of brands plucked from burning – they were the Baluchis.

Time passed... one lost the thread, and when one found it, it was to see the proprietor striding menacingly behind the chicken whose throat he wanted to slit, his hands flickering like sparks behind the terrified bird.

Then one became absorbed in the pile of the rug under one's shoulder, or in that little muscle contracting in the jaw like an animal caught in a trap. Later, as nerves relaxed and the sun went down, that fulfilling tiredness welled up, that desire to worship and to take on one's destiny – a feeling which takes hold of you all of a sudden and sets you free at a depth that is usually neglected: it brings a surfeit of life which one doesn't know how to use. If you were capable of moving an inch, you would break into a dance. Soon the heart – that pump of the emotions – calms down; you feel its more expansive beat, faithful in its place, a large muscle now fortified.

Later

Drove from six to midnight across anthracite-coloured mountains to get to Zahedan: thin eucalyptuses, a stage-set moon and, at the centre of a sandy crossroad, a policeman – who wouldn't get over the spectacle, at that hour and at the end of the world, of a car coming out of nowhere, with no lights, but the neck of a guitar and a bottle sticking out of the window, and driven by two ghosts who looked as though they'd just emerged from brine.

Zahedan, evening, July 20th

The only mechanic in the town was a sort of majestic hermit who spent his days sitting cross-legged in the corner of the bazaar, where he also sold a few vegetables. He briefly examined our broken gear-wheel, which shone like a jewel against his immaculate robe. I looked at the well-fed, Christ-like face, his brown toes as clean and fleshy as a baby's. It seemed inconceivable that this saint should concern himself with things mechanical. He finally gave it back to us: *Quetta doros miché* (They can repair it in Quetta). The little North-Western Railway Co., which did the Quetta-Zahedan run once a week with three wagons of drinking-water, asked a fantastic thousand silver rupees for transporting the car, and we didn't even have one. So we would have to cover the four hundred and thirty-five miles of the Baluchi desert in second gear. We worked all day on our backs, taking out the engine and stripping down the gearbox. We would reassemble it the next day. Meanwhile, we could lay down our arms.

We returned to the Chalchidis inn; once again, it was run by a Greek. In a very soft light, the owner and his family – a large mother, her white hair in a chignon, and two little girls – were dining under a walnut tree in the courtyard and peeling pistachios. They were speaking Greek; the *phi, psi* and *theta* hummed around the table and unrolled in the warm air, cut across by more boastful *omegas* which bounced off the sky-blue barrel of drinking-water. A branch of dried olive leant against the door, and several worn wooden tables stood against the white walls. An ash-coloured Baluchi servant girl was washing a cooking-pot near the well. Everything seemed lightly balanced, as though held in suspension: this courtyard, under its patch of sky turning to night, was a fragment of Thessaly. *A melon, some eggs, a sheep's foot, beer and tea.* The spoon shifting in my glass stirred up tiredness as well as memories. I deliberately forgot the threat of the road to Quetta and gave in to the sirens. A little taverna lost in a province of Asia, frequented by trucks or triremes, without a doubt just like the one Jason frequented in the Crimea long ago.

Mirjaveh customs, evening, July 21st
The customs building surrounded a sandy esplanade where a few unkempt soldiers and a customs officer with a quivering moustache urged us to be patient while waiting for their superior. None of them dared go in search of this satrap, whose activities we soon stopped asking about: a serving-girl laden with bottles crossed the courtyard; the face of a haggard, dishevelled woman had appeared at the casement of a room lit by an oil lamp and then unlikely moans of pleasure began to rise into the night.

What a customs-post! The wild cries were like those of a sleeper beginning a bad dream. No women lived there. I thought of the hours she must have spent in a truck, and the dust, and the flies, all for her wages and the pleasure of this one, withered old man who mustn't be disturbed at any cost. What strange destinies are accomplished beneath the sun!

Later, the officer joined us, wiping his mouth with one hand, setting things to rights with the other. We signed a black register as big as a tombstone, a few lines below Aurel Stein, who had passed that way thirty years before. We drank the tea the old man graciously offered us. When I inquired about the road, he replied serenely that it had been wiped out for four miles and he doubted whether it was passable. We couldn't go back, however, once our setting out had been registered, and the first Pakistani post was sixty miles east. If we hadn't asked, the captain wouldn't even have warned us. He was still in the grip of excitement. It took endless discussion to get him to let the soldiers go with us and help us push.

…We found ourselves alone beneath thousands of stars confronting the wide Baluchi desert. We couldn't do any more. It was the end of the night. We detested Iran almost as much as, under other circumstances, we might have loved it. Iran, that sick old man who had created so much, loved so many things, sinned so much through pride, fooled so many, and suffered so much. An old aristocrat with ivory hands, capable of bewitching charm in his lucid moments, at others, sliding into a deathly torpor of fading memories. By now he had fallen into the hands of creditors stronger and less refined than himself. One shouldn't be harsh towards dotards. One doesn't blame sick old men for being old and sick, but when the moment comes, what a relief to leave them behind.

Baluchi desert

The night was blue, the black desert as perfectly silent as we were, sitting on the roadside, when a truck from Iran drew up beside us. We exchanged greetings and chatted. One of the men travelling on top of the sacks tumbled off, clutching a fibre suitcase. He opened it and offered us each a packet of thin Ghorband cigarettes, with pale Persian lettering near the tip – they had a delicate taste, with a touch of harshness and a small, distinct flavour of mourning, wear and tear, and forgetfulness, like Persia itself.

Two days away from the border we thought of it with renewed tenderness; we saw Persia as a large, nocturnal space in its soft, sympathetic shades of blue. Already we could do it justice.

Around the Saki Bar

THE NOTICE WE CAME across at dawn announced 'Asphalt road begins here'. We thought we'd made it, but beyond Nushki there was a pass consisting of steep, dust-laden slopes, which we could only cross yard by yard with the help of chocks under the wheels. It drove us to dope ourselves. At midday, we passed the Quetta barrier, and white poplars and plots of melon surrounded by thorn bushes replaced the desert. The track became a road and then an avenue beneath waving boughs of enormous eucalyptus trees. Around us, the town laid out at intervals the little it was made up of: patches of cool shade, teams of grey buffaloes, a few gateways in the Victorian style, flanked by warriors and bronze cannon, and little sandy streets where old, turbaned men with great presence floated along on handsome bicycles that were well-oiled and silent. A sparse town, as fragile as a dream, full of repose, shoddy goods as light as smoke, and watery fruit. We too were pretty light by now. Our combined weight was no more than 220 lbs. We pinched ourselves so as not to fall asleep; as the drug wore off, a kind of night spread over the heart of the day.

White-washed, as crooked as a wedding-cake, built round a century-old mulberry tree, the little Station View hotel was just what we wanted. The proprietor, dark as an icon and wearing an Astrakhan hat, was seated at the entrance to his little courtyard behind an embossed brass cash register, whose frail tinkling woke us before cockcrow. The tiny room opened on to one of those rudimentary water closets – a tap and a hole in the damp earth – which belonged to bygone India, where one washed in a tub opposite a monumental commode with softly gleaming, polished armrests.

There was also a roof terrace where, the night we arrived, we were seated to drown the desert. We had really reached a town, and that night our beds there were made. The whiskies washed over us in compassionate waves, and the evil spells of the Lut seemed to have been spirited away. We could hear the mulberries dropping into the courtyard where two guests, sitting cross-legged on their beds, exchanged occasional, circumspect remarks from beneath their mosquito nets. An exhausted happiness kept us quiet. Everywhere branches were rustling; the world was full of trees. Between our glasses a handful of letters, *care of Quetta's postmaster*, awaited our pleasure.

'You can have the table,' said Thierry. 'I'll paint in the bathroom.'

But I was in no hurry to write. For several days 'having reached Quetta' sufficed as an occupation.

The hotel was turned upside down by the arrival of a very famous holy man from Kabul. Rooms and galleries swarmed with the devout. As soon as breakfast was over, the dining-room was transformed into an oratory where the mullah, seated between a heap of English illustrated papers and hastily served sweetmeats, received believers. A queue of the faithful in their Sunday-best waited for hours on end to kiss hands, to be blessed, healed, advised or to set one of those theological posers so dear to Muslims. We heard laughter, the click of cigarette-lighters, the continual recitation of *suras*, the disturbing 'plop' of bottles of fizzy water; even though bloated with tea, we were still thirsty. After the desert, these sociable noises made me giddy. We had to resume our town life with care.

Opposite the entrance to the Station View a very robust beggar was stretched out in the shade of a plane tree on a folded newspaper, which he changed every morning. Full-time sleeping is a delicate undertaking; despite a long career as a sleeper, our neighbour was still looking for the ideal position, which very few people attain in their lifetimes. Depending on the temperature or the flies, he tried out variants, evoking in turn breastfeeding, the high-jump, a pogrom and love-making. He was a courteous man when he was awake, without that gnawed, prophetic air that Indian beggars so often have. There was little misery here, and much of that frugality which makes life finer and lighter than ash.

To the right of the door, in front of a fruiterer's stall, a completely naked man was attached by his foot to a ring fastened to the wall. He sang while pulling at his tether, traced figures in the dust, nibbled on wheat stalks or smoked the already lighted cigarettes which the shopkeeper came out to put between his lips.

'No, he's not being punished, he's mad,' the shopkeeper told me. 'When they let him go, he ran away and went hungry, so one day they put him here, another day somewhere else, so as not to lose him. Quite reasonable, don't you think?'

We still felt weary from crossing the Lut. We fell asleep everywhere – at the barber's, leaning against the post office counter, trotting along in the yellow droshkies which serve for taxis in Quetta; in the cane seats of the little Cristal cinema, soothed by our neighbours' fans, we dozed off, saucers of tea on our knees, while Elizabeth Taylor – rendered darker and more beautiful by an underpowered projector – was discovering love. Then we spent the night in pursuit of sleep; sheet over eyes, the horrible song of the car in second filled our ears and we crossed the desert till morning.

Worn out, yawning beneath the already hot sun, we would set off to potter about the town.

On May 31st, 1935 an earthquake had razed the town completely, killing a third of the inhabitants. But the trees had held good and hereabouts water and shade are enough to create a place. The Quettans had rebuilt the rest as people resolved not to be caught out again: no foundations, no rubble. Adobe walls stuffed with straw, graceful arrangements of wood, matting, tin and rugs in faded colours. In the Baluchi quarter there were stalls so meagre and fragile that a strong man could have carried them away on his back. Even Jinnah Road, the 'modern' street and backbone of the town, floated along with its single-storey buildings and façades of varnished wood. It was the backdrop for a Western, put up overnight. Only the big trees, the pumpkins leaning over the dung-heap in the small courtyards, and the bronze doors of Grindlays Bank seemed at all permanent or serious. There was a tremendous profusion of notices, signs, untimely injunctions, advertisements ...*Cornflakes*... *Be happy*... *Smoke Capstan*... *Keep Left*... *Dead Slow*... smothering this frugal town life. Despite the rhetoric scrawled in aniline, the town weighed nothing. There was no glue – a strong wind could carry it away. Its fragility gave it great charm.

Quetta: altitude 5,900 feet; 80,000 souls; 20,000 camels. About five hundred miles west, at the end of the railway, Persia slept under its mantle of sand. It was the other side of the world and there was nothing – apart perhaps from contraband – to remind us of it here.

North of the town, a narrow military road crosses the area under cultivation, runs across an arid plain and then rises up to the Khojak Pass and the massif of the Afghan frontier, where Quetta's neighbouring tribes have their summer pastures. Despite the excellent road from the border to Kandahar, traffic is almost non-existent and the little customs-post of Chaman is an oven where nothing goes by except time.

North-eastwards, a branch of the asphalt road goes on to Fort Sandeman at the foot of the Waziristan Mountains. The Pathan tribes who live there – Massuds and Waziris – are the most hardened of the whole frontier; they are so aggressive, expert at plundering and quick to break their word that their neighbours unanimously refuse to acknowledge them as Muslims. It took fourteen punitive expeditions to convince them that they were no longer on the winning side.

Finally, southwards, the main line running alongside a bad road goes down to the Indus Plain and Karachi via the Bolan Pass which, when the flocks change pasture, is clogged with vast herds of frozen camels fanning out towards warmth and autumn grasses.

So much for the cardinal points. They are distant. They pinpoint but do not weigh on the town, which lives for itself between its station – like a vision of the Second Empire – and its silted-up canal, humming with mosquitoes, and the garrison quarter where the skirl of bagpipes heralds the morning.

After ten hours work amid the dismembered trucks of the Ramzan Garage, we finished putting our engine back together. Evening fell. The boy from the tea-house next door ferreted among the jacks to find our dirty glasses. When he finished, the mechanics scooped him up and with friendly great thumps passed him from hand to hand like a ball. Then they put on their funny red Baluchi skullcaps and

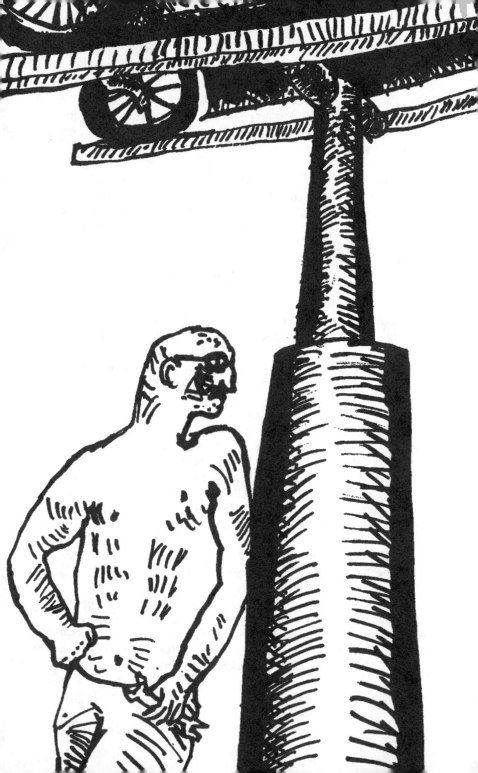

left the courtyard in a cloud of red dust, trailing their slippers. Our hair sticky with grease, we emerged from under the chassis and the night watchman offered us a rag soaked with petrol to clean our faces and hands. (We didn't try out the engine then and there; we didn't want to push our luck, and it would work better the next day).

In his glass cage, Ramzan Sahib sorted invoices and sang in a high-pitched voice. He was a giant, black as pitch, with rosy palms, a leonine mane and regular, haughty features. He was also an ace mechanic, who could cut through gunmetal as though it were nougat, and a resourceful man. His Khyber Pass Mechanical Shop – a hanger made from oil drums, with a small courtyard and a lift – was worthy of its lordly name: Ramzan and his team repaired anything and everything, and reigned unchallenged over a two hundred and fifty mile area. From Afghanistan, from Fort Sandeman, from Sibi, they sent him cars which expended their last ounces of strength to cross the passes and came to be revived at the garage.

There, where they use machines until they're ruined and don't have the worry of re-selling them, the garage men know nothing of that repertory of gestures of consternation or scorn which, at home, shame the owner of an old crock and force him into buying something new. They are craftsmen not salesmen. A bust cylinder head, a splintered camshaft, a sump full of a sort of steel flour – it took more than that to worry them. The healthy parts – lights, doors that close, a solid chassis – are what they notice first; as for the rest, well, that's exactly what they're there to fix. They take to pieces the most discouraging old crocks, reinforce them with parts taken from trucks, and transform them into tanks that will never wear out. The way they improvise is admirable, and never the same. Sometimes they indicate a particularly successful bit of patching by signing it with their screwdrivers. They don't get bored; they're well paid; while soldering and adjusting they brown toast over the charcoal forge, nibble at pistachio nuts and spit out the shells all over the workbench, and a boiling teapot is never far away. Most of the mechanics are former truck-drivers who have seen the country; their stops, their memories, their loves are spread across a vast province and this makes for an enlightened group of people who are prone to laughter. It is impossible to work alongside them without making friends.

Cleaned up, our hearts swelling within bodies drained by the Lut, we put away our tools and went to sit in one of the tea-houses in the red-light district. Sitting in front of a booth, a milky cup on our knees, we watched the three little streets come alive after evening prayer. They had gently rounded paving-stones half covered in sand, shops the size of cupboards selling brown sugar, soap, a handful of apricots laid out on silver paper, horoscopes and little cigars. A few slender silhouettes took the air in front of their houses, erect in their red and gold saris. There were also blue doors with grilles let into them, where young faces veiled in black waited for clients. A discreet conversation would ensue across this judas-hole, then the flap would half open for the suitor who, if he were feeling generous, would order a tray of tea and a musician. The lute floated out from behind closed doors, and the stars rose above this rustic quarter where hefty, peaceable scoundrels who'd come from the desert to do their shopping sauntered along, hands behind their backs, a wild rose in their caps, sniffing the night scents and directing their steps in accordance with calls from darkened portals.

There was no glitter here, no sign of haste; people were looking for leisure rather than pleasure. I thought of the neon signs, the fat paving-stones, the brick-coloured revellers bent on what a certain Europe calls 'a binge'. That's for the rabble. The Baluchi have too much space around them, too much natural distinction for that; everything about them – even love for sale – is redolent of a certain finesse and lack of show.

Mechanical work gives you a thirst; we spent our last rupees on tea, mango juice and lemon juice. We caught up on the world from an old *Paris-Match*, and sent off by registered post our requests for five or six visas for mountainous lands covered in snow. Quetta was just a crossroad: we could choose what came next. We gobbled fiery curries until the sweat stood on our foreheads and allowed ourselves all sorts of sweets. We needed to stuff ourselves before taking to the autumn roads, to fill out our dwindled shadows, to hear our steps sounding on the sand. Health is like money: you have to have spent it to appreciate it.

Sitting in front of the hotel, I would see the pancake vendors go by, their ovens on their shoulders; then the flute seller, his cheeks distended with strident scales; and the camel-drivers, who would tether their animals in tearing haste to go in avid search of a single cigarette. The Baluchi kept me happy.

According to the etymology suggested by Balsan in *Recherches au Baloutchistan persan*, Ba-luch signifies misfortune, which one is thus enabled to avert. Similarly the Tibetans give their infants names such as Scabby, Dejection and Bitterness in order to keep those spirits at bay until the child is weaned. There is a great deal of optimism and courage in dealing with misfortune this way. You reserve a beautiful omniscience for God, and attribute little intelligence to demons if you hope to fool them with such artless antiphrasis. The method has succeeded very well with the Baluchi; I know few people who are further from suggesting a jinx.

The Baluchi is quite sure of himself. His moral ease bursts out in the smile floating at beard-level, and in the fold and fall of his old but always spotless clothes. He is very hospitable and rarely troublesome. For example, fifty of them don't come and stand round, laughing stupidly at a stranger changing a wheel; on the contrary, they offer tea and plums and then go off to look for an interpreter and ply you with judicious questions.

Not particularly fond of work, he is always ready to smuggle things across the Persian border and to let off green rockets to attract the patrols of the marvellous Chagai Frontier Corps, while sacks are changing hands under God's eye at the other end of the desert.

Here, when it's time for the evening prayer, the lawns are strewn with forms prostrate alongside their bundles: vigorous devotions do not exclude tall tales. The Baluchi are good Sunni Muslims, without a trace of fanaticism. A Christian will be as well received as a co-religionist; what's more, with a touch of interest, and questions, because the Baluchi are as curious as weasels. They are not inclined to bigotry, turning up their noses, or striking attitudes. Whether nomads, *sardars* graduated from Oxford or cobblers, they don't stand upon ceremony and are very receptive to anything comical. Lieutenant Pottinger of the British India Company who, in Bonaparte's time, travelled the country in a disguise which only the

Baluchi could see through, saved his life several times by making them laugh. Such gaiety is one of the cardinal virtues. Several times in Quetta I saw extremely noble old men fall off their Raleigh bikes, doubled up with laughter, because a joke tossed from a shop had tickled their fancy.

The gearwheel in third that had been ground down in the Khyber Pass garage broke when tested. Ramzan turned over in his hands the scrap of mutilated steel which was keeping us in town. He didn't understand; he had fashioned it out of armour-plating 'borrowed' from the garrison's stocks. He offered to re-do it, watching over the tempering himself, but that would lose us another week and it risked a new break. We telephoned Karachi to order the part; squeezed into a telephone-box, its floor stained with betel juice, we heard a nasal voice five hundred miles away quoting a price which would put an end to our holiday. We would have to leave the hotel; we had still not fully recovered and this time, poverty frightened me.

Black with grease and heads down, we were on our way back from the post office when two journalists in search of copy cut across our path. We smoked a cigarette under the tamarisks while we explained our anxieties.

'Go to the Lourdes Hotel then, the owner will house travellers from Persia for nothing; he's just opened, and that's his way of advertising. You'll be very well looked after.'

And, made voluble with the pleasure of doing us a good turn, they expanded on the menu we'd be offered. They were right: his large body encased in a superb salt-and-pepper worsted and his mahogany face beaded with perspiration, the manager indicated the time for dinner and opened up a room shaded by a eucalyptus. An hour later, we'd made ourselves at home. Thierry had a canvas on his stretcher; in front of the table I unrolled the rug received one night in Persia – orange and lemon seedlings scattered over a slate-grey background – and went back to Ramzan with my typewriter under my arm, to solder a few capital letters. The same evening we sold our services – guitar, accordion, popular dances and waltzes – to the boss of the only bar in town, and life took a different turn.

I shall always remember the Saki Bar and its boss, Terence, who employed us for three weeks. Ever since we had news of his disappearance, I've been expecting him to turn up, with his baggy flannels, his patient eyes, his metal-rimmed spectacles and the leathery tan of homosexuals who retain two red blotches on their cheekbones, betraying their emotions. He was a distracted, kindly man, with an air of something both luminous and shattered. Although he was not at all forthcoming about it, he seemed to suffer from a tendency to which several in this town nevertheless succumbed – a little Pathan song which Saadik the cook hummed while poking the fire was charming witness to it:

> ...A young man crosses the river
> his face is like a flower
> his bottom like a peach
> But alas! I cannot swim...

Terence himself lovingly prepared excellent food: pepper soups, grilled steaks, and chocolate soufflés which he whipped up with a spatula heated over the fire. He finished them off with inspired touches, dispensing spices and chopped herbs with sober passion. His menus were redolent of the Wizard of Oz and the amorous gypsy, and the female side of his nature was most obvious when he was absorbed in cooking, along with a yearning for excellence – to do what he did perfectly – which sometimes lent an air of liberation and conquest to his various mishaps.

Saki is the Ganymede of Persian poetry, the cupbearer of Paradise, the introducer of delights beautifully portrayed on the sign above the entrance: a long-necked flask of wine, a hookah, a lute and a bunch of grapes – each one shining like a clean window – painted in muted, exquisite colours. Behind this panel began the surprising domain of the Saki Bar, where Terence ruled over his dusky, langorous kitchen boys.

It was a cool, narrow room with a white-washed terrace along its length, where the town dreamers came to sit of an evening beneath the scented laurel trees and where, from nine to midnight, under the misleading title of *Continental artists*, we gallantly strummed away.

Terence had tried to transform his courtyard into a French-style arbour: two trees in pots, a dance floor covered by a moth-eaten umbrella, rattan chairs, a piano with twisted candle-brackets, and on the walls, four front pages of *La Vie Parisienne* featuring women with gorgeous breasts and masses of curls, winking away. But such distant, outmoded souvenirs made this a mere sketch of an open-air café, like an abstract, and the blonde images warped by the sun were not enough to ward off all the surrounding aridity and whiteness. Terence sensed his defeat; the bare wall forming the courtyard bothered him and made him thirsty. On the first night, he suggested that we might fresco the whole surface: fish, shoals of sardines, little waves – something watery and blue. But how? Going back to the hotel at dawn, we tried to remember the look of the last fish we'd seen: the colourless, whiskery Siluridae which had risen from the centre of the earth in a vein of pure water in that tea-house at Abagou. But the next day, the shells and the dolphins had dissolved as in a dream. Terence had had callers after we left. He seemed worried; he had forgotten all about his fresco and formed a new plan: to leave Quetta.

Terence had known other ways of life, because almost all his customers – Baluchi or Pathan chiefs, Afghan liberals in exile, Punjabi businessmen, Scots officers in the service of Pakistan – seemed to have known him before, and they called him 'Colonel'. Piecing together the stories we heard while waiting for dawn, we could imagine something like this: that he had grown up in southern Persia, where his father had been British consul; had won his spurs in a Guards regiment in England; and had used up his share of the inheritance in the Paris of the *Ballets Russes* and Delage sports cars. He'd spent a few years in Abyssinia until the arrival of the Italians dislodged him. After some tribulations, which he passed over in silence, he found himself a colonel in Peshawar and 'political agent' for the Pathan area, which meant being responsible for about sixty miles of almost inaccessible mountains, of a decidedly independent nature and bristling with guns. Indian independence and the Partition troubles had caught him on this explosive yet salubrious frontier, whose map he could have drawn in his sleep. The little Kashmir war had enabled him to use his skills a bit longer... And now: cordon-bleu, boss of a bar in a sandy cul-de-sac between a

Franco-Indian photographer's shop and a Sikh bicycle dealer's, sighing with relief when the last customer left, and postponing the moment of going to bed as if he feared that while sleeping, he would miss a rendezvous for which he had come a long way...

When we asked Terence how the very beautiful girls in the red-light district were recruited, he mumbled a few embarrassed words about the Pathan procurers who came to drink at the Saki, then, thinking that we wanted to talk about girls and fearing that he might be seeming to shy away, he leapt back thirty years and told us the story of a certain Mrs Fitz. This lady kept a high-toned, select establishment in South Audley Street, London, which the cadets in his regiment praised in tones of hushed respect. One May evening, a very happy, very drunk Terence found his unsteady way to her address. It was a wealthy neighbourhood; the door gave nothing away, and a housekeeper opened it a crack to ask what he wanted. With considerable effort he straightened his face, held out his card and that of his 'sponsor'. After waiting beneath some handsome, aristocratic engravings, he was admitted to Mrs Fitz. She was a sweet old lady in a lacy bedjacket, sitting up very straight in a four-poster bed. Terence was intimidated; he was questioned about his family, his regiment, the schools he'd been to and then, in the same even and distant tone, about his preferences – an Annamite? a girl from Alsace?... the maternal sort? Or lubricious? Mrs Fitz also gave him to understand that she was expecting payment. She didn't mention a sum: if he were a man of the world, he would know how the favours of such a distinguished house were rewarded. He didn't know. He took a chance and wrote a cheque for ten pounds, proffering it uncertainly.

'Perfect, my young friend, but could you make that guineas?'

'*Guineas*! Just imagine!' Terence said to us.

He had not returned. I didn't know England, and to me this passion for 'social standing' in such an earthy transaction, this taste for social nuances even down to small change, seemed as singular as sacrificing a cock under the full moon, or the whirling of Dervishes. Under the magnifying glass of the Baluchi sun, we discovered England in Quetta in much the same way as the Gallo-Romans had found Greece in Marseilles: an enlarged and simplified version of a particular cast of mind – and lifted from its context of bricks and fog, it was more disconcerting, somehow, than anything we had encountered. If we got bored with Turkestan, there was always the possibility of living in Plymouth.

From this background, Terence had salvaged the most portable virtues: humour, discretion, great self-possession. He had sloughed off the rest in order to follow his own path and had reached, after who knows what reverses, what he called his true vocation of 'clown-restaurateur', living for the day, working without a safety-net and, like all his competitors, obliged to come to terms with the whims of a corrupt administration. All this gave weight to his opinions and his tastes. You truly love only the things you depend on: for three weeks we depended on the Saki Bar, and loved it. Terence depended on the Asia to which he was committed; he dreamed of tearing himself away, but he loved it and had paid dearly to experience that deep and bitter pleasure – nourished by the pattern of a rug or by Persian poetry – which only those with fearful troubles know.

Far too light-hearted to succeed in big business, the Baluchi had abandoned the shops on Jinnah Road to a few big-bottomed and self-important Punjabi businessmen in Astrakhan hats, who pinned a picture of Queen Elizabeth above the counter and rode about pompously in little Standard cars with large wheels. Those who frequented the Saki offered us drinks, assuring us that from Peshawar to Lahore their houses would be ours and begging us, meanwhile, to look in at their stores.

Close up, these shops in Jinnah Road were a distressing sight. Not a trace of craftsmanship. Borne on a majestic wave, the spray of western junk had reached and ruined local trade: lethal combs, celluloid Jesuses, ballpoint pens, mouth organs, tin toys lighter than straw – wretched samples that made one ashamed to be European. Not to mention the dreadful abuse of the chord of the major third – proof of the Anglicans' scant regard for beauty – which, starting from the harmonium in the garrison chapel, had even infected the strolling musicians; and not to mention the unwieldy and vastly over-priced bicycles on which the Baluchi pedalled about unsteadily, their voluminous robes all over the place. But that's how markets are created.

I consoled myself with the thought that, in this respect at least, India had got her own back – by recycling all its rubbish to Europeans: 'the Tonic Balm of the Brahmins', tin-pan gurus, fake fakirs, and the latest fads in yoga. Tit for tat.

Terence, who wished us well and tried to market our skills, introduced us to Braganza, boss of the Gran Stanley Café. Ablaze with gold teeth, in a billowing dhoti and carrying a fly-switch, Braganza was a Christian from Goa and belonged to one of those Portuguese ascendancy families which, over several generations and in panic and frustration, turned from coffee-colour to mahogany. He ran a sombre tea room opposite the Saki, with forty or so tables, where his Pathan customers relaxed, twiddled their toes and drank fizzy drinks. He offered us a hundred and twenty-five rupees to decorate two walls of his establishment: he wanted an exotic theme – French, perhaps – that would encourage eating and drinking. In order not to interrupt his business, he would leave the room to us between midnight and seven in the morning. Braganza showed us round the place; passing through the back kitchen, he opened a larder to reveal several doughnuts with flies in attendance... 'Plenty of oil, they'll do you good. Help yourselves.'

The same evening Thierry came up with two plans: for the righthand wall, an open-air café with Chinese lanterns, where aristocrats offered champagne to giddy girls; for the left, a Spanish bar where hidalgos and gypsies were contorted in lascivious *habaneras*. The whole to be resolutely figurative and redolent of the kind of thing evoked in an exhausted reveller by the cry of 'Montmartre!' or 'Olé!' I could lend a hand with the two large surfaces in flat colour – a big drum and a mare's hindquarters. Braganza said it sounded delightful. So, after work at Terence's, we spent several nights in his boiling hot café, slapping on colours and smoking little cigarettes to counteract the reek of curry from the stained tablecloths. While I stirred glue over the primus, Thierry stood facing his embodiments of the tango and the English waltz, which the poisonous colours from the local hardware shop rendered pleasingly satanic. Dripping with sweat, we took breaks to brew tea with large black leaves. The mutterings of the Baluchi cook who was dreaming, stretched out on his mat, rose from behind the counter.

The night wore on at a marvellously slow pace. We began to unwind on those evenings, worn out and immensely happy. Behind Braganza's rupees I saw our departure, Kandahar and autumn. We could sleep when we got to Afghanistan.

We went home like sleepwalkers. The scent of the eucalyptus drifted in waves along the narrow streets of sand like watered silk. In front of closed shops, little black goats tugged at their tethers. We followed the dry canal, passed Grindlays bank where the Pathan nightwatchman, a rifle across his knees, slept under sweeping moustaches like a furled umbrella. Arriving at the bridge, we gave the doughnuts (removed from the larder) to a beggar we met every sunrise at the same place, curled up like a dog. Only his greedy glance and a pair of quick hands distinguished this bundle of rags from a carcass. He was too miserable to be surprised by anything; these thin, paint-spattered foreigners who appeared at daybreak with pastries wrapped up in newspaper didn't wrest a syllable from him. He put out his hand and closed it, mute as a carp. When he had finished chewing and swallowing, he put his head back on his only possession: a dirty little cushion, embroidered with *Sweet Dreams* in Gothic cross stitch.

With light steps we walked beneath the great trees as the first mosquitoes sang. A red sun rose in a grey sky. We had just stretched out on our beds when the bagpipes from the barracks burst over the gentle dust with their strident, redemptive tones – as if Jericho had to be taken all over again. These Victorian fanfares from the North sound very good out there all the same.

Besides their sense of humour, a certain taste for Old Testament life must have attached those Scottish Presbyterians to such faraway sands.

The car that was costing us so dear had lost its number plate in the deserts of Iran; its import-license was out of date – legally speaking, it no longer existed. We went to a small villa next to the station to beg the Superintendent of Customs to sort it all out. He was a black, porcine man, his ears sprouting long, silky tufts. Beneath a fan that stirred the boiling air, he battled against a dreadful desire for sleep, and his sweating palms left damp moons on his blotting-paper. With two thumps of his rubber stamp he put an end to our worries, not without pointing out how much simpler it was in Quetta than in Persia; he praised the frescoes in the Gran Stanley Café. Finally, in a naughty boy's voice, he asked Thierry for a few nudes for his 'collection', and invited us to tea the next day.

It wasn't a bad trade-off: at ten rupees apiece there would be enough to buy four new tyres. Up at daybreak, we set to work copying from a *Vie Parisienne* borrowed from Terence. The year was 1920: eyes outlined in kohl, orchid mouths in tiny, heavily-powdered faces, jutting chins; dresses were waistless and fringed, revealing vulnerable shoulders; the shoes had high insteps. Heavens what a winning brood! I had misjudged the period. Having been surrounded by women enveloped in white veils, clouds rising from studded slippers, the graces of the flappers knocked us sideways. But that wasn't our concern. To gain time, I scribbled on a few sheets myself, but couldn't rise above the level of caricature or graffiti. Knowing how to draw a body should be as natural as speaking precisely. Instead of racking my brains over Ulpian and Beccaria's commentaries,* I would have done better learning how to draw. Not to be able to depict what one loves is a serious failing, and an embarrassing disability. In half an hour, Thierry had created three nymphs in provocative positions, and I coloured them in to order: straw-blonde hair and periwinkle-blue eyes, all the exoticism of the West. The early hour and the melancholy happiness aroused by the old magazines resulted in a mood that was more elegiac than saucy. Would the Superintendent see something in it? I doubted whether anything could move that mountain, but we were too young to do better – pornography is an old man's need.

On the threshold of a dark room decorated with peacock feathers, the Superintendent took forever to shake hands. He seemed embarrassed by the previous day's request and, to prove that he wasn't the libertine we might have thought, he insisted on introducing his children: three black, knock-kneed little girls in flounced dresses, who giggled and looked down at their bare feet when asked about school. At a table loaded with pralines, sugared almonds and sticky cakes, we spun out a languishing conversation.

---

* Ulpian (d AD 228), the Roman jurist and Cesare Beccaria (1738-94), Italian reforming criminologist. – Trs.

Then our host chased away his progeny and examined our creations with heart-rending sighs. Our hands on our knees and our mouths full, we did not disturb his contemplation; thirty rupees would do us nicely.

'Have you any others? More...'

'No.'

'None at all?'

He picked up the drawings and, having imprinted them on his mind, handed them back, covered in greasy fingermarks.

'They're too... artistic, you know, I... but help yourselves all the same,' he added, piling our plates.

Feeling humiliated, we went home on foot, bearing the large portfolio. It took us at least an hour, with the sun directly overhead and our pockets full of sweetmeats. So, I thought, that's where studying gets you. Thierry pondered: 'Not to have sold my pictures – others, yes, but *those!*' So we asked Saadik, the barman at the Saki, to circulate them discreetly amongst the Pathan bookies who came to have a little drink in his kitchen. Instead of which, for three days he hawked them round our friends, waving them under their noses and explaining them to the indifferent or shy customers.

'Nice lady to f——, sir', and cocking a thumb at Thierry, 'he did, sir.'

The British had spent a great deal of time in Quetta. In the nineteenth century, to guard the south Afghanistan passes and the Pathan mountains, they bought it from a local potentate when it was no more than a large village; extended the railway line from Karachi with vast effort; planted hundreds of trees; asphalted some streets, and put ten thousand troops in the barracks, with brass bands, a chapel and polo ponies. This installation was the work of first-class negotiators such as Pottinger and Sandeman, who effortlessly reached an understanding with the Baluchi and, far from disturbing their happy equilibrium, guaranteed it by reinforcing the tribal structure and awarding diplomas of good and loyal service to the Sardars on behalf of faraway Queen Victoria. If the Baluchi – excellent horsemen and capable of winging a skylark with a single shot from their ancient peashooters – were not rebellious, it was because there was something in it for them: selling their ponies, their fruit and their cattle to these regiments come from the other end of the earth in order to suppress their turbulent Pathan neighbours. The common love of horses, of the comical aspects of life, and of sensible arrangements, had succeeded in transforming this 'Protectorate' into one of the few idylls in colonial history. Under the shade of the eucalyptus, between the sand and the letters from home and the raucous summons of the bagpipes, many a Tom and Johnny had found a new kind of happiness. They had departed with the end of British India, and sometimes this light town seemed swollen with all the nostalgia that converged there.

Those who had remained in the service of Pakistan came to the Saki in white dinner-jackets every night: a few majors, two grizzled colonels with blue, whisky-soaked eyes, who politely exclaimed over the chocolate soufflé, applauded our renditions of *Gloomy Sunday* or *Fallen Leaves*, and sang us, in voices thinner than glass, old Highland ballads to widen our repertoire. They all spoke a bit of Urdu, loved their regiment and preferred the East to Britain. But the East had changed. In the republic which was barely seven years old, their former administrators were now their employers. The suzerains had become subordinates. Such transitions are always fraught. Discrimination founded on tradition becomes unacceptable from one day to the next; one is obliged to improvise new relations, and to develop them requires more than simple goodwill. To create the bridge you need imagination, and outsiders like Terence. The Saki courtyard was the source of a folklore for which he set the tone. It was enough for him to move between the tables, glass in hand, in his weary, relaxed style, for the small company of drinkers to feel in harmony with one another. At opportune moments he would leave his sauces in order to inspect his courtyard, as though lifting up a net; he would have a game of chess with a local horse-dealer, who would give him a racing tip, or greet one of the former Pathan irregulars whom he had only watched through binoculars when he was still in charge, and whom he now found seated peacefully over a glass of lemonade.

Despite the law in force, Terence served alcohol to Muslims without ever watering it down, and with a tact that his clientele entirely appreciated. When a glass of tea replaced the third order for whisky, far from protesting, they were grateful to be the object of such subtle diagnosis, and of a control all the more necessary because night patrols invariably detained Believers with suspect breath. Sometimes, people as important as the station master or the postmaster, who had eluded his surveillance and had slightly overstepped the mark, remained in a corner of the courtyard well beyond closing time, chewing coffee beans before risking their steadier steps in the deserted lanes.

In Quetta, where the icing criss-crossing the confectioner's tarts, colour photos of Jinnah, and stiff, shiny cats painted on velvet cushions were the limits of decorative invention, the personalities appearing over two nights on the walls of the Gran Stanley Café had attracted the curious. Braganza cashed in on this attention, and asked for more. He removed the bottles from the end wall, and for thirty rupees ordered atolls, coconut palms and Tahitians bathing. The subject was especially suitable as we had lots of blue left over. It was done in a night: cerulean sky, ultramarine waves where tobacco-coloured sirens combed their hair, and in a corner, to finish up the paint tins, a variegated steamer. It was as reassuring and fresh as the splendid, plumed savages on cigar-boxes and meant that the beggar by the canal got a last helping of doughnuts. Braganza was very pleased with the sea, having been dubious at first, but indicated with the end of his switch that the bathers should be more rounded, as they weren't plump enough for local taste. With three brushstrokes, Thierry transformed their posteriors into worthy targets, and calmly went back to the picture of Iran – a patch of lean desert beneath shreds of cloud – which he had already started.

Emerging from Ramzan's garage in the evening, I would spend a while with Tellier, the photographer, learning how to develop photos. Tellier, whose shop was next to the Saki Bar, had settled there before the earthquake and taught himself his trade. For the British clientele in this garrison town he specialised in 'haze' and 'blurred backgrounds', and in a chic *moiré* effect that came off perfectly in the terrific heat of his darkroom. But it was on the portraits of officers' wives that he really went to town; blonde women with faded features and special hair-dos, wearing their pearls. A drop of gum arabic gave the eyes a romantic shine, and with zinc white and little tweezers, Tellier touched up their necklaces which took on a magic, snowy brilliance. At night, in his dark window, you could see them gleaming beneath the scarcely visible faces, like thin crescent moons.

Independence and the departure of the British had reversed his technique; a dark clientele had replaced his erstwhile pale pink, over-exposed looking sitters; he now printed in black on a light background, and on smooth paper. The younger sons who – in default of a girlfriend – pinned up several langorous examples of their own portraits around their beds, hung about in front of his window, straightening their partings.

The printing paper he got from Karachi caused him problems, and he asked me to order some from Switzerland, for which he'd pay me back. I ordered fifty rupees' worth. Later on there were various occasions on which that amount would have worked wonders, and I would write *please, Mr Tellier...* or *s'il vous plaît, mon cher Tellier* – he was a native of Pont-Saint-Esprit. Tellier played dead, and I was reduced to cursing him in various chop-houses from Kabul to Colombo. No doubt he'd never received the paper; the envelope marked 'open in the dark' would have passed through the hands of our lustful friend the Superintendent who, suspecting an obscene parcel, had probably opened it in the privacy of his office, only to see those pure, virgin sheets turn an accusing, icy grey under his very eyes.

The three Saki boys belonged to that flighty species who hum and roll wandering eyes, walk around barefoot and carry their worldly goods in a handkerchief. A fortnight was long enough for them to fall in love, quarrel and recover. Flights, tiffs, burning ardour, sulks, partings – even Saadik the barman, who was both gullible and matter-of-fact, didn't eat for a week when he was 'dropped'. On these nights of crisis the distraught Terence was up to his eyes and never left the ovens except to catch a breath of fresh air on the terrace, his face dripping with sweat...

'Quick, play me that little number – you know the one...' It was a Serbian song:

I have a red flower in my bosom
and that flower gazes at the world...

or a perhaps Persian one, but always something heartbreaking. Once or twice we even saw him in tears.

Such work, after all, with its highs and lows, the town which was so light and so far from everything, the swindling suppliers – all these were too much for a man of his age. He gave the impression of being stuck, of wasting his talents there. Sometimes, going along to the station to see whether our parts had arrived, we would see him pacing up and down his little courtyard, reprimanding the boys in a stern voice, digging his fists into the pockets that Saadik's patching had stretched to his knees. You would have thought that he was about to butt someone with his head, but it wasn't that – it was just the way his isolation affected him, and Asia, too, so good for the heart and so bad for the nerves.

Terence often questioned us about France, where he dreamed of opening an inn one day – half hidden among the leaves, with oak panelling, a discotheque and horses for hire. We advised him to try Haute-Provence, where land could be got for nothing, or Savoy – as it was busier – of which Terence had found an excellent Michelin map in his shack. Once the last customer was shown to the door and our instruments propped against the wall, we pored over river-banks and red roofs, familiar patches of woodland, praising the elegance of its foliage, the austere melancholy of roughcast walls and a certain veiled hedonism that was very 'Terence'; over-praising them a bit, in order to encourage him, but also because the names Thoiry, Nernier or Yvoire recalled the lilacs and the wrought-iron café tables where the plans for our journey had matured before we set out.

For several nights in a row, waiting for dawn beneath the branching stars, we kept this piece of the province, in all its freshest green, spread out between our three glasses. Terence asked questions, carefully annotating this Land of Heart's Desire which helped him to give precision to his dreams, to create hideaways far from the habits and creditors that kept him in Quetta. We found it the next day, lying forgotten on the bar, with areas shaded in red, crosses marking villages and even, next to a few isolated farms – did the inhabitants guess how lucky they were – exclamation marks.

In a cubbyhole under the iron staircase linking the bar to the roof-terrace, Terence had stored away the things that had followed him around in his trials: the photograph of a litter of setters in front of a

pinnacled façade, some volumes of Tennyson, Proust in its green leather binding, three years of the *Vie parisienne* and ninety pounds of old HMV recordings: Alfred Cortot, Gluck's *Orphée, The Magic Flute*. Sometimes he went off to play a record, and disappeared amongst the bric-a-brac. Beneath the music you could hear him rifling through his odds and ends, talking to himself as he unpiled them, reading old letters, and you wouldn't see him again that afternoon. He would go up to the lean-to he used as his bedroom to be alone with his memories, and sleep would overtake him there. One day when an insistent Pathan was asking for him at the bar, I found him in his shack, sleeping on a rickety camp bed, all huddled up, with an attentive expression as though he were following some interior journey at a stiff pace. His big artillery binoculars were lying at his side. I wondered what on earth he could watch from his terrace, and went down on tiptoes to tell the importunate client to come back in the evening.

At slack times, filling in his betting slips, Terence would put the speaker in the courtyard so that he could listen to his favourite arias. They were excellent pre-war pressings, well worn by sun and sand, with some surprises in store: the violins, woodwind and a famous female voice would soar above a sort of gunfire, then suddenly the needle would veer towards the middle with a terrible squeal and the phrase, cut off clean – as enigmatic as fragments from oracles whose meanings are ambivalent   would float over the Saki. Terence would give a start as though he had been fired at point-blank range, and turned to us as witnesses; the way things wear out and age behind our backs affected him greatly.

In another pile, destined for the bar, we found sentimental, velvety and glittering American songs by Doris Day, Lena Horne, which I couldn't hear without lapsing into a dream about dough. I imagined young women with perfect faces behind simmering percolators, starched shirts, the money with which to seduce such sirens. I dreamed of selling it by the yard, like ribbon, this new liberty which was still so fragile. It didn't last. It was just that I was exhausted, and needed to sleep.

Waiting for me outside the post office, Thierry chatted to the man sweeping up the first fallen leaves. Then he walked round the building and came across his interlocutor again who, not recognising him, called out: 'The friend you're looking for has gone that way.' When I arrived, he had been going round after himself for a while. It seemed natural, everything was going round: little by little, weariness and lack of sleep had introduced the merry-go-round of dreams into our lives. There was no way we could sleep, what with the blazing light and the flies; we talked on and on from our beds, we sweated and stayed awake and the very substance of life was reduced; we ended up living in profile. The slightest emotion – a smile, a glint on a cheek, the end of a song – was enough to pierce us to the quick. Malarial fever also came round every four or five days: a kind of weakness and shivering which made me slide out from under the car with a feeling that my body was covered in leaves and dirty water. It was nothing serious, but a distraction.

Working in the garage, and for Terence, and at night amidst the paintpots… We would return to the Lourdes Hotel mute and exhausted: not the attitude one wants to see in those one is doing a favour. Metta, the proprietor, was in a fix: we added no lustre to his place. He was afraid that he would be lumbered with us forever, and replied absently to our greetings in the morning. It would be better to settle on the Saki's roof until we left – Saadik and the kitchen-boys slept up there on heaps of old newspapers.

While packing, I noticed that my whole winter's work had disappeared; the boy had swept it up. (I'd put a large envelope of it on the floor, to make room on the table.) It was midday, the sun was filtering through the trees and everyone was resting. With trembling hands I rummaged through the kitchen rubbish bin, crossed the office – sighs and groans rising up on all sides – and found the boy sleeping under a dirty tablecloth. He remembered, he'd thought… Rubbing his eyes, he took me as far as the rubbish dump by the main road. It was empty; the refuse truck and its skeletal attendants, masked in black felt, had gone by at dawn in a plume of dust, disappearing with my manuscript. No one at the hotel knew where they went. I would have to get on the next truck, find the place and search through it. While waiting, there was time to kill that I fervently wished I could turn back and retrieve my property. I began by throwing up, then went to work on our engine. While dismembering the bolts that had jammed, I saw that five-ton truck bumping over a rutted track, scattering my papers in the dust along with unmentionable muck and cauliflower stalks. I reconstructed the first page, the paragraphs, the paler lines where my fingers had gone numb as they typed, Tabriz, the poplars' shadow over icy ground, the passing silhouettes of scoundrels in caps, coming to the Armenian café to drink away the money from their shady deals. That whole steaming, darkened, irretrievable winter, written down by gas-lamp or on tables in the bazaar where partridges fought in their cages, by someone I no longer was.

That night at the Saki, Thierry did all the work. Terence kindly brought over glass after glass. He understood: there was almost nothing he couldn't understand. But I held back from drinking for fear of missing the truck the next day and seeing my slim chances buried under a new load of rubbish. I spent the night in an armchair in the gallery, tossing cigarette-butts on the ground, and no premonitory dream came to reveal the whereabouts of my wad of paper. At five o'clock the sky spread out in apple-green and the eucalyptus leaves gleamed like mercury; then the sun drowned everything in its heartless flood. The boss brought us two spades. He knew all about it, and even volunteered an anecdote: one of his friends had lost a manuscript in the Partition massacres.

'He spent years reconstructing it, remembering it, rewriting it... and believe me, it wasn't much good.'

Stomachs swollen with boiling tea and spades across our knees, we sat by the roadside to wait for the rubbish trucks. I tried to read Proust, filched from Terence, but the misfortunes of Albertine didn't work and anyway that day the road offered plenty of other distractions. It was the anniversary of national independence; a crowd dressed in their Sunday best flowed towards the festive square: beaming, bearded men given lifts on the crossbars of multicoloured bicycles; fierce smiles, turbans with aigrettes; squealing children, their chins covered in sugar, milling round a bear-leader, and peasants in fits of laughter making their buffalo lie down between the cannons of the siege of Kabul. It was a morning of real jubilation. We were bombarded with surprised but cordial greetings. The truck didn't arrive: the refuse-collectors had joined the fête. A policeman on horseback directed us towards the dump: it lay about eight miles along the Pichin road; the smell made it impossible to miss.

By midday, in the heart of a circle of bald mountains, on a plain black with filth and scattered with glinting fragments of broken glass, we were ready to get down to work. Enormous gusts of noxious air, as regular as a sleeper's breathing, vibrated upwards towards the sun, and clouded the horizon. A troop of threadbare donkeys was roaming about, butting at things or rolling round in revolting little hollows, with harrowing brays. All alone in the centre of this plague-spot, a completely naked man sifted through the ashes. We asked him about the previous day's truck, but as he was dumb he couldn't tell us much. At each of our questions he would put his dirty finger into his mouth and shrug his shoulders. The vultures and brown eagles directed us to the most recent intake. There were at least a hundred of them, perched around their latest quarry, digesting, excreting and belching. We threw clinker, bones and rusty cans at them. They dodged these with ridiculous sidesteps then, not understanding our quarrel with them at all, folded their wings again and stretched out their necks, which looked like rotting meat. We charged at them, yelling and brandishing our spades. They all took off, flapping like dirty washing, and settled a bit further away, watching us as we worked.

Seen at close quarters, the rubbish was a curious revelation of scarcity; successive removals – by domestics, rag-and-bone men, sick beggars, dogs and crows – had skimmed it off completely. Postage-stamps, fag ends, chewing gum and bits of wood had made other people happy long before the truck came along. Only the unnameable and the shapeless had reached this spot, reduced – after the vultures' final pickings – to a dead, ashy and acidic paste, full of traitorous snags which the spades hit. Bare-chested, with gags across our mouths, our noses in close proximity to broken light bulbs, melon rinds scraped down to the last fibre, scraps of paper red with betel-juice and half-burned sanitary towels, we held our breath and searched along a row. In this detritus you could find what was, in effect, a pale image of the layout of the town. Poverty doesn't produce the same waste as wealth; each level had its muck, and there were slight indications even here of transitory inequality. We changed neighbourhood with each spadeful; after the pink tickets from the Cristal cinema, an old bit of film mixed in with prawns indicated Tellier's and the Saki Bar. A few yards further on, Thierry explored the more prosperous seam of the Chilton Club – foreign papers, airmail envelopes, packets of Camel cigarettes eaten away by fermentation – and cautiously dug in the direction of our hotel. The heat, the murderous stench and above all the vultures prevented our working at top speed; as soon as we paused to breathe and leaned on our spades, the vultures, attracted by the promising stillness, shuffled towards us with cries of loathsome sweetness, until a well-aimed clod let them know that they were mistaken. Others sailed slowly overhead, projecting across our trench a shadow the size of a calf, which we could have done without. We understood their impatience; judging by what we were turning up, they weren't spoiled. In the mid-afternoon, Thierry let out a yell and all the carrion crows flew off together. He brandished an envelope – soiled and boiling, but empty. After a frantic hour's work, we found four torn fragments of the first page, then the spades came upon a black, poverty-stricken medley. We were far from the Lourdes Hotel. It was useless to look any further: fifty large sheets of strong paper represented capital that had no place here.

Exhausted, trailing our spades, we went back to the car with the shitty envelope and the four scraps of paper, which seemed to have been scorched. On the last you could read '...November snow which seals mouths and sends us to sleep'. Everything was simmering, the steering wheel burned our palms, our arms and faces were covered with salt from perspiration. And memory was a shadowy oblivion: the weight of cold, Tabriz, the heart of winter?!... I must have dreamed it all.

At six o'clock the fête was suspended for evening prayer. The town rested in a luscious light. All along the canal idlers mumbled their prayers, prostrated between their upside-down bicycles.

Terence was counting on the evening to make his till ring. Feverishly he looped light bulbs and little flags across the terrace. A slate leaning against the door announced: Treasure-Hunt with Prize – The Merrymakers' Band (three Pathan musicians loaned by Braganza) – and us, boastfully presented as *Genuine artists from Paris*.

We opened fire with the Pakistani anthem: a series of straightforward thirds which we had learned for the occasion. There was a crowd, and new faces; a table of exiled Afghans and an old, slightly drunk Armenian woman in a spangled dress, who danced alone with large, unsteady steps, head on the shoulder of an imaginary partner while passers-by in the next lane crowded round to enjoy the sight. We were at home. When we flagged, the Merrymakers' Band supported us with nice drumming effects and then took over. Everybody kept asking for 'Cherry Time':

cherries of love	*cerises d'amour*
in ruby clothes	*aux robes vermeilles*
falling on the moss	*tombant sur la mousse*
like drops of blood...	*en gouttes de sang*

Terence translated for his neighbours; replacing 'cherries' with 'pomegranates' almost gave the effect of Omar Khayyam. This faint sadness charmed the Baluchi. Saadik constantly filled our glasses, indicating spruce old men who bowed from their tables, hand over heart. A little breeze got up; the Armenian had sat down again, rubbing her eyes with a grubby palm. The Saki was awash with sighs of pleasure, well-trimmed beards, new turbans and cool feet.

Without the smell, I might have forgotten the day. But despite soap, a shower and a clean shirt, I stank of refuse. With each breath I saw that steaming black plain, freed of its remaining unstable molecules by gusts of air which made them one with elemental inertia and repose; matter at the end of its tribulations, in its last reincarnation, out of which a hundred years of monsoons and sunshine hadn't coaxed a single blade of grass. The vultures who pecked over that nothingness had not lost their nerve; the succulence of carrion flesh had long since deserted their memory. Colour, taste, even form – the fruit of delightful if fleeting associations – were not often on the menu. Neglecting such transient efflorescences, perched there in all their permanence and torpor, they digested Democritus' tough axiom: neither sweet nor bitter exists, but only atoms and the space between atoms.

In order not to antagonize the gods of whom he expected so much, Terence sometimes had a fit of realism: faced up to problems, made a slightly shady deal, made the most of an opportunity... He would organize a fête, transporting the whole of the Saki Bar – the

'orchestra', two boys, several cases of soft drinks and a block of ice –
to the racecourse, six miles away, for the Sunday Grand Derby. These
were poignant expeditions; we squeezed into a yellow *droshky*, a
guitar between our legs, on our knees a parcel of steaks for grilling,
wrapped up in old *Karachi Tribunes*. The boys, jammed together,
nibbled each other gently; the cabman made his brass bell ring, as
pure and melancholy a sound as the bell in a provincial grocer's shop;
and we jogged along to the racecourse over crumbling dirt paths
bordered by poplars.

We set up our refreshment stall under a ring of eucalyptus trees,
near the weigh-in. In the shade, where the horses' coats gleamed, the
Quetta 'horse-people' took up their positions: large Pakistani
landowners with faces pitted by smallpox, who had exchanged
turbans for riding-caps, and their amber worry beads for binoculars.
The last haggling, in nasal English accents, went on around the
striped silks of the jockeys. Further along, the punters swarmed
round the tote, while we unloaded our bottles in the centre of this
Moghul miniature, retouched by Dufy. The spectacle was handsome,
and the races were rigged. Sometimes, the best horse having
thoughtlessly overtaken the 'winner', his jockey reined him in so hard
that the judges burst out laughing. This in no way lessened the
interest in the bets; they were placed on the owners, which required
extra finesse and perception.

I don't recall that the *Continental artists* pulled in the crowds. The
boy massaged his ankles, singing. Terence re-read his gin-spattered
copy of *Le Côté des Guermantes*, politely pretending to be surprised
by tangos we had serenaded him with a hundred times, or clapping
along with them as though carried away, in the hope of attracting a
customer. In vain: our takings were further reduced by the march
past of the Baluchi Regiment at the thirstiest hour. No one wanted to
miss that. A carrot-haired Scottish bandmaster marched in front of
two rows of drummers dressed in tiger-skins, followed by forty
pipers black as ebony, in the kilts and plaids of Colonel Robertson's
tartan: he had founded the regiment. The troops came last, with their
impeccable swords and polished leather, in green turbans with silver
aigrettes. They marched with infectious gaiety, broad smiles splitting
their faces. There was none of that mulish pomp and circumstance of
marches past at home. When they paused, I examined the

inscriptions on their drums: *Delhi, Abyssinia, Afghanistan, China 1900, Ypres 1914, Messina, Burma, Egypt, Neuve-Chapelle, Kilimanjaro, Persia, the Ardennes,* and a number of other infamous places where the support of the bagpipes must have been welcome. It's invigorating music: taut, incisive, ironic, with no dubious whiff of holocausts. The British officers whom the Pakistanis had retained in their service looked happy as they marched at the head of the regiment, to whose fine organisation they devoted all their sober hours. The Saki Bar's best customers passed by in a haze of sunshine. ...Fireflies. The smell of leaves. A brief interval of coolness. Night was falling. The last thoroughbreds, wrapped in Persian horse-blankets, had taken the road back to Quetta. Drunk with sleep, our fingers tingling, we played very softly, like runners who still had a hundred yards to go before the race was over. Terence, sighing, counted up the unsold bottles. He was already reproaching himself for this foray into real life: it wasn't worth the bother. How had he let himself in for it? Round the racecourse, the gentle countryside criss-crossed by paths stretched as far as the desert. It was intersected by cactus hedges, and dotted with parasol trees in which green parakeets were sleeping.

Going back, I sat in the back of the cart, clutching a tub of dirty glasses. The horse was asleep on his feet, and paused from time to time. A plume of pearly steam rose above the station where the little North-Western Railway convoy, stuffed with tea, contraband and drinking water, was getting ready to leave for Zahedan.

'Terence, you're an Englishman ...'

'English? *I'd rather shoot myself...* I'm no shopkeeper, I'm Welsh – and *a very vicious man at that,*' he added calmly.

Indeed. For example, he had enough friends in the capital to crack down on his creditors, but he preferred to use such connections to obtain priority in Karachi for baskets of fresh prawns, half of which were eventually thrown away. To serve 'scampi' in the middle of all this sand to the strains of a dance hall accordion – that seemed to him worthy of his reputation. That was his idea of success; meanwhile, under his less than vicious management, the Saki Bar was in decline, like a civilisation too refined to last. Terence's friends at least paid for their drinks, but his friends' friends went off without settling their bills. Then there were the cops and the bookies who had to be treated carefully... then their friends, and at the end of the chain came the Pathan pimps and some unknowns in badly tied turbans who drank in the corner standing up.

I remember one night in particular. It was two a.m. The last drinker had long since left. Terence had grilled us a bit of meat, and we were eating at the bar when someone came striding through the door, brushed past without a greeting, and disappeared into the kitchen. Then there was complete silence. As he was very tall, and the ceiling very low, he must have been crouching in the dark, perfectly still. Terence hadn't even looked up from his book. I felt uneasy.

'Who was that?'

'How the devil should I know? He didn't even say good evening,' replied Terence, slightly irritated. He seemed more bemused than worried. Then we heard the little clink of a saucepan, and a chewing noise, and he broke into a smile.

Other half-starved, furtive shadows would follow, and soon the white dinner-jackets and Oxford accents would be no more than a memory. The Saki Bar was simply and inevitably being dragged down; Terence's taste for metamorphoses and surprises, and his gentleness born from a streak of abandon, were pushing him along with it.

The evening before we left, the Saki had no customers. We were going up to bed when two timid knocks sounded on the door. It was a Kuchi* musician, with a tiny harmonium under his arm. He was one of those wandering showmen who rove the subcontinent, a grey monkey on his shoulder, letting horses' blood, casting spells, living off windfalls, theft or songs, avoiding temples and mosques in the belief that man is born to 'wander, die, rot and be forgotten'. Even Braganza wouldn't take him in, but Terence invited him in and offered him a drink. He squatted in the centre of the courtyard to start up his instrument. With his left hand he worked a bellows on the side, while his right – a large hand blackened by the sun – went up and down a sweet-toned, two-octave keyboard. The equivocal, allusive, tremulous music scarcely rose above the puffing of the

---

* The Afghan name for the tribes of gypsy origin who had remained in their native region.

bellows; suspended phrases, shreds of music were crushed to nothing or, when his big fingers hit two keys at once, one note followed another like faithful shadows. Then, with his eyes lowered, he began to sing in a harsh voice that threaded like red wool between the nasal notes of the harmonium. There was a kind of singing sigh, too, strikingly reminiscent of the *sevda* songs of Bosnia. We recalled the smell of red peppers, the tables under the pine trees of Mostar or Sarajevo, and the gypsy orchestras in their threadbare suits, playing their instruments as if their urgency could remove an unbearable weight from the world. It was the same wild, fleeting sadness, inconstancy; seeds of hellebore.

In the town of Quetta – so a Persian legend goes – the Sassanian Bahram Gur recruited, just to amuse his court, ten thousand minstrels and gypsy musicians who, having received their pay, disappeared into the West to settle in that same Balkan countryside where, a year back, in the stork season, we had emptied so many glasses with their descendants.

After a tiring day at the garage, this return of memories was heaven. Our journey rose and spiralled back on itself. It gave us a sign, we had only to follow. Terence, who was very sensitive to happiness, uncorked his last bottle of Orvieto. The cork leapt out, increasing the Saki's liabilities by twenty-three rupees. What did he care? He had passed the point of efficiency, passed the point of being had. On half-pay, trapped in this disintegrating bar, burdened with the whole town's secrets, and with debts and old Mozart records, he travelled further and more freely than we did. Asia attracts those who like to sacrifice their careers to their fate. Once the sacrifice is made, the heart beats more generously, and many things become clearer. While the wine grew warm in our glasses and Terence, still and watchful as a night owl, gazed up at the stars, a couplet by Hafiz came back to me:

...If the mystic still doesn't know the secret of the World,
I wonder how the innkeeper came to learn it so well.

Afghanistan

The Road to Kabul

'THE KHOJAK PASS? That one's not for you.' 'It's very easy.' 'It's impossible with your car.' 'The road is excellent.' 'The road is execrable.' 'Take the turn-off to the right.' 'At all costs, avoid the right-hand turn-off!'

Those were a few of the opinions we had collected in Quetta about the route linking the town with the Afghan frontier. It was always the same: the Europeans who had made the road liked to exaggerate the difficulties; as for the Baluchi, they never gave displeasing information – it was not in their nature to be contradictory. It would be best to go and see for ourselves, and be prepared for the worst.

The Khojak Pass is carefully kept by the army, and is a hard climb between boiling hot patches of scree. At the bottom of the second slope the engine conked out. Really, one should only travel on foot! We ought to have given the car away... but to whom? There wasn't a soul around for thirty miles. Without much faith, we cleaned the distributor and the spark-plugs and adjusted the leads. The sun was at its zenith. We had no more cigarettes; moreover, fever made me so clumsy that I caught my left hand in the fan belt and gashed four fingers to the bone; it sent me hopping down the road, gasping with pain. Thierry wrapped my hand in towels to stop the bleeding, and it was the only time on the trip that the morphine we were carrying came in handy. It worked wonders: pushing, pulling, putting down chocks with that hand out of action seemed a joke. At five o'clock we reached the top. A fresh wind brushed our faces. From the summit we could see the leprous spot of the town of Chaman and the Afghan plateau, which spread northwards out of sight in a mist of light.

Laskur-Dong, Afghan border

It is still a privilege to visit Afghanistan. Not so long ago, it was an adventure. Unable to hold the country, the British army in India hermetically sealed off access in the east and south. For their part, the Afghans had sworn to keep their country from all Europeans. They almost kept their word, and were all the better for it. From 1800 to 1922 scarcely a dozen daredevils (deserters from the Bengal regiments, visionaries, agents of the Tsar or the Queen's spies dressed as pilgrims) managed to force the lock and travel round the country. Scholars were not so lucky. Unable to cross the Khyber Pass, the Indianist Darmestetter, a specialist in Pathan folklore, was reduced to searching out informants in the gaols of Attok and Peshawar. The archaeologist Aurel Stein waited twenty-one years for his visa for Kabul, and received it just in time to go there and die.

Today you can do it with a little tact and patience, but when we presented ourselves at nightfall at the border village of Laskur-Dong on the Quetta-Kandahar road, armed with the precious visa, there was no one to show it to. No office, no barrier, no control of any sort; just the white span of the track between the mud houses, and the wide open countryside. The three soldiers drinking in the tea-house in a cloud of moths had nothing to do with customs. As for the customs officer, apparently he had gone home for evening prayer.

Thierry went off to look for him. I stayed in the car, too worn out to stir. It was an interminable wait. The village was as black and as hot as an oven. I spent a moment looking at a truck piled high with basketwork which was manoeuvring on the square, directed by a child's voice, then I dozed off with my head between my knees. When the fever made me sit up, I saw pressed to the windowpane a soldier's pug-face, full of friendly amazement, and dropped back into yet deeper sleep...

The sound of the door made me jump: an old man was pushing a lantern under my nose and urging me in vehement Persian. He wore a white turban, a white robe, a well-trimmed beard and, round his neck, a silver seal as large as a fist. It took me a moment to realise that this was the customs officer. He had come along simply in order to wish us a good trip and to give me the address of a doctor in Kandahar. His dress, his presence and the welcoming note he brought to his job made him such a sympathetic figure that I stupidly pointed out – to prevent his getting into trouble – that our visas had expired six weeks previously. He had already noticed, and wasn't bothered. In Asia people don't keep to timetables, and anyway, why refuse in August the passage that would have been allowed in June? Men don't change much in two months.

Kandahar, 3 a.m.

Kandahar that night – with its cool, silent streets, its abandoned stalls, its plane trees, its twisted mulberry trees whose foliage made a warmer shadow amongst the shadows – was more like a dream than anything real… The town didn't so much as sigh. Here and there a *djou* shimmered, or a crow squawked, wakened by our headlights.

Sleep was what interested me most. As we cruised along at six miles an hour in search of an hotel, with the stars going out one by one, the word 'Kandahar' took on a succession of shapes: a pillow, an eiderdown, a bed as deep as the sea into which one could settle for, say, a hundred years…

Hotel Kandahar

I woke up when the doctor arrived: Graeco-Italian, I thought. I had imagined someone quite different! He was a tall, feverish Romeo in shorts and sandals, with one of those handsomely commanding masks that are so annoying when the expression beneath doesn't match them. One detected a thread of interior life some way behind the pompous façade, like a humble little courtyard tucked behind an imposing door. He seemed to feel awkward and constrained. He paced up and down the room, haughty and uncertain, grabbed hold of a chair, straddled it and said 'Well then!' in a marvellously resonant tone. I explained the situation with the economy that weariness imposes, but such calmness was not this doctor's style. The lack of drama disconcerted him. He had made his entrance in a manly, providential manner, and didn't know how to sustain this part if we didn't play along. He examined me brusquely: the hand? in two weeks I wouldn't notice it. The fever? simply malaria *vivax*, a joke, I would recover perfectly well, there was nothing to make a fuss about. You could get worse; he himself, more than once… When he saw that I was eyeing the curious scar at the base of his neck, he broke off, smiled and said ironically 'Too much violin', as a beggar showing an empty sleeve might have said 'Austerlitz', then stared at me with excessive intensity, as though he secretly hoped to be provoked, wounded in a sensitive spot unknown to us, and could then make his exit with the same flourish as he'd made his entrance. I was going to sleep for thirty hours, and had no intention of insulting anyone. Far from provoking him, we made a fuss of him, complimenting him on his French and offering him Baluchi cigars, while he hummed absent-mindedly and beat time on the chair.

What annoyed him about his self-imposed role was not knowing exactly whom he was dealing with. I sensed that he was trying to class us so that he could speak to us in the language he judged appropriate. I saw his eyes darting round the room, querying our luggage, lingering on the gear thrown on the foot of the bed and fearing that he had too quickly assumed a coarse, fawning or familiar tone. Some things – Thierry's easel, the tape recorder – unsettled him again and prevented his coming to a decision. Moreover, time was getting on; he'd been in the room ten minutes already. A sort of panic took hold of him; he gave up; suddenly the mask of Colleone gave way to a face of more modest dimensions, pierced by compassion, solitude and youth. Another personality appeared: competent, vulnerable, hungry for company; he spoke of lending us books, of coming to chat, of looking after me for nothing. Suddenly, everything seemed simple to him: he stopped fiddling with his cigarette, its smoke curling upwards in the rising sun. He took a blood sample and prepared slides without pausing in his monologue. Did we like Wilde? He was translating him into Italian in his spare time. And Corelli? The sweetness of his famous Christmas Concerto was often a balm to him. Well, he was an artist – had he mentioned that? He had an enormous record collection for which he had such a single-minded passion that his young wife had refused to join him in Kandahar. It was better that way: women knew nothing about extremes. He spent his nights alone at the top of his hospital, amidst floods of harmony, writing an Afghan novel – a vast psychological fresco which had such an ingenious plot that he hesitated to confide it to us. He had been working on it for years; he was tormented by it. Once it was finished, he would kill himself –

'Sorry?'

He would… exactly. He had no sooner uttered the word than he regretted it. But it was too late; he had seen the ghost of a smile and it plunged him back into his badinage. His chin jutted out; his face set. Returning to Mozart, he was under control again – pedantic, lightly humming the themes, tossing out Koechel numbers that meant nothing to us, quizzing us on minute details of orchestration: it was like an examination. We were pleasant, rash fools to be romping round Asia. It was all very well, but we mustn't forget that he, the doctor, had pushed his taste for Art and the violin so far as to scar his neck. And no ordinary violin at that! One of the five Italian *Amati*, which could only travel with an escort of *carabiniere*.

But time was passing, he had stayed far too long and work called – a few mountains to cut up, no doubt. He shot us a piercing glance, crossed the room as though stepping over a corpse at each stride, and left us with a brief smile.

'Let's hope for your sake that he doesn't write too fast,' said Thierry, closing the door.

All the same, he was a good doctor, and absolutely refused to hear of payment. He came back for several mornings afterwards, always in a whirlwind, feverish, holding the whole room with his unnecessary magnetism, his air of the thoroughbred harried by gadflies, and coursing with an energy that commanded respect, beyond the enigmatic, Nietzschean personality he so carefully cultivated. Doubtless he spent too much time on his own. I would have liked to see him in front of his mirror. Meanwhile, I watched him from my bed with a kind of envy. Other things being equal, his anxious narcissism was worth more than the apathy to which exhaustion had reduced me.

The fever came and went.

In the evening, my legs as unsteady as a drunk's, I went to sit at the edge of the main square. The steam from samovars and the smoke from hookahs rose up into the calm sky where a slant of yellow heralded autumn. The cool, echoing town overflowed like a basket with figs and grapes. It smelled of green tea and dried sweat in sheep's wool. The wasps, mad for sugar, lined the shade of the tea-houses above the shaven heads, turbans, Astrakhan skullcaps, and the angry and peremptory expressions. From time to time, a herd of goats or a jonquil-yellow fiacre crossed the square in a cloud of dust. The town was a bit of oriental Persia, plus the stubborn drive of mountain-dwellers, and, to a lesser extent, the lassitude that Persians feel on account of their all too lengthy past – a sort of moral erosion that reins in ambition, takes the edge off vigour and ends up by wearying God himself.

Night fell, and the fever returned. Voices, shops, silhouettes and lights began to revolve like the sail of a windmill, swiftly bearing away the table on which I leant with my ears buzzing, a pool of sweat under each elbow, too fragile to impose on my impressions the resistance which enables them to leave a mark on the memory. Nevertheless, I can see very clearly the little monument in the centre of the square and all around it the white crowd of people strolling to and fro, with a self-contained lightness, in front of six cannon 'captured from the English'.

Malaria is no more dangerous than a bad case of flu, as the first doctor you call will confirm. All the same, it lives up to one's rather different idea of it. It makes you shake and feel feeble; you want things to be made as easy as possible. You think of nothing but sleep; a bed is perfect. But then there are the flies...

For a long time I lived without hating anything much. Today, I positively hate flies. Even thinking about them brings tears to my eyes. A life entirely devoted to wiping them out seems to me a great destiny. I mean the flies of Asia; those who have never been out of Europe are no judges of the matter. In Europe flies keep to windows, to sticky liquids, to the shade of corridors. Sometimes they even wander on to a flower. They are no more than shadows of themselves, exorcised – that is to say, innocent. In Asia they are spoilt by the abundance of the dead and the abandon of the living, and they have a sinister insouciance. Tough and relentless, smuts from some horrible material, they are up with the sun and the world is theirs. Once it is daylight, sleep is impossible. At the slightest hint of repose, they take you for a dead horse and attack their favourite morsels: the corners of the lips, around the eyes, the eardrums. You find yourself asleep? They venture forth, get in a panic, and in their inimitable manner buzz up channels of the most sensitive mucus membranes in the nose, at which point you leap to your feet, retching. But if there is a cut, an ulcer or a spot that hasn't yet healed over, you could perhaps doze off for a bit because they will make a beeline for that, and their tipsy immobility then – replacing their odious agitation – has to be seen to be believed. You can then observe one at leisure: it has no obvious appeal, is not exactly streamlined, and its broken, erratic, absurd flight, designed to get on one's nerves, is beneath contempt. The mosquito, which one would happily do without, is an artist by comparison.

Cockroaches, rats, ravens, thirty-three pound vultures who haven't the brain to kill a quail – there exists a predatory world between-worlds, all in greys and chewed-over browns, industrious in their loathsome colours, their underlings' liveries, always ready to see you on your way. The domestic ones have their weak points – the rat fears the light, the cockroach is timid, even the vulture is afraid to stand on your outstretched palm – but the fly effortlessly rises above this rank and file. Nothing stops it, and I am convinced that if you passed the ether through a sieve, you would still find flies in it.

Everywhere life comes and goes, the busy fly is there in nasty swarms, preaching the gospel of Less – give in, give up the silly effort to breathe, let the great sun do its job – with the devotion of the nurse, cleaning itself with its cursed legs.

Man is too demanding: he dreams of a chosen death, something finished and personal, its outline complementing that of his life. He works at it and sometimes he achieves it. The fly of Asia doesn't make these distinctions. Dead or alive is all the same to that vile creature, and it's enough to see the children asleep in the bazaars (the sleep of the dead under their calm, black swarms) to understand that it's all one to the fly where its pleasure is concerned – a perfect servant of the formless.

The ancients, who saw them clearly, always thought flies the progeny of Evil. They have all the attributes: the deceptive insignificance, the ubiquity, the stunning ability to proliferate; and they're more faithful than a hound. (Many will abandon you, but the flies always remain).

Flies have their gods: *Baal-Zebub* (Beelzebub) in Syria, *Melkart* in Phoenicia, Zeus Apomyios of Elis, to which sacrifices were offered with fervent prayers that they would pasture their herds elsewhere. The Middle Ages believed that they were born from droppings and revived from ashes, and they saw them flying out of the mouths of sinners. From the height of his throne, St Bernard of Clairvaux swatted clusters of them before celebrating mass. Luther himself maintained, in one of his letters, that the Devil had sent his flies to 'shit on my paper'.

In the great era of the Chinese empire, they legislated against flies, and I am quite sure that all vigorous states have been concerned with this enemy in one way or another. We legitimately – and also because it's fashionable – mock the Americans' pathological concern with hygiene. All the same, the day when a flight loaded with DDT bombs killed off all the flies of Athens in one swoop, their planes were flying directly in the wake of the combative St George.

The Mukur road

Afghanistan hasn't a railway, just several roads of beaten earth which it's usual to malign. I don't subscribe to this attitude. The one from Kandahar to Kabul is strewn with fresh dung, clog-marks and camel prints, which look like large, four-leaf clovers in the dust. It travels between broad slopes, spread out in the mountain air. The September air was transparent, the view was clear for miles, and the dominant tone was a vivid mountain brown, cut across here and there by a pheasant's flight, a stand of poplars with each leaf distinct, or the smoke from a village. In places where there was some water, shrivelled trees bordered the road, so we rolled along on a carpet of medlars and little faded pears, crushing them and smelling the pungent scent that was enough to transform the wilderness into countryside.

Not that it was absolutely solitary. You smelled nature before men, but no hour went by without crossing the path of one of those high trucks painted like a toy in periwinkle blue or pistachio green, shining in a world of brown; a peasant on a donkey, the sickle under his arm hot from the sun; perhaps a porcupine. Or a troop of Kuchi gypsies, settled under a willow with their bear and their parrots, two monkeys in red vests stitched with little bells, while their women – large, vociferous, blowsy besoms – busied themselves around a fire that wouldn't catch. We stopped, as entertained by them as they were by us, then moved on.

These meetings were very conveniently spaced, and the road was not really so bad; we could drive along at twenty miles an hour without worrying. Besides, we weren't in a hurry and it was wonderful to be idling along on a fine morning, with the roof down and elbows out the window, not talking much, drinking in the rustic wilderness.

At that pace, if all went well, we would only have one pass to cross after nightfall. But that filled our minds. It had become a sort of possession. At dinner we discussed it again. We slept on it and dreamed about it. In the middle of the night the caravan we had passed on the way up arrived, and we were woken by the hubbub of voices and lanterns as they argued: they were also concerned about the pass. Yet it wasn't even marked on the map and all mountains worthy of the name were further north. It turned out to be no more than forty loops or so in the heart of yellowed mountain pastures; at the top there was a drystone mosque, with a green flag that snapped like a musket in the wind. All the same, we had spent the whole journey waiting for it, crossing it, and finally appropriating it. Taking your time was the best way not to lose it.

Sarai

The person who had the tenancy of the Sarai tea-house displayed an advertisement you couldn't miss: a log across the road. We stopped – you had to – and then perceived beneath the canopy of dry leaves two steaming samovars between garlands of onions and teapots decorated with roses lined up on the brazier; inside we joined several other victims of the tree trunk, who acknowledged us politely and at once turned back to their siesta, their game of chess or their meal.

You have to be familiar with the terrible lack of discretion that is the rule in other parts of Asia to appreciate how exceptional and welcome this restraint was. There, they believe that showing too much interest or bonhomie spoils hospitality. According to a popular Afghan song, the freak is he who receives his guest by asking where he has come from, then 'kills him with questions from head to foot'. The Afghans don't change their ways for Westerners. There was no trace of the spinelessness some second-rate Indians greet you with, or of the phony psychic powers some of them claim. Is it the effect of the mountains? No, it's rather that the Afghans have never been colonised. Twice the British beat them, forced their way across the Khyber Pass and occupied Kabul. Twice the Afghans memorably rebuffed the same British, and they were back where they had started. Thus there is no affront to wash away, no complex to heal. A foreigner? A *firanghi*? Simply a man. One makes room for him, makes sure that he's served, then everyone goes about his own business.

As for the log, which permitted no hesitation, it was good sense itself. How could one resist such a joke? We were even ready to pay a stiff price for it. But there was no question of that: the tea was boiling, the melon just ripe, the bill reasonable; and when we got up to leave, the proprietor rose and courteously removed his barrier.

Kabul

WHEN THE TRAVELLER from the south sees Kabul in its belt of poplars, its mauve mountains lightly sprinkled with snow, and the kites billowing in the autumn sky above the bazaar, he congratulates himself on arriving at the end of the world. On the contrary: he has just reached its centre; this was maintained by a great emperor:

> The country of Kabul is situate in the fourth climate, in the midst of the inhabited part of the world... Caravans from Ferghana, Turkestan, Samarkand, Balkh, Bokhara, Hissar and Badakhshan, all resort to Kabul; while those from Khorasan repair to Kandahar. The country lies between Hindustan and Khorasan. It is an excellent and profitable market for commodities. Were the merchants to carry their goods as far as Khita [Northern China and its dependencies] or Rum [Turkey], they would scarcely get the same profit on them ... There are many merchants that are not satisfied with getting thirty or forty for ten ...
>
> The fruits of the cold districts in Kabul are grapes, pomegranates, apricots, peaches, pears, apples, quinces, jujubes, damsons, almonds and walnuts; all of which are found in great abundance ... There is a species of grape which they call the water-grape, that is very delicious; its wines are strong and intoxicating ...
>
> The climate is extremely delightful, and in this respect there is no such place in the known world ... Samarkand and Tabriz are celebrated for their fine climate, but the cold there is extreme beyond measure ...
>
> In the country of Kabul there are many and various tribes. Its valleys and plains are inhabited by Turks, Aimaks and Arabs. In the city and the greater part of the villages, the population consists of Tajiks. Many other of the villages and districts are occupied by Pashais, Parachis, Tajiks, Berekis, and Afghans ... There are eleven

or twelve different languages spoken in Kabul: Arabic, Persian, Turki, Moghuli, Hindi, Afghani, Pashai, Geberi, Bereki and Lamghani. It is doubtful whether so many distinct races, and different languages, could be found in any other country.*

While he was there, Babur even counted thirty-three kinds of wild tulip on the hills surrounding the town, and a number of streams which he lists in terms of mills, half a mill, a quarter of a mill. He doesn't stop at that – his inventory of minutiae runs to at least ten pages in his memoirs, which he composed in one of the Turkish dialects of Central Asia after he had taken refuge in the land of Kabul in 1501 and then seized power with scarcely a shot fired. At that stage he wasn't yet twenty, and dogged by failure: his relations had deprived him of all his privileges at Fergana. The Uzbek princes of Samarkand were after him. For years he'd been involved in weaving futile plans, gathering adherents, constant fighting and flight, sleeping under the stars and the breath of a few horses, in the company of the handful who stayed loyal.

In Kabul, for the first time, he could sleep in peace. He fell in love with the place at once. He repaired the town wall, laid out gardens, increased the hammams, dug pools – the Muslims have a passion for running water – and planted vines to cater for the drinking bouts in which he gallantly indulged.

He must have spent many a day on horseback, a falcon on his wrist, in the orchards of Kabulistan, which are full of partridges and thrushes, and even more enjoyable evenings under an apple tree or on the flat roof of a dovecote, smoking hashish as he waited for nightfall, swapping riddles and epigrams with his brightest companions, or in elaborate versifying – the taste for ornamental knowledge was typical of the Timurids – to spare his blushes before his neighbour, the prince of Herat, whose court was so literate 'that you couldn't stick out your foot without touching a poet's backside'. These memories were affectionate, and when Babur carved a fitting empire out of India, his revenue of two billion five hundred million

---

* Emperor Zahir-ol-Din Babur (the tiger), founder of the Mogul dynasty in India. *Memoirs of Babur*, translated by John Leyden and William Erskine; annotated and revised by Sir Lucas King, 2 vols (Oxford University Press, 1921), I, pp 216-25.

rupees – one's eyes widen here – could not make up for having left Kabul. His whole army, himself above all, was bored. So he hastened to send two riders to measure the precise distance from Agra to Kabul, and to set up post horses and camels along the way so that he could make the journey as fast as possible. For years he was thus able to bring wine from Afghanistan to his new capital, and the melons whose scent always made him cry. But he was too busy in India to be able to get back to Kabul. He returned only when he was dead. You can find his tomb in a garden west of the bazaar, in the shade of gigantic plane trees.

It is a certificate of merit for a town, to have won such a man's extravagant devotion. Although he was usually circumspect, he naïvely took down all the fables about it: Cain built it with his own hands; Lamech, father of Noah, was buried there; Pharaoh had peopled it with his progeny...

But as to its being the 'centre of the world', one must admit that he was right. Such a claim is made all over the world, only in this case it is actually justified. For centuries the province of Kabul, which commands the passes of the Hindu Kush and those going down to the Indus plain, has functioned as a sieve for the cultures of India, of Hellenised Iran, and of China via Central Asia. It was not by chance that the *diadochoi*, who held on there for so long, worshipped a 'three-headed Hecate', goddess of the crossroads; and when, at the dawn of the Christian era, Hermaios, the last Greek petty king of Afghanistan, struck his coins with Indic script on one side and Chinese on the other, it had truly become the crossroads of the known world.

Moreover, since the time of Alexander's Macedonians – who cried 'Dionysus!' at the sight of every new vineyard and thought they had somehow already arrived home – what comings and goings! The five hundred elephants that Seleucus Nicator had bought in India to hammer his western rivals; the caravans laden with carved ivory, Tyrian glassware, Persian perfumes and cosmetics, the naughty statuettes of Silenus or Bacchus mass-produced in the workshops of Asia Minor; the money changers, the usurers and the gypsies; Caspar the Magus, perhaps – an Indo-Parthian king from the Punjab whose name was mangled by the writers of the *Acts of St Thomas*; the Scythian or Kuchi nomads, chased out of Central Asia, arriving at full tilt and each foolishly burying their nice little piles of money for lucky numismatists and archaeologists later on. More merchants. A person who was simply inquisitive – there always are such people – followed by a servant taking notes (perhaps yet to be discovered). No historians, alas. Chinese Buddhists, who returned complaining of their perilous Indian pilgrimage, their knapsacks stuffed with sacred texts. Then more nomads, this time the Huns, who made a brutish impression on the first lot who had civilised themselves in the interim...

Then in the seventh century came hard Islam, with no memories. After that, the crossroads saw many others, but I'll stop there. Today's traveller, who comes on the heels of so many others, should present himself with appropriate modesty, and not hope to surprise anyone. He will then be made perfectly welcome by the Afghans who, for the most part, have completely forgotten their own history.

The Afghans maintain a fine independence of mind with regard to the West and its attractions. They consider it with roughly the same cautious interest as we consider Afghanistan, valuing it but not letting it impose itself on them.

There is an excellent little museum in Kabul where they display the finds of the French archaeologists who have been digging in Afghanistan since it became independent. There are other things, too – a little of everything: fragments of collections, a stuffed weasel, coins found when the sewers were repaired, rock crystal. On the ground floor, in a recessed case devoted to costumes, you could see in 1954, between a Maori feather cloak and a shepherd's cloak from Sinkiang, a common enough sweater bearing the label 'Ireland', or perhaps 'Balkans'. It was dyed red, no doubt hand-knitted, but was merely a sweater! The kind you'd see on people in trams in October at home. Was it put there by mistake? I rather hope not! I looked at it for a long time, with fresh eyes, and from an objective point of view I admit that the civilisation represented by this wine-coloured top made a poor show next to the plumage from paradise and the Kazak cloak. One could only despair. In any case, you wouldn't be at all tempted to go and see the country where that was what they wore.

I was enchanted by the display, and had the impression that one of those Swiftian reversals had taken place which makes the heart beat faster and steals a march on your understanding. Anyway, a pinch of Afghan-centrism was welcome after twenty-four years of a Europe that had made us study the Crusades without mentioning the Mameluks, found Original Sin in mythologies where it had no place, and only interested us in India from the moment and to the extent that the merchant companies and a few brave rascals from the West had begun to finger it.

A week after we arrived, we both fell ill. Crossing the Lut, the wear and tear on our nerves in Quetta and those evenings in the Saki Bar had finally caught up with us. We had no taste for anything, no inner resources and felt utterly lacklustre. We were prone to see everything in the blackest colours, and had an eye only for what went wrong. The idea of sallying forth importuning people, trying to arrange lectures or display watercolours – none of that gladdened our hearts. Indeed, our hearts were in our boots when chance threw us in the way of a Swiss doctor, a UN expert, who was living on his own in Kabul and offered to have us as lodgers for as long as it took – a considerable time – to set us on our feet again. He was a man who was open to everything, generous, delicate, attentive despite an air of perpetual distraction, and he seemed almost embarrassed by his own niceness. He was the exact opposite of the doctor in Kandahar and all his poses. This one, when he spoke, had a way of inclining his head as though he were speaking into his breast pocket, with strong reservations about his own remarks. He loved to laugh, and took marvellous care of us: in short, he was a friend.

Aided by this providence, my memories of Kabul approach the delightful portrait drawn by Babur, with one reservation: the odour of mutton-fat (used in all Afghan cooking) that impregnates the town, unbearable if you feel at all liverish. And one revision: the wine. In Babur's time it flowed like water; the Law was broken every day and drunks slept on the short grass, their turbans unravelled, out for the count. Today, with the best grapes in the world, the Afghans have returned to abstinence: there isn't a drop of alcohol in the whole of Kabul. Only the diplomats have permission to import it; other foreigners are reduced to buying grapes by the hundredweight in the bazaar and preparing their own vintage. The French launched this fashion and the Austrians followed suit. When

September comes, geologists, teachers and doctors are transformed into wine-makers.

Neighbours join forces to press the bunches and tip the must in earthenware jars. At dinner, bottles of white wine sealed with wax appear on the table; they have a taste of manzanilla, and are quite drinkable, sometimes a bit dry, but in any case – someone will whisper in your ear while refilling your glass – superior to dear Z's, or poor B's. The best bottles are still those of the chaplain to the Italian ambassador, who for years has had practice making his wine for mass; he gives the most deserving the bottles he has neglected to bless.

Having handsomely pillaged their neighbours, the Afghans long suspected foreigners of wanting to do the same to them – and they were not far wrong. They had shot at the Europeans in the nineteenth century; it wasn't until 1922 that the door was half-opened to let in a few. Being choosy had its advantages, because where the West couldn't impose its merchandise, its underlings and its rubbish, it had to resign itself to sending clever men – diplomats, Orientalists, doctors – who were curious and tactful, and understood very well how to behave like Afghans.

The little Western colony in Kabul offered a great deal of variety, charm and resource: Danish ethnologists who found themselves two days away from a valley town where no Westerner had ever set foot; the British, very much at ease in their role as former enemies, which they were accustomed to playing in Asia; a number of UN experts; and above all the French, who provided this society with its centre and its gaiety. The French – perhaps forty of them – had a sort of club at the bottom of a priest's garden, where you could go once a week to drink cool drinks, listen to records, borrow from the library, and meet extraordinary men who knew the country like the back of their hands and could talk about it without being pedantic. It was a charming, lively, gracious welcome. After fourteen months on the road, without lectures, I rediscovered the pleasure, for example, of listening to an archaeologist back from his dig in Arachosia or Bactria, warming to his subject, glass in hand, and getting carried away in marvellous digressions on the inscriptions on coins or the plaster of a statuette. There were a few witty women, some other pretty ones whom we looked at very attentively, and also – provincial life never loses its claims – some of those ladies dourly disposed to argue over precedence, knitting patterns and tartlets as though they still lived in Montargis or Pont-à-Mousson. In short, it was a lively, amusing, interesting world, in which individuals had enough liberty and space to assert themselves. It might have come out of Beaumarchais, Giraudoux or Feydeau.

Sometimes there was a bout of Bovaryism, of amused rumours, and the guilty parties would go for their fling – there was such a lot of gossip in that microcosm – to Lahore or Peshawar, atoning for their distractions in advance on the two hundred miles of dreadful road which separated them from the border.

Ideological conflicts were reduced to a provincial level in Kabul, and the Russian diplomats were less buttoned-up there than elsewhere; this may have been linked with the image of the great, easy-going agricultural neighbour that they tried to create on the frontier of the Oxus. You could see them on a group trip to the barber, opposite the only cinema in town, bouncing over the potholes in an old Ziss with lemon stripes, raising a cloud of dust. Under the snip of the scissors they relaxed a bit and dared to venture a few remarks. Serious and stubborn with their straw hats sitting squarely over their eyes and ties with fist-sized knots, they clumsily sought some elementary sympathy that no one would dream of denying them.

You would also meet them at J's, the German dentist, whose wife was so gorgeous that, despite his pedal drill and his rudimentary equipment, his surgery was always crowded. But there they were on their guard: the conciliatory atmosphere and neutral territory of the Afghan shop was lacking. This antechamber was already the West, with all its snares. So they never took their noses out of the copies of *Ogonyok* left on the table for them, never skipped anything, carefully read the advertisements, the housewife's diary and the doctrinal columns in order to reach, finally, like a well-deserved oasis, the colour photos of a Turcoman collective worker or a peasant in costume and shining boots, wheeling their tractors round in front of the camera and smiling at the reader, baring all their teeth. After a minute, you would feel a sympathetic interest in these people who had forgotten how to laugh and therefore seemed so impoverished.

You couldn't imagine giving the powerful women a few fashion tips, or telling the brown men, 'Look, skip the advertisements, it doesn't matter – cheer up, have a cigarette and a chat! Twelve hundred miles away, in the most extraordinary country in the world, that couldn't do anyone any harm.' Perhaps they simply didn't see us. Perhaps they had thoughts like ours, but we could try making contact and they couldn't, and it was a precious distinction.

The youngest ones sometimes came for a furtive drink at the *Maison Française*: stocky men arriving in pairs, with sinewy faces and squeezed into suits that were too small for them. They spoke a little French learnt at an artillery school or a flying school or in minesweeping classes, never just 'at school'. They were well received and quizzed about everything and nothing – mostly about nothing, as all subjects other than Gorky, Khatchaturian and the Hermitage smacked of heresy. There were always a few of them there, circumspect but pleasant, their champagne glasses invisible in their enormous hands; not too much like fish out of water, because they had read in their textbooks that Diderot was the father of agrarian reform, Molière the sworn enemy of the bourgeoisie, and Thorez* a delicate stylist.

In 1868, the Amir Abdur Rahman had already adopted a sanctimonious tone in speaking of 'the poor Afghan goat, caught between the Russian bear and the British lion'. Under his rule, however, the Afghan goat had often managed to dupe both neighbours by playing them off against each other, and his political skill in this game had become an accepted technique. They were used to these prickly neighbours, and the Revolution had not made much difference. They were not troubled, either, by contradictions between principles and facts because, as good Orientals, they didn't believe in principles. Nobody was surprised when this socialist, secular republic offered eight horses to the sovereign of a kingdom where Islam was the state religion; it was known that the present was the bait for a request and that, if need be, the Russians would have offered to build a mosque.

* Maurice Thorez, Secretary General of the Parti communiste française 1930-64. – Trs.

As for the Americans, you saw even less of them. They lived on the outskirts, as usual, learning about the country from books, not mixing much and drinking only boiled water, in terror of viruses and illnesses which they still didn't manage to avoid.

We didn't either. Thierry just had time to exhibit and sell a few paintings before he got jaundice, from which it took him several weeks to recover. Without our friend Claude, the doctor, and without the kindness we met with everywhere, I don't know how he would have got over it. In mid-November, he took the plane for New Delhi, intending to travel on by train to Ceylon in preparation for Flo's arrival. He was in too much of a hurry to meet this deadline to wait for me to get back on my feet, and still too weak to go over the passes by car and endure the wear and tear of going down to India by road. I was to meet them there a few months later, with the luggage and the car, in time to celebrate the wedding.

Civil aviation in Afghanistan consisted entirely in a little enterprise called 'Indomer', which carried pilgrims to Mecca and derived the greater part of its income from smuggling carpets; the ever-cautious state kept one of the airline administrators permanently imprisoned. As for the airport, it was a field with markings, humbly submissive to the bad weather and closed as soon as it snowed; the twin-engined planes of Air India or KLM used it when weather permitted.

I went there with Thierry at dawn. It was cold, and the long, brown, fallow fields which spread out south of the town were covered in white ice, recalling our first months in Tabriz. The Indian machine, piloted by a bearded Sikh, was already on the runway. Before he passed the barrier, we split the money that Thierry had earned in Kabul, where I hadn't made a sou.

Back by jeep. The rising sun brushed the top of the poplars and the snow on the Suleiman Mountains, making the harvested barley shine where it lay on the flat roofs of the bazaar. Halfway back to town, a blue and green bus – those colours always combine brilliantly – was upside down in a ditch. Passengers were squatting all around it, smoking; others were strolling about as though they had not expected anything less. I liked this country. I was also thinking about Thierry: time flowed more amply in Asia than at home, and our perfect companionship seemed to have lasted ten years.

A few days later, Claude went off to south Afghanistan where his work called him. I went northwards, across the mountain to Bactria, where French archaeologists had offered me some work.

The Hindu Kush

ABOUT FORTY miles north of Kabul stretched the ranges of the Hindu Kush. At a mean altitude of some thirteen thousand feet, they cross Afghanistan from east to west, lifting the glaciers of Nuristan to nineteen thousand feet and separating two worlds.

On the south side: a burnt plateau, intersected by garden valleys and stretching as far as the mountains on the Baluchi frontier. The sun is strong, beards black, noses hooked. They speak and think in Pashto (the language of the Pathans) or in Persian. On the north side: light is filtered through the mists off the steppe, there are round faces, blue eyes, quilted coats on Uzbek horsemen trotting towards their yurt villages. Wild boars, bustards and disappearing watercourses are scattered across the rushy plain, which slopes gently down to the Oxus and the Aral Sea. People are taciturn. They speak the sober Turkish dialects of Central Asia. The horses do the thinking.

On November evenings the north wind gusts down to Kabul, driving away the stench of the bazaar from the streets and leaving a fine tang of the heights. It is a sign from the Hindu Kush. You can't see it, but you smell it beyond the first hills, spread out like a cloak in the night. It takes up the whole sky – and the mind, too. After a week your head is full of the mountains and the country that stretches beyond them, and thinking of it, you have to set off.

To cross the Hindu Kush and reach Afghan Turkmenistan – formerly Bactria – you need a pass from the Kabul police and a seat in the *Afghan Mail* bus, or in one of the trucks going up north. Permission is often denied, but if you give a simple, straightforward reason that appeals to the man you're talking to – to see the country, to wander around – then the police are as good as gold. All Muslims, even cops, are potential nomads. Mention *djahan* (the world) or *shah rah* (the open road), and they picture themselves freed of everything and in search of Truth, scuffing the dust beneath a thin crescent moon. By adding that I was in no hurry, I got my permit straight away.

The Kabul bazaar: stone weights clink in the balances and fighting pheasants poke their beaks through their willow cages. In the ironmongers' souk, trucks are parked with their noses in the forges. While the white-hot metal cools, the drivers squat on their heels and gossip. A hookah passes from hand to hand, messages and information resound in the chilly air... the Kunduz bus has fallen into the river... the Lataband Pass is full of red pheasants... digging a well, they found treasure at Gardez. New arrivals join the company, each with his anecdote or bit of news, and hour after hour the spoken newspaper of the kingdom rises up with the smoke between the dark mass of trucks.

A word about these trucks. The Afghan takes ages to make a decision, but once it's made, he gets carried away. If he buys a truck, he dreams of gigantic loads that will astound the bazaar. He'll make his fortune in four or five trips. Everyone will be talking about him. His sixteen-ton Mack or Internash hardly satisfies his ambition. The engine and chassis will do at a pinch, but the loading deck seems a bit mean. He sells it for firewood and in its place fixes a sort of open-topped room, big enough for a dozen draught-horses to roll around. Then he looks for a painter. Every inch of Afghan trucks is decorated with a small brush: minarets, hands coming out of the sky, aces of spades, daggers piercing a surrealist breast, surrounded by quotations from the Koran which coil in all directions, because the artist works with his nose to the sheet, his aim being to fill the space rather than to organise it. Once the work is completed, the truck disappears beneath its light-hearted decorations; what remains is a cross between an icon and an 'Old Berlin' chocolate box.

Then the driver loads up. This done, he runs over the route in his mind: if the lowest branches of the walnut trees are twenty-three feet off the road, he'll go up to twenty. At first his truck moves at a good speed, but he can hardly extricate it from the clay of the souks. Can he keep it up? It's unlikely: he stops in the suburbs, picks up passengers going north at fifty *afghanis* a ride, and puts them in the back with the sacks. Then he rattles off to the Hindu Kush, to Mazar or Kunduz, *insh'allah*, and two, five or eight days later there he is, thanks to a series of miracles which surprise no one, since God is Afghan and Muslim. Unless, that is, the truck remains somewhere at the very bottom of a ravine.

I went by the ironmongers' souk at nightfall. Pieces lifted out of the forge with tongs were ringed with an eye-catching red halo. Voices were rare: the drivers still at work left at night or early in the morning. I had no trouble finding a lift north. The next morning I was up at dawn, putting on clothes that hadn't been unpacked since Tabriz and greasing my boots as I listened to the singing coffee pot. The town was freezing. Through groves of sorb-apples encrusted with dust, I went on to the outer orchards, where two apple-thieves with smiles as wide as their sacks slid along the walls. No sound of engines came from the bazaar, where the first smoke was rising. The man had said seven o'clock, without feeling tied to it. Words counted less than the thought, and who could guarantee what he might think the next day? Time belongs only to God, and the Afghans don't readily make promises that impinge on the future. Tomorrow morning… tomorrow evening, or in three days, or never. I went ahead. The sun was high when the truck overtook me, sounding its horn. I clambered on top of the load, with a handful of very lively old people, and ended the morning lying on the spare tyre, hands behind my neck. With each swerve, the thin legs, slippers and beards of my neighbours lurched across my view of the sky. We crossed the little pass separating the valley of Kabul from the valley of Charikar.

I had midday rice and tea at Charikar with the people from the truck. The king was expected, on his way back from hunting, and the place had been turned upside down. Soldiers had blocked off the road with branches, and had stopped all traffic to the Hindu Kush until the convoy should arrive. This was no business of the truck-driver, who had washed his hands in a ewer and was drying them in the wind, turning them over and thinking. He had discovered among the guards a cousin who would take the wheel and, after a discreet manoeuvre, the truck was found on the other side of the barricade. Cousins are easy to find in Afghanistan, which comes in handy.

The sun was beginning to set when the truck turned west to enter the Ghorband Valley: a long stretch of black soil planted with chestnut trees, walnuts and vines, where surfeited starlings and thrushes rose up in clouds with a noise like hail. Everything along the king's route breathed expectancy. All the tea-houses had been swept, tables laden with pears had been set up in the courtyards, and places set on white linen scattered with vanilla orchids and a type of chrysanthemum. Squatting behind steaming teapots, the tenants scrunched up their toes inside their slippers, looking out at the dust of the royal convoy descending slowly into the night: blessed if the king chose their courtyard, doubly blessed should he sit down, triply if his chamberlain dreamed of paying as they departed.

Halfway up the valley we passed the small caravan, which had halted under a chestnut tree. A few men on horseback, carbines slung across their chests and lances fixed in their stirrups, flanked the royal jeep and the trailer full of still warm moufflon, deer and bustards, whose black blood dripped on to the road. The king was seated on a bench in front, between two officers. All three were wearing exactly the same olive-green tunics and, as their faces were in shadow, I could hardly make out the fine features that pictures in the bazaar had made so familiar. The escort, unsettled to find this rogue truck beyond the barriers, brusquely questioned the driver and shoved their horses against the doors as they suspiciously looked inside the cabin. Despite the tons of bristles and feathers, there was none of that tired arrogance which usually accompanies the return of the hunt. The riders' shouted questions, the nervous horses and the three motionless, watchful silhouettes suggested rather the cautious bearing of a group of travellers at an uncertain frontier. The valley, however, was peaceful and the kingdom more tranquil than ever; but ever since the Afghan throne had existed, such precautions had been taken and had enabled one king in three to die in his bed. In such a country, where passions ran high, where the taste for land, inter-tribal rivalry and the burden of vendettas had guns blazing in a trice, it was difficult to reign without some 'anticipation', and the elimination of each adversary threw you into the arms of a whole clan of avengers. Since King Nadir, his father, had been killed at point-blank range by the page of an ousted general, and his child had died under torture without saying a word, King Mohammed Zahir protected himself on all sides and slept with one ear cocked. 'Ten dervishes can easily sleep under one worn-out cape, but the world isn't big enough for two Padishah', the proverb runs. This bucolic fief offered even less space; all the same, there was enough to make it coveted.

At nightfall we reached the bottom of the village of Chardeh Ghorband, the southern entrance to the Shibar Pass. Vines as thick as thighs tapped against the cob houses and arched over the little street. Between bunches you could see the forbidding rock-face towering over the village, and the first stars. We had climbed a long way, and the cold was biting. A caravan just down from the pass occupied the little square: twenty or so camels from Central Asia with thick, curly fleeces were steaming around the water-trough. Behind his animals, the Turcoman driver, standing up in his saddle and with the reins held high, was making his horse pirouette, goading it on by a sort of chirping. His slanting eyes gleamed in his red face and his cloak fanned out around him. He informed the drivers in bad Persian: eight trucks from Russia, kept on the other side during the royal hunt, would pass through that night; there was no fresh snow on the heights. Blowing on our fingers, we had taken refuge in the tea-house where the truck-driver, in good spirits after hearing the news, offered sugar and tea all round. Hard biscuits were extracted from the bundles, and at first you heard nothing but chewing and sighing, then, as your ears got attuned to it, the noise of the river ever closer. The manager, who knew everyone who used the pass, had taken up conversation with the team where they last left off. While speaking, he turned up the flame of the acetylene lamp so that light crept over the room; when it reached me, he interrupted himself to ask where the stranger came from.

'From Switzerland, on my way to Mazar.'

Switzerland? He could picture it well. He often had in the courtyard a truck from Kabul with a Swiss castle painted on it. This impregnable castle was mirrored in a lake surrounded by rock; on the blue water sailed boats with crossed lateen yards like the craft off the coast of Oman. The motif must have been one of those dearest to the bazaar painters' hearts, because of the water, which was very difficult to render, especially the waves, which many only knew of by hearsay. In Switzerland, he added, the mountains were like needles and they were so high, and the valleys so deep, that you couldn't tell night from day down there. Also Swiss watches were luminous. They asked me what they would think of Swiss roses and Swiss melons. The roses are superb, but as for the melons, nothing touches the melons of Kabul. Everyone was delighted. From Turkistan to the Caucasus, the fortunes of a patch of land are gauged by the quality of its melons. It is a subject of debate, pride and prestige. Throats are cut over melons, and respected men would willingly undertake a week's journey to taste the famous white melons of Bokhara. My declaration was intended to give pleasure. I was about to mention the gun and forty cartridges that every Swiss soldier keeps at home – a delicious privilege – but the company had lost sight of the West, spread out their mattresses and yielded to sleep. The stink of badly tanned leather, an honest stench but a stench all the same, drove me into the courtyard.

The night was glacial. The full moon illumined the cliffs and the village on its rocky shelf, as well as garlands of peppers hung up in the galleries of the houses. Above us, vast expanses of mountain crackled with solitude and cold. There was no sound of an engine; the pass gave no sign of life, but you sensed it patiently breaching the night.

Despite competing passes (Salang, and particularly Hawak, to the east of Shibar, a higher pass which was formerly used more often), Shibar had never lacked customers. On their return to India, the Chinese Buddhists had climbed it (*snow flew over a thousand li*) to make a pilgrimage to the sanctuaries of Bamiyan. Babur had crossed it several times, his frozen ears swelling up 'as big as an apple'. For a long time no one risked it without being in a group and armed, because of the Hazara bandits* – schismatics, drinkers of arak, holed up in the western ranges – who pounced on any traffic. Then there was mountain guerilla fighting between the people of the two sides, with betrayals, climbing, and musket fire magnified a hundred times by the echo. And there were punitive expeditions as well, camels tamping down the snow to let the cannon pass. That was in the past: today, all is calm. The Hazara, converted to reason, sell their local wine from under their cloaks in the Kabul bazaar, and those who drive up to the summit in trucks have only chilblains, squalls and avalanches to fear.

---

* A Central Asian people, once believed to be descendants of Genghis Khan, grouped in thousands (*hazara* = thousand in Persian). It is now thought that they are a remnant of the ancient Sino-Tibetan population of the Pamir mountains.

Like a fish-laden river, the Shibar feeds its tributaries. The owner of the staging-post at Ghorband knew a thing or two. He was located exactly at the pivot of the route: the trucks coming from the north feasted there because they had made it thus far; those from the south because they needed fresh heart for the climb. The teams and caravans exchanged goods, gossip and news in his courtyard, and by means of these nomads, without stepping over his threshold, he kept an eye on the world. His pile of *afghanis*, roubles and rupees, his curry from Lahore and his stove made in Russia, his pilgrimage to Mecca, his social ease and his general knowledge picked up in passing – all these he owed to the Shibar Pass. He spoke of it reverently. He didn't speak so highly of the Soviet mail-plane from Tashkent to Kabul, which he heard on certain summer mornings as it passed, high in the eastern sky. He had even drawn it in a fresco on the tea-house wall: a machine which, in sum, ignored the mountain and threatened his livelihood – not at all to its advantage. It looked like a sort of fly, lost amid the sharp peaks; to judge by the angle of the machine and the flames licking round it, it looked as though the mountain still had the upper hand.

I went as far as the drinking-trough, softly, so as not to wake the dogs. Rolled up in his old goatskin, the Turcoman was sleeping on the ground beside his animals. The village was silent but the Shibar was about to emerge from its muteness: as high as the stars, the intermittent sound of an engine in first was coming down towards us. I went back, numbed. I put my money in my boots, my boots under my head, and fell asleep with my feet in my neighbour's beard.

Morning: the drivers from Russia had arrived in the night and were lying between the sleepers, so we woke among strangers. They were Tajik Muslims, dressed in dusty blouses and knee-length black boots. They had left Stalinabad four days previously, crossed the Oxus by ferry at Termez and come down to deliver the new trucks to Kabul. Small, alert and taciturn, they seemed very much at ease and returned *salaam* for *salaam*, rubbing the sleep from their large eyes.

A thousand miles of border in common and tight economic interdependence obliged the Afghans to handle their neighbours carefully. The Iron Curtain opens to allow passage of petrol, cement and Soviet tobacco in one direction; in the other, dried fruit and especially the raw Afghan cotton which is processed in Tajikistan. It also opens for certain nomadic tribes whose summer pastures are in the Hindu Kush and whose transhumance is regulated by treaty. Less officially, there are Tajik deserters who cross the Oxus to take refuge in Afghanistan. After a year of surveillance, these immigrants are assimilated and establish themselves as growers in the great Bactrian plain where, for several years, their villages have been springing up like mushrooms. Despite these illegal comings and goings, and the skirmishes that sometimes result between the Uzbek 'smugglers' and Communist border guards, relations between the two sides are extraordinarily relaxed. The Afghans show neither fear nor hatred nor attraction towards the USSR, and maintain a status as self-determining neighbours only equalled by Finland.*

The Tajiks naturally joined us round a hookah. Men and doctrine are no barriers between Muslim truckdrivers, and the pipe passed from mouth to mouth without pausing. The Afghans teased their poor fellow-believers who had to work during the fast of Ramadan and were not allowed to go on pilgrimage any further than Bokhara. On both sides questions were asked to which honesty demanded plain answers. As they were leaving, the Tajiks – as if they were unwillingly obeying a misguided order from on high – distributed a few coarse biscuits mixed with political slogans, then started up their machines and made off for Kabul in a cloud of dust.

The owner of the staging-post examined our load with a puzzled expression. It wasn't bad, of course, but a shrewd driver could do better still. Indeed, he found himself with several bundles destined for Mazar-e-Sharif, as he confided to the driver. His hands emphasized his overtures, flying in seductive circles round the driver, who gradually began to see the advantages of adding to his cargo. By midday they were still negotiating, and the process promised to be too enjoyable to settle before night. I set off by myself. I listened out for them for a mile or two as I climbed, but I never saw them again.

All afternoon I walked along the pass, sniffing the iron scent of November. When evening came, I sat on a drystone wall and ate the Russian biscuit. I was weary, and the mountain hadn't come a scrap

---

* This was written, of course, some years before the Soviet invasion of Afghanistan in 1979. – Trs.

closer. The road went through large patches of snow which the night was rapidly obscuring, but above seventeen thousand feet the high slopes of Koh-i-Baba were still splashed with sunlight. I dozed off for a moment, then was woken by the noise of a climbing truck, knocking and whistling. It wasn't my truck, but it slowed down and indicated that I should get in. I hung on to the back and scrambled up.

I gingerly poked the load: dew-damp rolls of carpet – what luck! Nothing going through the Hindu Kush is so attractive. You could chance on barrels of Russian petrol, stinking and clanging, or on sacks of cement which would chill you to the bone. At the front, where it was less bumpy, two muffled forms already occupied the best places. A toothless old man, emerging from a bundle of wollen rags, asked me the ritual question: '*Kodja miri insh' Allah?*' – where are you going, God willing? The other passenger had entirely disappeared beneath a carpet, from which his studded slippers stuck out, trembling continually. But his belongings gave him away: a Koran, a flint and steel lighter, a melon and an umbrella with steel-rimmed spectacles fastened to the handle by elastic, viz, a mullah. He was going as far as Zebak. He would be shaken all the way: from there to Kunduz was a day's journey at least, then the road turns east, reaching Faizabad, whence a bad road joins Zebak: two or three days, if all went well. At Zebak there was a clay and straw mosque and about twenty dilapidated houses, filled with smoke by the mounted patrol who guarded access to the upper Wakan and the Chinese border.* Beyond that there was nothing apart from the solitary slopes of the Pamirs, where a handful of trappers hunted the blue fox and the snow leopard. A journey you wouldn't wish on anyone: to the end of the world. Zebak is Piogre.**

The truck climbed across slopes of dirty snow, shaking horribly. The narrowing of the pass was heralded by short, nasty inclines that tilted the chassis as though to overturn it. Drivers maintained the lowest

---

* The post was located sixteen and a half thousand feet up. No one passed that way.

** Piogre is an imaginary town in Swiss folklore. If someone impertinently asks you where you are going, you might reply, 'I'm going to Piogre to shoe flies.' – Trs.

speeds, changing gears abruptly and grindingly. In the cabin, attention mounted; not alarm, because everything was already written, but watchfulness and a great capacity for endurance and resignation that would stand them in good stead for the breakdowns, changes of gradient, landslides and tumbles that the Shibar Pass holds in store for its regulars.

All the long-distance lorries in Asia carry more or less the same team. The actual owner of the vehicle is Allah, and the inscriptions all over its body remind him of his responsibilities. The earthly possessor is called *Motar-sahib*. It is he who chooses what is to be carried, takes the wheel during difficult crossings, decides on the itinerary, the stages, the meals, or the sudden halts in the middle of the steppe to shoot at any bustard pecking within range. The blunderbuss, the backgammon set and the prayer-rug stored under the seat belong to him. His second and lieutenant is called the *Mesteri*. He is an electrician-mechanic-smith and repairs anything anywhere, with whatever comes to hand. When the damage is serious he takes command, stops colleagues' trucks, passes on messages to nearby smithies, negotiates the exchange of money or help. Each evening he takes out the distributor and the spark-plugs and goes off to the tea-house, a greasy carton under his arm. This is partly caution – no one will steal a truck without the ignition – and partly to keep his hands busy. Once he has had tea, he spends the evening polishing the electrodes and the plates, all those small surfaces that produce light or sparks and are the soul of the truck. This daily commerce with magnetism gives him a great deal of pleasure and imparts a sort of radiance. After several years on the road, when the Mesteri has enough to buy an old chassis, and enough pieces here and there to complete it, he himself becomes a Motar-sahib. This stage is sometimes accelerated by marrying the boss's daughter, as he is in a strong bargaining position during those long stretches of the night when so much depends on him.

Conspirator number three, and by no means the least, is a young, badly dressed underdog called the *Kilinar* – a corruption of the English 'cleaner'. He makes sure that there's enough petrol and oil, makes the tea when they stop, and carefully sponges down the decorated panels every day. In the passes, he travels clinging on to the back of the truck, his face screwed up against the cold, his hand clutching the heavy piece of wood which is used to wedge the back wheel on the slopes and twists. He spends whole nights like this, shaken until his bones rattle, whipped by an icy wind which shreds his cigarette butt and blows it in his eyes, while instructions from the cabin reach him in gusts, mixed with the warm smell of furlined coats. At fifteen, the Kilinars are all muscle, bone and temper. They are the toughest souls in the country – and you can't wring a smile from their wolf-faces. They live on the margins of society.

At the staging-posts, these boys unroll their mattresses in some dark corner, and you should hear them bawl out the managers if they don't serve them at once. The Kilinars also have their moments of power: on the cliff roads, on the hairpin bends that take three shots to negotiate, they direct the operation – 'A bit further... slow down ...*brake*! you dumb mother-fucker...' – and take advantage of the situation to give hell to the ones travelling soft in the cabin. They have no choice, for without the Kilinar and his wedge, the always overloaded lorries would tip over a precipice, and their landing would not be gentle.

In the Hindu Kush it is rare for a Kilinar to make his fortune. Most stick to their path out of sheer determination for four or five years of a life that matures too early, and then they collapse one evening without warning on the ledge of a tea-house. For the first time in their lives – a late but incomparable surprise – they are surrounded by care and warmth, then they take leave of this transitory world, not having lasted as long as the wooden wedge handed on to their successor.

Midnight or one o'clock. We were coming down. A stream murmured below us, its icy waters on their way to join the Oxus, ending up in the Aral Sea, in the middle of Central Asia. We were about to change worlds. The road entered a dizzying gully, blacker than the night; in places it had dropped away into the river, leaving only a narrow, sloping causeway. The Motar-sahib stopped the truck and got down, muttering, to test the ground underfoot. In first gear, the truck ventured into the mud, leaning towards the water into which clumps loosened by the wheels fell with a distant sound; then inch by inch, regained firm land and straightened up, while a calm but relieved flow of comments rose from the cabin.

...Breakdown. For at least two hours we heard the Mesteri curse and swear from under the chassis. The wind cut right across us on our perch. The old man, clambering across the bundles, came to share my blanket. He had disentangled from the load a bunch of dead chickens tied by the legs, still warm, which served him as a muff. I pulled my fur cap over my ears, clasped my hands between my thighs and closed my eyes, trying to summon up all the warmth that I had ever given or received. It didn't work. No doubt I'd never given out enough. Deep in my boots my feet had long since given up; my lips were completely numb though a cigarette still warmed my mouth. Lying back on the damp carpets, I dreamed in snatches – of mulled wine, of buckets of charcoal, of chestnuts popping over a brazier – brief dozes from which the sharp smell of the poultry or the cigarette butt burning my lip jerked me awake.

The moon shone bright; a wall of black and red rock rose up around us in spurts of three hundred yards. Leaning right back, you could see as though from the bottom of a well, the heights of Koh-i-Baba sticking up into the coping of the sky where the stars almost seemed to be breathing. Eventually, I had to give in to the numbing effect of wintry nature. I didn't feel the truck starting up again.

I woke as the sun rose, to the hoarse cries of pheasants and hoopoes. We had stopped, having come down a long way as I slept. The stream had turned into a thin, lazy, meandering river. Here and there beside the road, eroded moraine sloped gently towards the plain. The team had dismounted and was collecting armfuls of twigs for a fire. I jumped down from the truck and joined the circle of silhouettes squatting down and stretching out their chapped hands to the brazier. The Kilinar filled the teapot. As for the mullah... having seen his skinny legs and his specs, I had imagined an old man: he was lad of twenty, his round head shaven, who looked me over curiously. It wasn't every day you saw a foreign traveller on top of a truck – and a Christian to boot. He opened out his knife, offered me a slice of melon, and accepted a cigarette, which he smoked sitting back on his heels, continuing to stare at me. He was puzzled, but he must have been more at ease with me than with those Hindus in the Kabul bazaar who cherished gods by the hundred. After all, we were among the 'people of the Book', believers in One God, and cousins in religion. That we had slaughtered each other for a thousand years

301

didn't matter much, especially in Afghanistan, where there was a lot of internecine killing and where the same word – *tarbour* – means both cousin and enemy.

Our gods, willy-nilly, have a long history in common. Afghan folklore swarms with biblical references and the Old Testament, in effect, is stuffed with their daily life. We know that Cain founded Kabul, and that Solomon had his throne on a mountain south of the Khyber Pass. As for Issa – Christ – they know him better than we know Moses or Jeremiah. On the day of death, they even count him among their intercessors and, in a funeral lament they sing in Pathan lands, the dying 'say to Noah, Moses, Jesus and Ibrahim (friend of Mohammed): according to your wisdom, who else but you would still come to our aid?'

This Issa, whose coloured picture you sometimes find in the bazaar for ten afghanis – not crucified, of course, but floating amidst well-armed archangels, or ripening for his grave and generous fate on the back of a jerkily trotting young donkey – is more familiar in their houses than in ours. Everyone there knows his pitiful story, but no one is really upset by it. He is a gentle sort, Issa, astray in a hard world, with the police against him and hares for companions – only fit for sleeping, betraying him and bolting when they catch sight of the soldiers' torches. Perhaps he is too gentle; there, where *doing good to the wicked is like doing ill to the good*, there are indulgences they can't understand. The way he disarmed Peter in the Garden of Olives, for example, passes their understanding. Perhaps a son of God is allowed to push mercy to that extreme, but Peter, who was just a man, certainly should have been able to turn a deaf ear. If he'd had a few Pathans at Gethsemane, the police wouldn't have won the day, nor Judas received his thirty pieces.

So they sympathise with Issa, and respect him, but wouldn't dream of following his example. Look at Mohammed! Also a just man, but more than that: a good general, a leader of men and the head of his clan. Preaching God, conquering and having a family: there's a chief who puts heart into you. But Issa? Who would want to live alone in this world, ending up nailed to a couple of beams between two thieves, without even a brother to avenge you? Moreover, if Issa had been the victim of a family conspiracy, in one of those affairs where the eldest sells the youngest for a bit of vineyard or a few head of cattle, then that would have won their attention. The opposite is the case: he ignores his earthly family – they disappear into obscurity, and when he does happen to mention them, the tone is harsh. Not a word about Mary, his mother, who followed him to the end, and above all, nothing about Joseph, who had plodded so far to provide shelter, and accepted such strange events without a murmur; nothing at all about the male side, the interesting one.

You shouldn't think, though, that Islam in those remote highlands is attached to earthly things and to success. There is an appetite for what is essential, constantly fostered by the spectacle of nature in which man appears as a humble accident, by the subtleties and slowness of a life in which frugality kills off pettiness. The god of the Hindu Kush is not, like that of Bethlehem, in love with man; he is his merciful and great creator. The credo is simple but striking. People there put it to a harder and more stringent test than we do ours. *Allah ou Akbar* – everything hangs on that: the magic of this Name is enough to transform empty interiors into space, and this divine largesse, through being inscribed on tombs with chalk or shouted from the top of minarets, becomes the true property of everyone – a wealth of which their faces bear fleeting but incontestable traces. Of course this doesn't rule out cunning, nor bouts of violence, nor stop salacious laughter from flowering light-heartedly among their beards.

On an even track, scattered with fresh dung, the truck overtook a large troop of horsemen, parting them like water. We were in Turcoman country, with the mountain far behind us. The Motarsahib sang as he drove; he was through with gorges and abysses, and the truck had only to keep going down to reach Kunduz before night. The mullah no longer thought of God or the Devil, and was cracking nuts between his hands. The old man, his clothes all soiled with chicken droppings, slept across the bundles with his mouth open, the sun from the steppe stroking his shoulder. About midday, at the Pul-i-Khumri fork, I left the truck to go north. The village was full of pretty, straw-coloured horses, their harnesses buffed to a shine. All you could hear was their pawing the ground and neighing. I had lunch in a tea-house which smelled of hay, and set off again on foot.

I wasn't very far from the French dig: just two or three hours' walk on the old Mazar road. It crossed a plain of peat-bogs, where white poplars lifted their rustling leaves. You could see the little owls perched in the forks of willow trees, and a number of voles sunning themselves beside their holes. I cut a club from a spruce tree, and gathered a few stones for warding off dogs. It was a fine day. I was drunk with exhaustion. Crossing the broad, gently sloping land, where autumn had found a voice, I wondered whether Euthydemos, Demetrios or Menander, the Greek kings of Bactria, had greatly missed their olive trees, their salty beaches and their dolphins.

The Pagans' Castle

After an hour and a half at a good pace, you cross a pretty poplar spinney, the very place for a siesta after walking ten miles from the canal which feeds the mill at Pul-i-Khumri. Then you're back on the road, and when you ask some horsemen the way, they point towards a hill to the north-west: Kafir Khale – the Pagans' Castle.* You go on for nearly an hour and reach the foot of the hill, convinced that you're mistaken: the slope under excavation is invisible from this part of the road, and you can't make out any sign of occupation nor hear a single voice. Then you see the tyre-marks which loop here and there across the steep slope of yellow earth, and say to yourself: 'It must be here.' You shout then wait, and against the grey sky small silhouettes appear on the crest, cupping their hands to their mouths and shouting – 'Have you got the post?'

'No!'

'Ahhh...' and they vanish.

I climbed on, and then understood that what I had taken to be the top was only the ridge of a breastwork which protected the place from the wind. It sheltered five large military tents laid out like the camp of a Shakespearean king, the tea-table still set in the open air – tea, black bread and French honey – and a kiosk which could only be a shower. To the right of the level area was lean-to where the Muslim cook was busy among his pails and steaming pots.

We shook hands.

'So you're here. But what about the van? And all the stuff?'

'It had broken down when I left Kabul, but the driver swore he would leave the same night and would be here before me. I came by truck and foot, that's why I haven't brought anything.'

'Ah!'

Once autumn comes, the post isn't regular in the world beyond Kabul. It is even less so between Kabul and Pul-i-Khumri (because of the mountain, the state of the passes, accidents and breakdowns), so they have to go there and look for it every three or four days.

'However I did collect some papers that had just arrived at your office.'

* For the Afghan peasant, Greeks, Parthians, Kuchi, Sassanid and everything preceding Islam is covered by *Kafir* – pagan.

Professor Daniel Schlumberger (head of the French Archaeological Delegation in Afghanistan) and his colleagues were cheered up by the *Figaro littéraire*, five issues of *Le Monde*, and the Russian publications on the excavation in process in Tajikistan which had taken three months to reach them, via Tashkent-Moscow-Paris-Karachi-Kabul. Without the Iron Curtain, their Soviet colleagues' dig would have been scarcely two days drive by truck.

Although the sun was hidden, the view from the hill was splendid: you surveyed an immense expanse of rushes and swamps and ploughland covered in thorn bushes, with a stream snaking between the willows. To the south-east, you could see a mile or two of the road on which I'd come. I measured the disappointment of the excavators, who were hungry for letters and could see me approach from a long way off. To the east: two yurt villages the colour of wheat, drowned in clay and pools, with a few clumps of trees displaying all the hues of autumn. In this russet space, where a horseman sometimes left dusty traces, the present was diluted and lightweight. As for the past: the top of the hill, levelled out by the excavations, revealed the carefully disinterred foundations of a sort of *oppidum*, forming a long rectangle, with an enormous stairway, still partially covered, taking up the other slope and linking it with the level of the plain. It was a temple to fire, from the great Kushan dynasty. I felt an ignorant blockhead; they would have to explain it all to me the next day.

'Were you cold on the Shibar?'

'I think I'm lucky still to have ears.'

By five o'clock the mist from the plain reached the hill; at six the bell rang for dinner, assembling some familiar faces: the Belgian Orientalist I'd already met in Persia; the professor's Lebanese assistant, an ace mechanic to whose kindness I owed several rescues from breakdowns; and Dodo and Cendrat, two travellers like us who were working there. They advanced with the tired but satisfied gait of those who've worked in the open air all day, their fingernails black with dirt. Ashur was there too, the Algerian globetrotter we'd met briefly in Kabul, regaining the colour which he'd been drained of by two years of tribulations. He was the sole occupant of the tent I moved into: a gas-lamp, his red pirate scarf thrown on the bed with the canvas-backed notebook in which he kept his diary, a packet of Camels bought with his latest pay, an 'Opinel' knife, and an ocarina;

we never heard that, as he needed persuading and we didn't insist too much. He willingly sang, however, and most agreeably: *Le rossignol et puis la ro-o-ose,* or *Tu n'iras pas faire la guerre, Giroflée, Girofla...* some old 'anarchist' choruses that went back to Fort-Chabrol – where had he picked those up? – then back to *Le rossignol...* A bit monotonous, but all the same he had 'a real touch of artistic talent', as they say after dinner.

> *Picking up the threads,*
> *written six years later*

And yet what was the point of that excavation? Foreigners spend years – if you add up all the seasons – toiling like navvies in some solitary corner of the steppe, in order to bring the Magi back to life or resuscitate dynasties that have been dead for eighteen centuries; and those Kushan temple-builders from the north-east, of whom we know almost nothing since they disappeared from the Chinese annals when they reached the banks of the Oxus.* One can't help brooding on such a situation. Is there a methodical way of putting down what is known about such a place, all the facts in order of importance? No doubt there is – I have laboured over it, but I can't get it right although I have covered twenty pages with reflections on the archaeologist's craft and on dating, on those yellow onion-skin sheets I use for drafts. Moreover, as the years go by, I feel less and less confident about the whole business. Why add stale words to fresh things that can get along perfectly well without them? It's as though one were a shopkeeper, this urge to get something out of everything, not to let anything go... and even though you're painfully aware of that, you keep on taking the trouble, coaxing, struggling against the vast, insistent, chilling effect of life.

But then why insist on talking about this journey? What bearing does it have on my life at present? None; anyway, I no longer have a present. The pages accumulate, I deplete the money I've been given, I might as well be dead as far as my wife is concerned – it's good of her not to have put the key under the mat and left. I move on from sterile

---

* The Kushan are only known from the coins they struck, Indian inscriptions and bits of widely scattered, marginal evidence which are difficult to piece together – worn down fragments of bone, for example, a bit like pot shards without a base. No doubt the base will turn up in Bactria, where we were excavating for the first time a monument attributed to the Kushan.

*dreaming to panic, giving up nothing, not able to do anything more,
and refusing to do anything else for fear of compromising this ghostly
narrative which devours me without getting fatter, and about which
some people sometimes inquire impatiently, or even with a hint of
derision. If only I could give it all my flesh at a stroke, and it were
finished! But that kind of deal is impossible; the ability to submit and
endure is no substitute, I know, for the ability to invent. (I have more
endurance than I need: a mean gift from the fairies.) It has to proceed
by accretion, bit by bit, patiently linking cause and effect. No, back to the
Pagans' Castle, back to that hole in my memory, to those slopes of now
faded yellow clay, to the feeble echo and tatters of ideas which slip away
as I try to grasp them; to that tough, happy autumn when my life
seemed so well defined; back to the restless, lively Frenchmen on top of
the hill, who made me so welcome and uncovered a world to me, fed me
with the results of their fishing and hunting. Return, yes, but more than
that; I must dig up the terrifying weight of earth that separates me from
it all. (That, too, is archaeology! The shards and the ruins are different,
but it is equally disastrous when something of the personal past is lost.)
I must bore through this indifference which erases, disfigures and kills,
and recover the verve of that time, the elasticity of spirit, the flexibility,
the nuances, the ripples of life, the rich chances, the way music fell on
the ear, the precious relationship with the material world and the
pleasure one took in it.*

*Instead of which: this desert place my head has become, the corrosive
silence of memory, this perpetual distraction which isn't attention to
anything else (not even to the most tenuous of inner voices), this
imposed solitude which is a lie, my companions for whom I am no
company, this work which is no longer work, and these memories which
have withered on the stalk, as though some malevolent power has
severed them from their roots, thus cutting me off from so many of the
things I loved.*

*Once more: back to the excavation. I can see a hundred details again,
but none of them comes to life. So I must describe the actors, motionless
round the table at night, in the large tent where we dined.*

*The professor sits at the top end, in his yellow woollen hat pointed
above the ears and forehead, such as the Reformation leaders wore. His
wife is on his left. His nine-year-old daughter – who sometimes appears
in photographs to provide the scale – has already gone to bed, carrying*

the 'doubtful' (i.e. not Kushan) human skull which is her favourite toy. The architect, a Breton who is worth his weight in gold, sits on the professor's right. The Belgian philologist sits at the other end, his Tutankhamen mask illuminated by the slanting light from the gaslamp. The rest of us are in the middle. The cook has just brought in a pot of meat and lentils which, after it has gone round the table, is hung, still boiling, from the tent-pole. While the spoons scrape on the enamel plates, I read the thoughts written in a circle above each head, as in some Byzantine icons. The professor thinks that in two days the picks will reach the base wall of the second flight of steps, and that on its vast, vertical surface – insh'Allah, insh'Allah, insh'Allah – he will find the foundation inscription that he has been looking for over three digs: a few lines in that bizarre jigsaw of a Greek alphabet used by the Kushan, perhaps enough of a text to allow him to understand the as yet incomprehensible dialect of outer Iran.* Cendrat is thinking of the wild boar he had killed the day before, almost by chance, with the very first shot he had ever fired. He'd hauled it up with great effort and then – because the Muslim cook refused to skin an impure carcass – had to lug it back to rot in the swamp. Antoine, a French traveller visiting like me, is stubbornly praising Malraux to the professor, as though he were trying to sell him. He is devilishly didactic, doesn't pay attention to any objections, and with his obtuse enthusiasm sterilises a whole corner of the conversation. I would much rather he left the talking to his neighbour opposite. I'm with Gorky in seeking my university on the roads, but when you come across a real scholar, it's very wrong not to take advantage of it. Especially this one, who always takes the trouble to answer questions, to inform, and is so animated that he comes right up to his interlocutor as though he wished to eat him up. He has that passion for the past he reconstructs without which historians are merely clerks, and true knowledge impossible. As for me, I'm thinking about the Kushan, who are the reason for our presence; a fine, obscure and ambiguous name, redolent of leather and fur. I think of Ceylon, where Thierry and Flo wash in water drawn from a well in huge buckets, against a background of bananas and palms. I think of the walk I'll be

---

* The inscription was discovered two and a half years later, nearly a hundred feet lower down: some twenty-five lines, intact as though incised yesterday, much more than they had dared hope.

*taking with Antoine, who badgers me all the time, proving that my ideas
are false and that I'm travelling in the wrong way. He has already driven
a long way and knows a great deal, but there's a school prefect inside
him who is never satisfied. I once brought the subject round to women,
to give his monologue a livelier turn. He said to me, 'Have you tried the
Iranians? I have... they're great.' The word 'tried' discouraged me, so I
left it at that. He has seen all of Europe, Russia and Persia too, but has
refused to surrender an inch of his integrity. What a surprising
programme! Maintaining his integrity – remaining intrinsically the
same simpleton who first set out? He couldn't have seen very much,
then, because there isn't a single country – as I now know – which
doesn't exact its pound of flesh.*

Dodo

I don't know whether he got the nickname Dodo on the dig. His real
name escapes me. He was a native of Grenoble, about forty years old,
and had spent twenty of those on the road. Placid, a straight-faced
comic, more detached than a Dervish and blending in with things all
the better to observe them, he was very good company. Above all he
had that phlegmatic nature – which is no more than a form of the
greatest resistance – so necessary to a life of travel, where the over-
excited and irascible always end up bashing into the image they've
made of themselves. Dodo had lived everywhere for a while, left
many jobs just as they became profitable, had learnt a lot and
doubtless read a lot. He rarely talked about it all. He said '*voui*' for
'*oui*' on purpose, I imagine, and disguised his reading and his talents
beneath a rather slow, rustic exterior for fear of his services being too
much in demand: he liked to organise his own time. The only task to
which he was entirely devoted was the training of his teammate,
Cendrat, a likeable electrician cum watercolourist, at least fifteen
years his junior. When night fell round the tent they shared at one
end of the camp, and being certain that he would not be found in
flagrante delicto with his learning, Dodo summoned all his resources
to adorn the mind of his pupil. (One night, when I went to borrow
their storm-lantern, I heard through the canvas: 'And there, in the
middle, was a great family that pulled the strings – the Medicis...')

We had met them in Persia at the beginning of the year; they had
come from Egypt, where they'd been for some time. This time they

had arrived from India, which hadn't been too successful. They planned to return to Europe via Tashkent and Russia and, in order to prepare themselves, carried a tattered copy of Popatov's grammar everywhere they went. Responsible for adjoining works, they conjugated Russian verbs out loud, which their workers no doubt mistook for some sort of prayer; there again, it was Dodo who initiated his associate into the pitfalls of the participle and the pluperfect. I don't know how their plan worked out, but if the journey continued for as long as they intended, Cendrat would have become more refined than a hundred Jesuits. Dodo had another project which I trust was some way off: to die in Japan.

On Saturdays and Sundays, when we set off across the marshes on horseback, Dodo always chose the slowest mount: a cuddlesome, battered old nag, saddled with a sheaf of straw, which he had to tickle with a willow branch to get going. He chose it out of caution, but also for the pleasure of moving unhurriedly through the marvellous autumn landscape, mulling over his thoughts or singing passages from *La Belle Hélène* or *Lakmé*, which he knew pretty well by heart. I can see him so clearly, perpetually lagging behind among the rushes, his glasses glinting. To simplify his toilette, he had shaved his head and wore a shapeless grey felt hat which he ceremoniously lifted to greet the peasants. I couldn't see him bareheaded without laughing: perched on his little horse, with his shining cranium and thin, sardonic smile, he gave the impression of a crooked old judge, corrupted by bribes.

A man in his forties would usually have become disenchanted with the life of a vagabond, and gloom would have set in. Time to draw a line. You travel, subsist and are seasoned; the years mount up; the pursuit loses sight of its goal and turns into flight; the adventure, emptied of its content, is prolonged by a series of expedients but loses all impetus. You perceive that travels may have a formative effect on youth, but they also make it pass. In short, you turn sour.

But not Dodo: he was completely at ease in his frugal, nomadic life. His soul had been scoured by his trials, his spirit remained fresh and ready for anything. Sometimes there was a mild nostalgia for white wine and walnuts and camembert... but no desire to go home or to settle down.

'It's not so much out of laziness,' he would add, stretching out under the aspen to which he'd tethered his horse, 'more out of curiosity – *voui*, curiosity.' He sent smoke rings up into the sky, gradually drained of light.

These wanderings kept us out late. We would come back in the dead of night, our horses worn out. On the outskirts of the

excavation, the peasants spent the evenings in their fields, muskets between their knees, to scare off the wild boars which would destroy their crops. Even with a pipe and a teapot, the time dragged. From time to time you would catch a scrap of soliloquy or a long sigh rising up from a cucumber patch. The air was exquisitely fresh.

The Khyber Road

Return from the dig. Departure for India.
December 3rd – alone.

A T THAT TIME of year and in that corner of the country, you were woken every morning by an absent-minded downpour which struck the tea-house awning and pattered on the samovars. Then the slanting red sun would dispel the mist; the road, the rushes and the hills would glisten, and behind them the high white sierras of Nuristan. Smoke rose up from the braziers while the sleepers washed – a frantic dabbing of fingers, mouth and beard – then hurried through their prayers, and saddled up the hobbled camels whose coats steamed in the cold. Husky conversation started up over bowls of green tea.

I had slept well. I felt fit, and the grazes I'd got the previous evening while mending the front spring had healed over. I got dressed and went to recruit some 'pushers' from around the samovar, as the battery was dead. There were a dozen old men with slender hands, beating their arms to get warm, and two tanned, silent Pathans. They made room for me with knowing chuckles. I offered tea. Afterwards, naturally, they helped push. In a whirlwind of white robes, beards, slippers and muddy legs, the car took off for Jalalabad.

Afghan border. Khyber Pass
December 5th

In Kabul, the people I'd asked about the Khyber Pass could never find words to describe it: 'Unforgettable… it's the clarity, above all… or the scale… or perhaps the echo, how to put it?' Then they would tie themselves in knots, give up and, for a moment, I felt they had returned in spirit to the pass, gazing once more at the thousand facets and bulges of the mountain – astounded, transported and carried beyond themselves, as they had been the first time.

On December 5th, at midday, after travelling for a year and a half, I reached the foot of the pass. Light touched the base of the Suleiman Mountains and the Afghan customs house, surrounded by a cluster of willows which shone like scales in the sun. There were no uniforms on the road, barred by only a flimsy wooden gate. I approached the office, stepped over the goats blocking the threshold and went inside. It smelled of thyme and arnica, and was humming with wasps. The blue gleam of revolvers leaning against the wall was very cheerful. Sitting up straight at the table, behind a bottle of purple ink, an officer was facing me. His hooded eyes were closed. With each breath I heard the creak of his new leather belt: he was asleep. He was probably an Uzbek from Bactria, as foreign there as I was myself. I left my passport on the table and went off to lunch. I wasn't in a hurry – you aren't, when it's a matter of leaving a country like that. Feeding salt to the goats, I re-read the last letter from Thierry and Flo. They had settled in an old Dutch citadel in the south of Ceylon.

> *Galle, December 1st*
> …Just to tempt you, here are the names of the bastions of the fort: Star, Moon, Sun, Zwart, Aurora, Pointe d'Utrecht, Triton, Neptune, Clippenberg and Aeolus. In a place like this, where you might come across a bonze in brilliant saffron next to an old man in a violet sarong next to a young woman in a pink sari, all against a background of jade sea and the setting sun, you become a painter. A table is waiting for all your papers. In the evening you slosh water over each other under a ballet of fireflies. So, until we clink our fraternal coconuts…

It was another world. He hadn't left for nothing.

Then I smoked a hookah, gazing at the mountain. Beside that, the customs house, the black, red and green flag, the truck full of Pathan children with long rifles across their shoulders – indeed everything human – looked crude and diminished, separated by too much space as in children's drawings where the proportions go wrong. The mountain wouldn't waste itself in useless exertions: it rose from its powerful base, rested, and rose again, its flanks broad and its facets bevelled like jewels. On the lower peaks, the towers of Pathan strongholds shone as though rubbed with oil; the higher, chamois-coloured slopes rose up behind them and broke off in shadowy circles into which drifting eagles disappeared in silence. Then there were pieces of black rock where clouds snagged like wool. Towards the top, sixty-five thousand feet from the bank where I was standing, there were narrow, gentle plateaux splashed with sunlight. The air was extraordinarily transparent. Voices carried. I could hear children shouting, far up on the old nomads' road, and the light footfall of invisible goats resounding down the whole pass with a crystalline echo. I spent a good hour without moving, drunk on this Apollonian landscape. Confronted by this prodigious anvil of earth and rock, the world of anecdote might never have existed. The mountain stretching out, the clear December air, the midday warmth, the sputter of the hookah – everything right down to the small change chinking in my pockets had become elements of a plot in which I had arrived, after many obstacles, in time to play my part. 'Durability... transparent proof of the world... peaceful belonging...' No, I couldn't do it either, couldn't find the words, for as Plotinus said:

> A tangent is a contact which one can
> neither conceive nor formulate.

Ten years of travelling would not be able to pay for this.

That day, I really believed that I had grasped something and that henceforth my life would be changed. But insights cannot be held for ever. Like water, the world ripples across you and for a while you take on its colours. Then it recedes, and leaves you face to face with the void you carry inside yourself, confronting that central inadequacy of soul which you must learn to rub shoulders with and to combat, and which, paradoxically, may be our surest impetus.

I picked up my stamped passport and left Afghanistan. It had cost me. The road is good on both sides of the pass. On days when the wind blows from the east, well before reaching the top the traveller meets gusts of the ripe and fiery scent of the Indian subcontinent...

And this benefit is real because we are entitled to these enlargements, and once having passed the bounds shall never again be quite the miserable pedants we were.

R. W. Emerson

TITLES IN SERIES

For a complete list of titles, visit www.nyrb.com or write to:
Catalog Requests, NYRB, 435 Hudson Street, New York, NY 10014